CW00797956

Exploring C

COMBATING MENACE OF PIRACY

Dear Readers, Publishers, Booksellers, all College & University Administrations, & Librarians,

The Federation of Publishers' & Book Sellers' Associations in India (FPBAI) would like to bring a matter of great importance to your urgent notice. Though possession of pirated copies is a cognizable and non-bailable offence, punishable by law and carries stiff penalties including imprisonment, it continues to thrive in markets, bookshops and photocopy shops. This is a matter of grave concern for all of us in the education and publishing community. Let us all do our bit in combating this crime against creation and spread of knowledge. If you come across a pirated book, photocopies pages from a book or are in any kind of doubt about the genuineness of a copy, please contact Chairman, Anti Piracy Committee, FPBAI, 84, Second Floor (Opp. Cambridge Primary School), Daryaganj, New Delhi-110 002.

Your co-operation and help in bringing the culprits to book will help the publishing industry combat piracy and facilitate the continued availability of good books of quality production at reasonable prices.

RELEVANT PORTIONS OF THE COPYRIGHT ACT ARE GIVEN BELOW:

INFRINGEMENT OF COPYRIGHT

The owner of the copyright has the exclusive right in respect of the reproduction of the work and such other acts which enables the owner to get the financial benefits by exercising such rights. If any of these acts relating to the work is carried out by a person other than the owner without a license from the owner or competent person/authority under the Copyright Act 1957, it constitutes infringement of copyright in the work.

PIRACY

It is a kind of illegal activity which has been caused by rapid technological advancement. Latest techniques of photocopying and printing have made it easy to produce unauthorized copies of a book within a short span of time at a relatively low cost on a large scale. This offence deprives the author of the work from getting his legitimate due and ultimately hampers the growth of original and creative work by the pursuit of hard work and intellectual skill and national economy as well.

COPYRIGHT LEGISLATION

The Principal Act (Copyright Act, 1957) was amended in 1984 to incorporate anti-piracy legislation to check widespread piracy of books, etc. and it has been made a cognizable and non-bailable offence.

The punishment for various offences have been enhanced by amending sections 63 and 65 and by inserting new sections 63A & 63B.

SECTION 63:

Any person who knowingly infringes or abets the infringement of the copyright work shall be punishable with:

    (i)   Imprisonment for a term which shall not be less than 6 months but which may be extended up to 3 years;

    (ii)   Fine of not less than Rs. 50,000/- but up to Rs. 2 lakhs.

SECTION 63A:

The quantum of enhanced penalty on second or subsequent conviction shall be:

    (i)   Imprisonment for not less than 1 year but up to 3 years; and

    (ii)   Fine of not less than rupees 1 lakh but may be extended up to Rs. 2 lakhs.

SECTION 63B:

The quantum penalty for the offence of knowing use of infringing copy of computer program shall be:

    (i)   Imprisonment for not less than 7 days but up to 3 years; and

    (ii)   Fine of not less than Rs. 50,000/- but may be extended up to Rs. 2 lakhs.

More powers have been given to the police for prompt action and speedy apprehension of the offender by amending section 64, as any police officer not below the rank of Sub-Inspector may seize without warrant all infringing copies or the work if he is satisfied that the offence is under section 63 in respect of the infringement of copyright. The Economic Offence (Inapplicability of Limitation) Act, 1974 was amended by incorporating in the Schedule the clause (a) of section 63 of the Copyright Act, 1957 which declared infringement of copyright as an economic offence.

Exploring C

Yashavant Kanetkar

BPB PUBLICATIONS

B-14, CONNAUGHT PLACE, NEW DELHI-110001

FIRST EDITION 1993, REPRINTED 2005

Distributors:

MICRO BOOK CENTRE
2, City Centre, CG Road,
Near Swastic Char Rasta,
AHMEDABAD-380009 Phone: 26421611

COMPUTER BOOK CENTRE
12, Shrungar Shopping Centre, M.G. Road,
BANGALORE-560001 Phone: 5587923, 5584641

MICRO BOOKS
Shanti Niketan Building, 8, Camac Street,
KOLKATTA-700017 Phone: 22826518, 22826519

BUSINESS PROMOTION BUREAU
8/1, Ritchie Street, Mount Road,
CHENNAI-600002 Phone: 28410796, 28550491

DECCAN AGENCIES
4-3-329, Bank Street,
HYDERABAD-500195 Phone: 24756400, 24756967

MICRO MEDIA
Shop No. 5, Mahendra Chambers, 150 D.N. Road,
Next to Capital Cinema V.T. (C.S.T.) Station,
MUMBAI-400001 Ph.: 22078296, 22078297

BPB PUBLICATIONS
B-14, Connaught Place, **NEW DELHI-110001**
Phone: 23325760, 23723393, 23737742

INFOTECH
G-2, Sidhartha Building, 96 Nehru Place,
NEW DELHI-110019
Phone: 26438245, 26415092, 26234208

INFOTECH
Shop No. 2, F-38, South Extension Part-1
NEW DELHI-110049
Phone: 24691288, 24641941

BPB BOOK CENTRE
376, Old Lajpat Rai Market,
DELHI-110006 PHONE: 23861747

Copyright © BPB PUBLICATIONS

All Rights Reserved. No part of this publication can be stored in any retrieval system or reproduced in any form or by any means without the prior written permission of the publishers.

LIMITS OF LIABILITY AND DISCLAIMER OF WARRANTY

The Author and Publisher of this book have tried their best to ensure that the programmes, procedures and functions contained in the book are correct. However, the author and the publishers make no warranty of any kind, expressed or implied, with regard to these programmes or the documentation contained in the book. The author and publishers shall not be liable in any event of any damages, incidental or consequential, in connection with, or arising out of the furnishing, performance or use of these programmes, procedures and functions. Product name mentioned are use for identifications purposes only and may be trademarks of their respective companies.

All trademarks referred to in the book are acknowledged as properties of their respective owners.

Price : Rs. 165/-

ISBN 81-7656-633-0

Published by Manish Jain for BPB Publications, B-14, Connaught Place, New Delhi-110 001 and Printed by him at Pressworks, Delhi.

Dedicated to
Prabhakar Kanetkar

About the Author

 Yashavant Prabhakar Kanetkar obtained his M. Tech. from IIT, Kanpur in 1987 and since then has been the Director of ICIT, a Training and Software development firm which he set up at Nagpur. Already an author of the books 'Let Us C' and 'Programming Expertise in Basic', these days he is writing a few more books on C and Unix with his team at ICIT. Mr. Kanetkar conducts a number of courses including those on C, C++, Unix Internals, Writing Vaccines & removing Viruses and Discrete Data Structures. Mr. Kanetkar writes 'The C Column' in Express Computer every week and is also the creator of COMPGARD anti-viral software.

Contents

Acknowledgments

It is a pleasure to be able to thank all the people who helped me turn this edition of Exploring C from a list of good ideas into a real book.

It is not always easy to accept the criticism of one's 'perfect' manuscript. However, I have been extremely lucky to have many technical reviewers whose comments, corrections and suggestions have enormously enriched this book.

I owe special thanks to Kirthiga Venkataraman, Niranjan Bakre and Sangeeta Karandikar, who played a major role in scripting this book.

Kirthiga has an uncanny knack of solving any problem that may occur - be it C or Ventura or what have you. She hopes to complete her Masters degree in Computer Science in the United States. The general opinion is that there isn't much that can come in her way.

Niranjan, an ice-cool person who has his own way of co-ordinating the multifarious activities that go into the production of a book - from cover design to page layout to font selection to technical content. He manned all these activities tirelessly.

Sangeeta arrived on the scene when I was already through with the first five chapters. But with her sponge-like brain, she quickly adapted herself and was soon writing and rewriting and reviewing the text as if she has been doing it all her life. She has a way with apostrophes and commas.

Anyone who has written a book knows the amount of time and effort that goes into such a project. Anyone who is related to the author can tell you at whose expense that time is spent. Mere thanks to Seema, Ammi, Dada and Aditya seem pretty small compared to the months of tremendous support and indulgence they gave. Without their cheerful support this book would not have seen the light of the day.

Introduction

If a hen and a half lays an egg and a half in a day and a half, how many and a half hens, who lay better by half, will lay half a score and a half in a week and a half? Foxed!? Well, this problem has been the inspiration behind this book. There are many good books available which would teach you C language. But I felt there was a dire need for a book which would solve for you twisted problems. A book which would take you to every nook and cranny of this language, exploring its subtleties, appreciating its elegance, making you realise why C stands a class apart.

The problems and programs in this book have been designed so as to challenge the reader's mastery of the basic rules of C and lead the reader into seldom accessed corners, beyond reasonable limits, and past a few open pits. The programs in the book should not be read as samples of good coding style. In fact, you may find some of the programs atrocious. But this is only to be expected, since the same qualities that make a crooked coding style often make an interesting program. I firmly believe that its only after soiling your hands in the murky depths do you get the rare glimpse into the actual working of C language.

While teaching C over the years I have realised that it doesn't nag you with strict rules, nor does it tie you down to mannerisms. It believes in the fact that two programmers never think alike and hence would come up with two totally different programs which essentially do the same thing. It is this tenet of C that I have attempted to unveil in this book.

What equipment you need to use this book

An ideal book is one which makes the instructor a redundant commodity. To that end, it has been my sincere effort to put to rest any doubts that may (and perhaps may not!) occur to you about how C behaves under any conceivable circumstances. So, if you possess a readiness to look further than the obvious, and think beyond the conventional, all you need is:

1. A PC, PC/XT, PC/AT or above
2. Any C compiler, preferably Turbo C
3. MS-DOS version 3.2 or above.

Chapter organisation

The serialisation of the chapters, as well as the programs within them has been done with easier ones first (from my viewpoint) and the more tricky ones towards the end. You would benefit if you follow this order. However, if you are impatient and want to try your hand at a particular example straightaway, go right ahead and have a go at it. You have nothing to lose except a lot of time, CRT phosphor and torn hair! The choice of course, is entirely yours. In each chapter there is a short explanation of the topics covered. I have attempted to keep this explanation as concise as possible. This is followed by an exercise which is intended to challenge your understanding of the concepts covered. Should you be able to solve it yourself, nothing like it. Otherwise you can avail of the solutions given at the end of each chapter.

Lastly, by the time you have reached the last chapter, if you are raring to teach us a thing or two, then I suppose the purpose of this book has been served.

1

The ABC of C

C was developed in 1972 by Dennis Ritchie at Bell Telephone Laboratories (now AT & T Bell Laboratories). It is an outgrowth of an earlier language called B, which was also developed at Bell Laboratories. C was largely confined to use within Bell Laboratories until 1978, when Brian Kernighan and Ritchie published a definitive description of the language. This description is often referred as "K & R C".

And after this there was no looking back, as more and more computer professionals switched over to C. Today there are C compilers available under every conceivable environment from DOS to Windows to Unix, and on all sizes of computers from micros to mainframes. Power, portability, performance and flexibility are possibly the four most important reasons for C's popularity. C has been designed to have a relatively good progamming efficiency as compared to Machine oriented languages like Assembly or Machine language, and a relatively good machine efficiency as compared to Problem oriented languages like COBOL and FORTRAN.

Variables and Constants in C

Simply put, a variable is a tool to reserve space in computer's memory. The reserved space is given a name, which we call a variable name. Constants are stored in this reserved space. The constants stored in the space reserved by the variable may vary from time to time, hence the name variable. The name once given to a location, however, remains unchanged. Thus in the statement,

    i = 5

5 is a constant which is being stored in a location which has been given a name **i**. So, **i** is a variable just as **a, x, note** or **str** are. They all designate memory locations that will hold different values assigned to these variables from time to time.

Depending on the purpose for which you want to utilize memory, C allows you to decide how much memory to allocate to a variable. Accordingly memory comes in three convenient versions: **char, int** and **float,** which occupy 1, 2 and 4 locations (bytes) respectively. A **char** can store values in the range -128 to +127, whereas an **int** can store values in the range -32768 to +32767. When do we use **float**? When we want to store numbers like 3.1415, or 0.0005672 in memory. A **float** can store values ranging from -3.4e+38 to +3.4e+38. Now that is certainly a very impressive range!

The memory occupied by each datatype can be found out using an operator called **sizeof**. For example, **sizeof (int)** would yield 2. Similarly, **sizeof (float)** would yield 4. The essence of these datatypes has been captured in Figure 1.1.

The **char**s and **int**s can also be expressed in hexadecimal and octal notations. For example, 16 can be expressed in hex as 0x10, and as 020 in octal. Similarly, 22 can be expressed in hex as 0x16, and as 026 in octal. A hex number is always preceded by 0x or 0X whereas an octal is preceded by 0 (zero, not o or O). C doesn't accept **float**s in hex or octal.

With constants out of the way, let us now take a look at the variables. Certain rules have been framed to create variable names. A variable name can be any combination of alphabets, digits and an underscore,

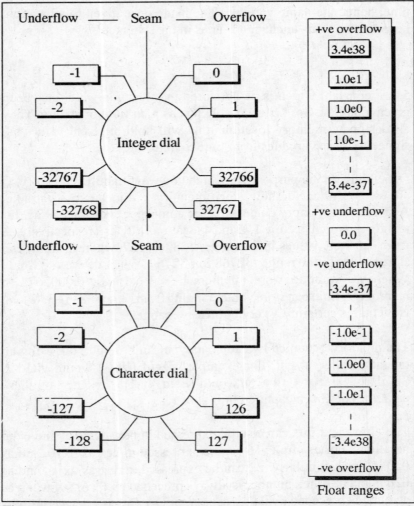

Figure 1.1 Integer, Character and Float ranges

with a proviso that the first character is an alphabet. The length of the variable is a compiler dependent feature. Turbo C accepts a variable name upto 32 characters.

Operations on Data

C programs are concise partly because of the large number of operators available with it. There are as many as 45 operators available in C. For starters we will concentrate only on arithmetic and assignment operators. These are shown in the Figure 1.2. Operators are classified as unary, binary or ternary depending on the number of operands they operate upon. For example, **+** is a binary operator since it operates on two operands that it adds.

Operators	Name	Type
-	Unary minus	Unary
+ - * / %	Arithmetic	Binary
=	Assignment	Binary

Figure 1.2 Arithmetic and Assignment Operators

Except for **%** the other operators are as usual. **%** is read as 'modulus' operator, and it returns the remainder on dividing an **int** with another. As against this, a **/** returns the quotient. While evaluating an expression, C gives priorities to some operators above the others. A unary minus has the highest priority, followed by arithmetic operators and lastly the assignment operator. Within arithmetic operators, *****, **/** and **%** enjoy a higher priority than **+** and **-**.

Integer and Float Conversions

It is important to understand the rules that govern the conversion of floating point and integer values in C. These are mentioned below.

(a)   An arithmetic operation between an integer and integer always yields an integer result.

(b)   An arithmetic operation between a **float** and **float** always yields a **float** result.

(c)   In an arithmetic operation between an integer and **float**, the integer is first promoted to **float** and then the operation is carried out. And hence it always yields a **float** result.

(d)   On assigning a **float** to an integer (using the = operator) the **float** is demoted to an integer.

(e)   On assigning an integer to a **float**, it is promoted to a **float**.

The following figure illustrates these conversions, demotions and promotions. Assume **i** to be an **int** and **a** to be a **float**.

Operation	Result	Operation	Result
i = 5 / 2	2	a = 5 / 2	2.0
i = 5.0 / 2	2	a = 5.0 / 2	2.5
i = 5 / 2.0	2	a = 5 / 2.0	2.5
i = 5.0 / 2.0	2	a = 5.0 / 2.0	2.5
i = 2 / 5	0	a = 2 / 5	0.0
i = 2.0 / 5	0	a = 2.0 / 5	0.4
i = 2 / 5.0	0	a = 2 / 5.0	0.4
i = 2.0 / 5.0	0	a = 2.0 / 5.0	0.4

Figure 1.3 Integer and Float Conversions

printf( ) and scanf( )

printf( ) is one of the most versatile statements in C. In fact, it is a standard library function used to display the output on the screen. The general form of **printf( )** looks like this...

```
printf ( "Format string", list of variables ) ;
```

And here are a few examples...

```
printf ( "%c %d %f", name, age, sal ) ;
printf ( "name = %c age = %d salary = %f", name, age, sal ) ;
printf ( "name = %c\nage = %d\nsalary = %f", name, age, sal ) ;
```

Assuming the value of **name** as 'A', that of **age** as 23, and that of **sal** as 1500.00, the output of the above **printf( )**s would be

```
A 23 1500.000000
name = A age = 23 salary = 1500.000000
name = A
age = 23
salary = 1500.000000
```

The first **printf( )** prints the values of the variables **name, age** and **sal**. As against this, the second would print messages against each value displayed. In the third **printf( )**, the **\n** is used to send the cursor to the next line, hence the three values are printed on three different lines.

Sometimes the list of variables may be dropped, as in,

```
printf ( "Enter values of a and b" ) ;
```

In this case everything enclosed within the pair of double quotes would be printed as it is on the screen.

Having imbibed those details, now let us switch over to **scanf( )**. **scanf( )** is once again a standard library function. It is used to receive values of variables from the keyboard. For example, the following **scanf( )** would let you supply the values of variables **a** and **b**.

```
scanf ( "%d %f", &a, &b ) ;
```

The general form of **scanf( )** is almost similar to **printf( )**, except for two important differences:

(a)   Within the pair of double quotes there should occur only format specifications like **%c, %d, %f** etc.

(b)   The variable names must always be preceded by the 'address of' operator **&**.

Exercise

[A]   Complete the following:

(1)   C has been developed by _____ in the year ___ while working at _____.

(2)   Binary equivalent of 762 is _____ , its octal equivalent is and its hex equivalent is ____.

(3)   Maximum allowable width of a variable in Turbo C is __ characters.

(4)   First character in any variable name must always be an a_____.

(5)   C variables are case _____ (sensitive / insensitive).

(6)   A character variable can at a time store __ character(s).

[B]   Point out which of the following variable names are invalid:

gross-salary
INTEREST
salary of emp
avg.
thereisagirlinmysoup

[C]   Point out which of the following C constants are invalid:

124.567
0001
0xbc40
0Xbc40
0x12.45
0xfgff

```
.001
-12e-12
```

[D]   What will be the output of the following programs:

(1)
```c
main( )
{
    printf ( "%d %d %d %d", 72, 072, 0x72, 0X72 ) ;
}
```

(2)
```c
main( )
{
    printf ( "%d %o %x", 72, 72, 72 ) ;
}
```

(3)
```c
main( )
{
    char ch ;
    int a ;
    float b ;
    printf ( "bytes occupied by ch = %d\n", sizeof ( ch ) ) ;
    printf ( "bytes occupied by a = %d\n", sizeof ( a ) ) ;
    printf ( "bytes occupied by b = %d\n", sizeof ( b ) ) ;
}
```

(4)
```c
main( )
{
    printf ( "char occupies %d bytes\n", sizeof ( char ) ) ;
    printf ( "int occupies %d bytes\n", sizeof ( int ) ) ;
    printf ( "float occupies %d bytes\n", sizeof ( float ) ) ;
}

main( )
{
    printf ( "bytes occupied by '7' = %d", sizeof ( '7' ) ) ;
    printf ( "bytes occupied by 7 = %d", sizeof ( 7 ) ) ;
```

```
          printf ( "bytes occupied by 7.0 = %d", sizeof ( 7.0 ) ) ;
      }
```

(6)   main( )
```
      {
          char ch = 291 ;
          printf ( "%d %d %c", 32770, ch, ch ) ;
      }
```

(7)   main( )
```
      {
          printf ( "%d %c\n" ) ;
          printf ( "%d %c\n" ) ;
      }
```

(8)   main( )
```
      {
          int a = 33000 ;
          float b = 3.4e100 ;
          printf ( "a = %d b = %f\n", a, b ) ;
          printf ( "%d %d", sizeof ( a ), sizeof ( b ) ) ;
      }
```

(9)   main( )
```
      {
          int a, b ;
          a = -3 - -3 ;
          b = -3 - -(-3) ;
          printf ( "a = %d b = %d", a, b ) ;
      }
```

(10)   main( )
```
      {
          int x ;
          x = 3 * 4 % 5 ;
          printf ( "x = %d", x ) ;
```

```
        }

(11)    main( )
        {
            int x ;
            x = 3 + 4 - 7 * 8 / 5 % 10 ;
            printf ( "x = %d", x ) ;
        }

(12)    main( )
        {
            int x ;
            x = -3 + 4 - 7 * 8 / 5 % 10 ;
            printf ( "x = %d", x ) ;
        }

(13)    main( )
        {
            int x ;
            x = 4 % 5 + 6 % 5 ;
            printf ( "x = %d", x ) ;
        }

(14)    main( )
        {
            int x ;
            x = -3 * -4 % -6 / -5 ;
            printf ( "x = %d", x ) ;
        }

(15)    main( )
        {
            printf ( "%d ", 4 / 3 ) ;
            printf ( "%d ", 4 / -3 ) ;
            printf ( "%d ", -4 / 3 ) ;
            printf ( "%d ", -4 / -3 ) ;
```

```
        }

(16)    main( )
        {
            printf ( "%d ", 4 % 3 ) ;
            printf ( "%d ", 4 % -3 ) ;
            printf ( "%d ", -4 % 3 ) ;
            printf ( "%d ", -4 % -3 ) ;
        }

(17)    main( )
        {
            float a = 5, b = 2 ;
            int c ;
            c = a % b ;
            printf ( "%d", c ) ;
        }

(18)    main( )
        {
            int x ;
            x = 3 ** 4 - 7 ^ 8 ;
            printf ( "x = %d", x ) ;
        }

(19)    main( )
        {
            int g = 300 * 300 / 300 ;
            printf ( "g = %d", g ) ;
        }

(20)    main( )
        {
            float a = 1.5 ;
            int b = 3 ;
            a = b / 2 + b * 8 / b - b + a / 3 ;
```

```
            printf ( "a = %f", a ) ;
      }


(21)  main( )
      {
            int i = 3, a = 4, n ;
            float t = 4.2 ;
            n = a * a / i + i / 2 * t + 2 + t ;
            printf ( "n = %d", n ) ;
      }


(22)  main( )
      {
            int q = 2, d = 3, st ;
            st = q * d / 4 - 12 / 12 + 12 / 3 * 16 / d ;
            printf ( "st = %d", st ) ;
      }


(23)  main( )
      {
            int a, b ;
            a = 5.999999 ;
            b = 5.000001 ;
            printf ( "a = %d b = %d", a, b ) ;
      }


(24)  main( )
      {
            float a ;
            a = 4 / 2 ;
            printf ( "%f %f", a, 4 / 2 ) ;
      }


(25)  main( )
      {
            printf ( "%d %f\n", 4, 4 ) ;
```

```
        printf ( "%d %f\n", 4.0, 4.0 ) ;
    }

(26)  main( )
    {
        float a = 4 ;
        int i = 2 ;
        printf ( "%f %d", i / a, i / a ) ;
        printf ( "%d %f", i / a, i / a ) ;
    }

(27)  main( )
    {
        printf ( "%d ", sizeof ( 4 ) / sizeof ( 2.0 ) ) ;
        printf ( "%d ", sizeof ( 2.0 ) / sizeof ( 4 ) ) ;
    }

(28)  main( )
    {
        printf ( "nn \n\n nn\n" ) ;
        printf ( "nn /n/n nn/n" ) ;
    }

(29)  main( )
    {
        int p, q ;
        scanf ( "Enter values of p and q %d %d", &p, &q ) ;
        printf ( "p = %d q = %d", p, q ) ;
    }

(30)  main( )
    {
        int a, b ;
        printf ( "Enter values of a and b " ) ;
        scanf ( " %d %d ", &a, &b ) ;
        printf ( "a = %d b = %d", a, b ) ;
```

```
        }

(31)    main( )
        {
                int p, q ;
                printf ( "Enter values of p and q " ) ;
                scanf ( "%d\n\n%d", &p, &q ) ;
                printf ( "p = %d q = %d", p, q ) ;
        }

(32)    main( )
        {
                int p, q ;
                printf ( "Enter values of p and q " ) ;
                scanf ( "%d %d", p, q ) ;
                printf ( "p = %d q = %d", p, q ) ;
        }

(33)    main( )
        {
                /* This program attempts to find what happens when
                integer range /* -32768 to +32767 */ is exceeded */

                int a = 330000 ;
                float b = 3.4e100 ;
                printf ( "a = %d b = %f\n", a, b ) ;
        }

(34)    main( )
        {
                printf ( "Menu is a list of options you have at a \
        particular point in a program. It is just \
        like a restaurant menu - everything has a \
        misleading name and what you want is never \
        available." ) ;
        }
```

[E]   Attempt the following:

(1)   Write a program to round off an integer **i** to the next largest multiple of another integer **j**. For example, 256 days when rounded off to the next largest multiple divisible by a week results into 259.

(2)   Temperature of a city in farenheit degrees is entered through the keyboard. Write a program to convert and print the temperature in centigrade degrees.

(3)   Two variables **a** and **b** contain values 10 and 20. Write a program to interchange the contents of **a** and **b** without using a third variable.

(4)   Write a program to find out how many days and how many weeks have passed between the dates 01/01/92 to 31/05/92. Also find out how many days could not get evened out into weeks.

Answers

Answers to [A]

(1)   Dennis Ritchie, 1972, American Telegraph & Telecommunication's Bell Laboratories

(2)   1011111010, 1372, 2FA

The way to convert a decimal number to binary, octal or hexadecimal is as shown in Figure 1.4. Take the case of conversion to binary first. Since binary numbering system is a base 2 numbering system, we carry out divisions successively by 2 till we get a zero. The remainders obtained, when written in reverse direction yield the binary equivalent. Similar procedure is carried out for conversion to octal and hexadecimal, only difference being instead of 2 we carry out divisions by 8 and 16 respectively for octal and hex. Also note that octal numbering system is a base 8 numbering system, and hence any number in this system is built as a combination of digits 0 to 7. Similarly, hex is a base 16 numbering system, and any number in hex is constructed using 16 digits 0 to 9 and A to F (A being 10 and F being 15).

Once we have obtained the binary equivalent there is a simpler and faster way of obtaining the octal and hexadecimal equivalent. Let us first convert 1011111010 to octal. All that we need to do is pick up 3 digits at a time (from right to left) and then go on writing their octal equivalents as shown below.

```
1 011 111 010
1  3   7   2
```

For example, octal equivalent of 010 is 2, whereas octal equivalent of 111 is 7 and so on.

The same method can be used to conver 011111010 to its
hex equivalent. Only difference being this time we would take
4 digits at a time. This is shown below.

10 1111 1010
2 F   A

2	762			8	762			16	762	
2	381	0		8	95	2		16	47	A
2	190	1		8	11	7		16	2	F
2	95	0		8	1	3			0	2
2	47	1			0	1				
2	23	1								
2	11	1								
2	5	1								
2	2	1								
2	1	0								
	0	1								

Figure 1.4

(3)   32 characters

This maximum allowable width changes from compiler to
compiler. Some compilers like Turbo C allow the user to set
this maximum width through its Integrated Development Environment (IDE) by selecting items from the menu in the
order: Options, Compiler, Source, Identifier length.

(4)   alphabet

(5)   sensitive. This means that variables **sal**, **Sal** and **SAL** would
be treated as different variables in C.

(6)   only one character. In fact, if we execute the following statements, what gets stored in variable **ch** is not really the character constant, but the ascii value of 'A', which is 65.

```
char ch ;
ch = 'A' ;
```

Answers to **[B]**

gross-salary   -   Because a minus (-) is not allowed in the variable name. However an underscore (_) is acceptable.

salary of emp   -   Because spaces are not allowed within a variable name. Thus, **salaryofemp** would have been acceptable.

avg.   -   Because a '.' is not allowed in the variable name.

Answers to **[C]**

0x12.45   -   Because C accepts only integers in octal and hexadecimal numbering systems, not **float**s.

0xfgff   -   Because 'g' cannot be a part of a hexadecimal number. Only alphabets allowed in a hex number are a to f, or A to F.

Answers to **[D]**

(1)   *Output*

72 58 114 114

Explanation

C accepts integer constants in three numbering systems - decimal, octal and hexadecimal. To differentiate between the three, C specifies that the octal integer must be preceded by a 0, whereas a hex integer must be preceded by 0x or 0X.

In this example, we are printing 072, 0x72 and 0X72 using **%d**. **%d** specifies that the value should be printed as a decimal numbering system integer (hence the **d**). Therefore, decimal equivalents of octal 072, hex 0x72 and 0X72 get printed.

(2)   *Output*

72 110 48

Explanation

Here **%d** prints out as a decimal number, whereas **%o** prints octal equivalent of 72 and **%x** prints hexadecimal equivalent of 72.

(3)   *Output*

```
bytes occupied by ch = 1
bytes occupied by a = 2
bytes occupied by b = 4
```

Explanation

sizeof is an operator which yields the memory occupied (in bytes) by its argument. In C, a **char** is always 1 byte long, an **int** is always 2 bytes long, and a **float** is always 4 bytes long. Hence the output.

(4)   *Output*

char occupies 1 bytes
int occupies 2 bytes
float occupies 4 bytes

Explanation

sizeof is an operator which yields the memory occupied by its argument in bytes. **sizeof** can take as its argument not only variables (as shown in the previous example), but also the datatypes themselves. Output, as expected, would be 1, 2 and 4, confirming the fact that in C, a **char** is always 1 byte long, an **int** is always 2 bytes long, and a **float** is always 4 bytes long.

(5)   *Output*

bytes occupied by '7' = 2
bytes occupied by 7 = 2
bytes occupied by 7.0 = 8

Explanation

A small surprise! Size of '7' is reported as 2. How come? Because when we say '7', we are really specifying the ascii value of 7, which is 55, an integer, and hence its size is 2. The second output is as expected - an integer 7 being reported as occupying 2 bytes in memory. Third output is of course unexpected. We were really expecting 4 instead of 8. This so happens because a floating point constant by default is stored as an 8 byte number. The same floating point constant, if stored in a **float** variable, would be stored as a 4 byte number. Consider the following example.

```
float a = 0.7 ;
printf ( "%d %d", sizeof ( a ), sizeof ( 0.7 ) ) ;
```

Here the output would be 4 and 8, confirming the fact mentioned above.

(6)   *Output*

-32766 35 #

Explanation

32770 falls outside the integer range (-32768 to +32767) hence goes to the other side and becomes an appropriate negative number (-32766) which gets printed.

Same thing happens to 291, which also falls outside the range of **char** (-128 to +127), hence goes to the other side and becomes 35, which is then printed. The third output is the hash character. This is nothing but the character corresponding to ascii value 35. %c always prints the character corresponding to the ascii value.

(7)   *Output*

-22 A
-22 A

Explanation

Here, even though we have not supplied any variables to **printf( )**, still some garbage integers (for %d) and characters (for %c) get printed. This is however true only of characters and integers. For example try the following statement:

```
printf ( "%f %f" ) ;
```

This statement gets compiled, but during run-time it flashes the error message: printf: floating point formats not linked, Abnormal program termination.

(8)   *Output*

```
a = -32536 b = +INF
2 4
```

Explanation

33000 exceeds the valid integer range, whereas 3.4e100 exceeds the valid float range. In the first case the number from the other side of the range is picked up, which in this case turns out to be -32536. However, in case of 3.4e100 the **printf( )** simply prints out +INF, which should be read as 'plus infinity', telling us that we are going beyond the valid **float** range on positive side. If we attempt to print out - 3.4e100, **printf( )** would output -INF.

Whether the range is exceeded or not, the number of bytes occupied by variables **a** and **b** in memory remains unchanged - 2 for an **int** and 4 for a **float**.

(9)   *Output*

```
a = 0 b = -6
```

Explanation

'Minus of minus is plus'. This is true in usual arithmetic, so also in C. Hence **-3 - -3** becomes **-3 + 3**, which is equal to 0, and is assigned to variable **a**. Similarly, while evaluating the next statement, **-(-3)** becomes **+3** and therefore the statement gets reduced to **-3 - +3**, which is equal to **-6**. This **-6** is assigned to variable **b**. The values of **a** and **b** are then outputted through **printf( )**.

(10) *Output*

    x = 2

Explanation

The first operation performed here is multiplication, which yields 12. And then **12 % 5** is performed, which yields the remainder 2. This 2 is assgined to the variable **x** and then printed out.

(11) *Output*

    x = 6

Explanation

While evaluating an expression, the order in which the operations are performed depends upon the priority of operators involved. In this example, the operations are performed in the order *****, **/**, **%**, **+** and **-**. Thus, the evaluation proceeds as follows:

x = 3 + 4 - 56 / 5 % 10	operation : *
x = 3 + 4 - 11 % 10	operation : /
x = 3 + 4 - 1	operation : %
x = 7 - 1	operation : +
x = 6	operation : -

Note that **56 / 5** yields 11, since 56 and 5 both are integers, and hence must yield an integer on performing any arithmetic operation on them.

(12) *Output*

x = 0

Explanation

Here, the unary - gets the highest priority while evaluation, followed by *****, **/**, **%**, **+** and the binary minus. Stepwise, these operations would be performed as follows:

x = -3 + 4 - 7 * 8 / 5 % 10	operation : unary minus
x = -3 + 4 - 56 / 5 % 10	operation : *
x = -3 + 4 - 11 % 10	operation : /
x = -3 + 4 - 1	operation : %
x = 1 - 1	operation : +
x = 0	operation : -

(13) *Output*

x = 5

Explanation

% has a higher priority than **+**. But in the above expression which **%** gets the priority? The one which occurs earlier. Thus **4 % 5** is performed before **6 % 5**. **4 % 5** yields 4, whereas **6 % 5** yields 1, which when added results into 5, which is assigned to **x**.

(14) *Output*

x = 0

Explanation

Going by priorities of evaluating arithmetic expressions, firstly the unary minuses are bound to their operands. This would make 3 as -3, 4 as -4, 6 as -6 and 5 as -5. This is followed by *, % and /. The step-by- step evaluation is shown below.

x = -3 * -4 % -6 / -5	operation : unary minuses
x = 12 % -6 / -5	operation : *
x = 0 / -5	operation : %
x = 0	operation : /

(15) *Output*

1 -1 -1 1

Explanation

On dividing two integers we always get an integer. If you imbibe this fact, then the above program is a breeze. **4 / 3** will result into 1, and not 1.333333. Whenever either the numerator or denominator is negative, the answer will be negative. If both are negative, then they cancel out, and the answer would be positive.

(16) *Output*

1 1 -1 -1

Explanation

% operator always returns the remainder on dividing the first integer by the second. If one of them is negative, then the result takes the sign of the numerator. Once these facts sink in, the above output is fairly straight-forward.

(17) *Output*

Error message: Illegal use of floating point in function main.

Explanation

The **%** operator works only on integers, never on **floats**. Here we are using it with **float**s **a** and **b**. Hence the error message.

(18) *Output*

Error message: Invalid indirection

Explanation

The culprits here are ****** and **^**. Unlike many other languages where exponentiation operator (usually ****** or **^**) is available, C doesn't offer this facility. An omission which seems all the more surprising when weighed against the fact that C offers as many as 45 operators!

(19) *Output*

g = 81

Explanation

On first analysis, we would have expected the output to be 300. But then the least that C langauge does is spring surprises on you when you least expect them.. forcing you to analyse things a little more carefully. Here, on actually carrying out the multiplication (**300 * 300**), the result exceeds the range of integers (-32768 to +32767), hence goes to the other side and becomes an appropriate number, which is certainly not 300. Hence, dividing this number by 300 doesn't yield 300.

(20)   *Output*

6.500000

Explanation

Steps involved in the evaluation of the expression are given below. Note the following points carefully:

(a)   An operation between an **int** and an **int** would result into an **int**. Thus, 3 / 2 would give 1 and not 1.5.

(b)   An operation between a **float** and an **int** would result into a **float**.

Let us first replace the variables in the expression by their values and then proceed with evaluation.

a = 3 / 2 + 3 * 8 / 3 - 3 + 1.5 / 3	
a = 1 + 3 * 8 / 3 - 3 + 1.5 / 3	operation : /
a = 1 + 24 / 3 - 3 + 1.5 / 3	operation : *
a = 1 + 8 - 3 + 1.5 / 3	operation : /
a = 1 + 8 - 3 + 0.5	operation : /
a = 9 - 3 + 0.5	operation : +
a = 6 + 0.5	operation : -
a = 6.5	operation : +

(21) *Output*

n = 15

Explanation

As in the previous example, let us first replace the variables with their actual values and then evaluate the expression step by step.

n = 4 * 4 / 3 + 3 / 2 * 4.2 + 2 + 4.2
n = 16 / 3 + 3 / 2 * 4.2 + 2 + 4.2   operation : *
n = 5 + 3 / 2 * 4.2 + 2 + 4.2   operation : /
n = 5 + 1 * 4.2 + 2 + 4.2   operation : /
n = 5 + 4.2 + 2 + 4.2   operation : *
n = 9.2 + 2 + 4.2   operation : +
n = 11.2 + 4.2   operation : +
n = 15.4   operation : +

When 15.4 is to be assigned to **n**, it is demoted to 15 before assignment, because **n** is an **int**, and hence can hold only integer values.

(22) *Output*

st = 21

Explanation

Replacing the values of variables in the expression, we get,

st = 2 * 3 / 4 - 12 / 12 + 12 / 3 * 16 / 3

Let us now evaluate the expression, keeping in mind the priorities of operators and integer and **float** conversion rules.

st = 6 / 4 - 12 / 12 + 12 / 3 * 16 / 3	operation : *
st = 1 - 12 / 12 + 12 / 3 * 16 / 3	operation : /
st = 1 - 1 + 12 / 3 * 16 / 3	operation : /
st = 1 - 1 + 4 * 16 / 3	operation : /
st = 1 - 1 + 64 / 3	operation : *
st = 1 - 1 + 21	operation : /
st = 0 + 21	operation : -
st = 21	operation : +

(23) *Output*

a = 5 b = 5

Explanation

Whenever a floating point value is assigned to an integer variable, the fractional part is always truncated, and never rounded off to the next integer. Thus, 5.999999 as well as 5.000001, both are truncated to 5 when assigned to integer variables, **a** and **b**, which are then printed out.

(24) *Output*

2.000000 -1.4746701e+308

Explanation

4 / 2 evaluates to ⌐, and when assigned to **a**, a **float** variable, is promoted to 2.000000. Value of **a** is printed correctly by **printf( )**. Where **printf( )** falters is while printing the result of **4 / 2**. The reason is, **4 / 2** evaluates to 2, which is an integer and we are attempting to print this integer using **%f**. Hence the erratic behaviour. Moral is, do not rely on the format specifications in **printf( )** to carry out the conversions. Do them explicitly through the assignment statements.

(25) *Output*

    4 512.000001
    0 4.000000

Explanation

In the first **printf( )**, the first output (i.e. 4) is alright but the second one, 512.000001, is unexpected. Reason is, we left it to **printf( )** to first convert 4 to 4.0 and then print it out as a **float** using **%f**. And here lies the mistake. The **printf( )** is not intelligent enough to perform this conversion properly, and hence we get the absurd result. Same is the story of the second **printf( )**. Here, the first output is faulty, whereas the second is as expected. Once again for the same reasons - a misplaced trust in **printf( )** to carry out the conversion before printing.

(26) *Output*

    0.500000 0
    0 0.000000

Explanation

When the first division in the **printf( )** takes place, since **i** is an integer and **a** a **float**, **i** is first promoted to **float**. Thus, the actual division takes place between 2.000000 and 4.000000, which yields 0.500000, which is printed out. In the second division also, the result is 0.500000, but since it is being printed out using **%d**, on conversion it turns out to be 0.

If the first **printf( )**'s output is 0.500000 and 0, then its natural for us to expect the second **printf( )**'s output to be 0 0.500000. However, the results above do not confirm this. The reason is, once **printf( )** messes up one conversion the output of the subsequent variables to be printed in that **printf( )** are likely to get messed up too.

(27) *Output*

0 4

Explanation

sizeof (4) would yield 2, whereas **sizeof (2.0)** would yield 8. Therefore, the **printf( )**s are reduced to,

printf ("%d ", 2 / 8) ;
printf ("%d ", 8 / 2) ;

which results into 0 and 4, which are then printed out. Notice that in **2/8**, since both are integers, the result is an integer.

Also notice that a **float** variable occupies 4 bytes in memory, whereas a floating point constant by default is stored as an 8 byte number.

(28) *Output*

nn

nn
nn /n/n nn/n

Explanation

The output highlights the difference between a **\n** and a **/n**. A **\n**, when used in **printf( )**, ensures that the subsequent output goes to the next line. As against this, a **/n** is treated as two ordinary characters, and if they occur in **printf( )**, they are outputted as they are on the screen. Once this difference is understood, the above output would appear quite logical.

(29) *Output*

p = 1562 q = 1686

Explanation

We got the above result when we entered 10 and 20 as values of **p** and **q**. Surprising? This so happens because of the message 'Enter val.... q' written inside the **scanf( )**, due to which it behaves erratically. To get rid of the problem, either we should drop the message from **scanf( )**, since it is serving no mean-ingful purpose, or while entering the values, before the values we must type the message through the keyboard as it is. For example, if we supply through the keyboard the following to **scanf( )**, it would match the message with the message in **scanf( )** and ignore it, whereas it would store 10 and 20 in **p** and **q**.

Enter values of p and q 10 20

(30) *Output*

No output

Explanation

The **scanf( )** just doesn't seem to work. Once again the reason is the spaces immediately after the '"' and the spaces immediately before the '"'. **scanf**( ) works in a peculiar way if you write anything other than format specifications like **%d %c %f** within the " ". If it finds anything other than format specfications (even spaces), then it expects the same characters to be typed through the keyboard, such that it can match them with the ones in the format string, and ignore them. Thus, if we supply the input as follows, the **scanf**( ) would work correctly.

\<space>\<space>10 20\<space>\<space>

Since this seems to be quite unnecessary, we can make a ground rule that in the format string of **scanf**( ), do not write anything except the format specifications. However, spaces, if they occur between two format specfications, do not create any kind of problem.

(31) *Output*

Enter values of p and q 10 20
p = 10 q = 20

Explanation

If between two format specifications of **scanf**( ), anything other than spaces, **\ns** or **\ts** occurs, then the **scanf**( ) doesn't work as expected. However, any number of spaces, **\ns** or **\ts** between two format specifications would not mess up the working of **scanf**( ), irrespective of whether we supply values in the same line, on different lines, separate them by tabs, or any other such format.

(32) *Output*

Enter values of p and q 11 12
p = 105 q = 1666

Explanation

When we supplied the values as 11 and 12, we got the above result. The reason for this absurd result is the missing **&** before the variables used in **scanf( )**. **&** before the variables is a must. The reason for this can be understood only after we learn pointers.

(33) *Output*

Error message: Expression syntax in function main

Explanation

A comment cannot occur within another comment. And this is what has been done in our program. Hence the compilation error. In other words, nested or embedded comments are not acceptable in C.

(34) *Output*

Menu is a list of options you have at a particular point in a program. It is just like a restaurant menu - everything has a misleading name and what you want is never available.

Explanation

printf( ) can be split over multiple lines. However, at the end of each line, it is necessary to give a '\', which tells the compiler that what follows on the next line is the continuation of the previous line.

Solutions to **[E]**

(1) *Program*

```
main( )
{
    int i, j, k ;

    printf ( "\nEnter values of i and j " ) ;
    scanf ( "%d %d", &i, &j ) ;

    k = i + j - i % j ;

    printf ( "\nNext largest multiple = %d", k ) ;
}
```

Sample run

```
Enter values of i and j 256 7
Next largest multiple = 259
```

Explanation

Suppose value of **i** and **j** are entered as 256 and 7, then **k** evaluates to 259 which is the next largest multiple of 7 after 256.

(2) *Program*

```
main( )
{
    float f, c ;

    printf ( "Enter temperature in farenheit degrees " ) ;
    scanf ( "%f", &f ) ;

    c = 5 / 9.0 * ( f - 32) ;
    printf ( "Temp. in centigrade degrees = %f", c ) ;
}
```

Sample run

```
Enter temperature in farenheit degrees 212
Temp. in centigrade degrees = 100.000000
```

Explanation

Once the temperature in farenheit degrees is entered through the keyboard, all that we have to do is apply the standard formula to get the temperature in centigrade degrees. The only catch here is, while using the formula is it necessary to use 9.0, or 9 would do? If we use 9, then irrespective of what is the value of **f**, **c** would always turn out to be 0. This is because 5 and 9 both are integers, and hence must always return an integer. Therefore **5 / 9** would yield 0. To avoid this integer division we use 9.0, such that before division 5 would get promoted to 5.0 and then **5.0 / 9.0** would be evaluated, which would return a **float** value. This **float** value is then multiplied by the result of (**f - 32**), and the answer is stored in **c**, which is ultimately printed out.

(3) *Program*

```
main( )
{
    int a = 10, b = 20 ;

    printf ( "Before interchanging\n" ) ;
    printf ( "a = %d b = %d", a, b ) ;

    a = a + b ;
    b = a - b ;
    a = a - b ;

    printf ( "\nAfter interchanging\n" ) ;
```

```
        printf ( "a = %d b = %d", a, b ) ;
}
```

Sample run

Before interchanging
a = 10 b = 20
After interchanging
a = 20 b = 10

Explanation

To begin with, we initialise variables **a** and **b** to values 10 and 20. The **printf( )** then prints out these values. Then come the three arithmetic statements. **a = a + b** stores 30 in **a**. Thus, the next statement **b = a - b** becomes **b = 30 - 20**, yielding 10, which is assigned to **b**. Then **a = a - b** is executed, which is equivalent to **a = 30 - 10**. Therefore 20 is assigned to **a**. Having thus interchanged the contents, the interchanged values are displayed using **printf( )**.

(4) *Program*

```
main( )
{
    int days, weeks, leftoverdays ;

    days = 31 + 29 + 31 + 30 + 31
    weeks = days / 7 ;
    leftoverdays = days % 7 ;

    printf ( "days = %d", days ) ;
    printf ( "weeks = %d", weeks ) ;
    printf ( "left over days = %d", leftoverdays ) ;
}
```

Sample run

```
days = 152
weeks = 21
left over days = 5
```

Explanation

Calculation of **days** is straightforward. To calculate **weeks**, we divide **days** by 7, whereas to calculate **leftoverdays**, we use the modulus operator. This is because while calculating **leftoverdays**, we are not interested in the quotient, but in the remainder.

2

Steering the Control

E veryone of us is called upon to take decisions in the face of changing circumstances. If there is a good movie on TV I would stay at home; if I get a visa I would fly next month; if you do it so would I. Put all these statements in spotlight and you will notice that the decisions depend on certain conditions being met.

C, too, must be able to perform different sets of actions depending on the circumstances. C has three major decision making media:

(a)   **if-else** statement
(b)   **switch** statement
(c)   Conditional operators

In this chapter we will examine the **if-else** and the conditional operators. Figure 2.1 shows the **if-else** at work. From the figure one can observe that if the condition after **if** is satisfied one set of statements gets executed, otherwise a different set of instructions gets executed.

But how do we express the condition itself in C? And how do we evaluate its truth or falsity? As a general rule, we express a condition using C's Relational operators. The relational operators allow us to compare two values to see whether they are equal to each other, unequal, or whether one is greater than the other. The various relational operators are shown in Figure 2.2.

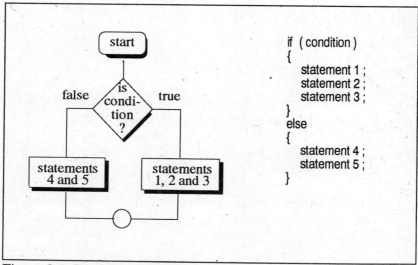

Figure 2.1 Working of **if-else**

this expression	is true if
x == y	x is equal to y
x != y	x is not equal to y
x < y	x is less than y
x > y	x is greater than y
x <= y	x is less than or equal to y
x >= y	x is greater than or equal to y

Figure 2.2 Relational operators

Points to Note

A few tips are in order:

(a) Whenever a condition is evaluated in C, it is given a value 1 if the condition is satisfied, and 0 if it is not satisfied.

(b) Any non-zero number is always treated as truth, whereas a zero is treated as falsity.

(c) The group of statements after the **if**, upto and not including the **else** is known as the "if block". Similary, the statements after the else form the "else block".

(d) If there is only one statement in the **if** block then the pair of braces can be dropped.

(e) If there is only one statement in the **else** block then the pair of braces can be dropped.

(f) If there is no statement to be executed in the **else** block then the keyword **else** can also be dropped.

(g) It is perfectly valid to write an entire **if-else** construct within an **if** block or an **else** block. This is called 'nesting'.

(h) More than one condition can be combined together using logical operators **&&** (AND), **||** (OR), **!** (NOT). For example,

```
if ( ( per >= 50 ) && ( per < 60 ) )
    printf ( "Second division" ) ;
```

On execution, 'Second division' would be printed if both conditions, (**per >= 50**) as well as (**per < 60**) evaluate to

true. Even if one of the conditions evaluates to false, then the
printf( ) would not be executed.

Let us look at another example:

```
if ( ( code >= i && key == 5 ) || ( code < 5 && val == 1 ) )
    printf ( "Whisky is Risky" ) ;
```

Here there are four conditions being checked. They have been
split into two groups by the || operator. "Whisky is Risky"
would be printed if any one group evaluates to true. In each
group there are two conditions separated by **&&** operator. For
each group to evaluate to true, both the conditions in the group
must be satisfied.

(i)   The **!** operator reverses the value of the expression it operates
on. It makes a true expression false and a false expression true.
Consider the following example.

```
! ( y < 10 )
```

This is read as "not y less than 10". In other words, if **y** is less
than 10, the expression will be false, since (**y < 10**) is true.
We can express the same condition as (**y >= 10**).

The **!** operator is often used to reverse the logical value of a
single variable, as in the expression,

```
if ( ! flag )
```

which is same as saying

```
if ( flag == 0 )
```

(j)   Your understanding of complex conditions using **&&, ||** and **!**
can be improved if you follow the following figure step by step.
It summarizes the usage of **&&, ||** and **!**.

Operands		Results			
x	y	!x	!y	x && y	x ‖ y
0	0	1	1	0	0
0	non-zero	1	0	0	0
non-zero	0	0	1	0	1
non-zero	non-zero	0	0	1	1

Figure 2.3 Logical operators

Hierarchy of Logical Operators

Since we have now added the logical operators to the list of operators that we know, it is probably time to review all these operators and their priorities. Figure 2.4 summarizes the operators we have learnt so far. The higher an operator is in the table, the higher is its priority. A full-fledged precedence table is given in Chapter 3.

But can arithmetic operators and logical operators be combined in a statement? Yes, as shown below:

```
a = ( y != 3 ) && ( 3 + 4 > x ) ;

if ( a == 4 || ( b = x + y > 3 ) )
    printf ( "C it for yourself" ) ;

if ( x || y && ( a + b >= c * d / e ) )
    printf ( "Foxed?" ) ;
```

Operators	Type
!	Logical NOT
* / %	Arithmetic and modulus
+ -	Arithmetic
< > <= >=	Relational
== !=	Relational
&& ||	Logical AND and OR
=	Assignment

Figure 2.4 Hierarchy of operators

The Conditional Operators

The conditional operators **?** and **:** are sometimes called ternary operators since they take three arguments. Their general form is:

```
expression 1 ? expression 2 : expression 3
```

What this expression says is: "if **expression 1** is true (that is, if its value is non-zero), then the value returned will be **expression 2**, otherwise the value returned will be **expression 3**".

Consider the following example.

```
y = ( x > 5 ? 3 : 4 ) ;
```

This statement will store 3 in **y** if **x** is greater than 5, otherwise it will store 4 in **y**.

The following points may be noted about the conditional operators:

(a)   Its not necessary that the conditional operators should be used only in arithmetic statements. This is illustrated in the following examples:

```
( k == 1 ? printf ( "Amit" ) : printf ( "All and sundry" ) ) ;
printf( "%c" , ( a >= 'a' ? a : '!') ) ;
```

(b)   The conditional operators can be nested.

```
big = ( a > b ? ( a > c ? 3 : 4 ) : ( b > c ? 6 : 8 ) ) ;
```

(c)   The limitation of the conditional operators is that after the **?** or after the **:** only one C statement can occur.

Exercise

[A] What will be the output of the following programs:

(1)
```
main( )
{
    int x = 10, y = 5, p, q ;
    p = x > 9 ;
    q = x > 3 && y != 3 ;
    printf ( "p = %d q = %d", p, q ) ;
}
```

(2)
```
main( )
{
    int a = 30, b = 40, x ;
    x = ( a != 10 ) && ( b = 50 ) ;
    printf ( "x = %d", x ) ;
}
```

(3)
```
main( )
{
    int a = 100, b = 200, c ;
    c = ( a == 100 || b > 200 ) ;
    printf ( "c = %d", c ) ;
}
```

(4)
```
main( )
{
    int x = 11, y = 6, z ;
    z = x == 5 || y != 4 ;
    printf ( "z = %d", z ) ;
}
```

(5)
```
main( )
{
```

```
        int a = 300, b = 10, c = 20 ;
        if ( !( a >= 400 ) )
            b = 300 ;
        c = 200 ;
        printf ( "b = %d c = %d", b, c ) ;
    }
```

(6)   main( )
```
    {
        int a = 500, b = 100, c ;
        if ( ! a >= 400 )
            b = 300 ;
        c = 200 ;
        printf ( "b = %d c = %d", b, c ) ;
    }
```

(7)   main( )
```
    {
        int x = 10, y = 100 % 90 ;
        if ( x != y ) ;
            printf ( "x = %d y = %d", x, y ) ;
    }
```

(8)   main( )
```
    {
        int x = 10, y = -20 ;
        x = !x ;
        y = !y ;
        printf ( "x = %d y = %d\n", x, y ) ;
    }
```

(9)   main( )
```
    {
        int x = 0, y = 1 ;
        y = !x ;
        x = !y ;
```

```
            printf ( "x = %d y = %d\n", x, y ) ;
        }

(10)    main( )
        {
            if ( ! 3.14 )
                printf ( "I have robbed and killed..." ) ;
            else
                printf ( "Until my evil purse was filled" ) ;
        }

(11)    main( )
        {
            int x = 3, y = 4, z = 4 ;
            printf ( "ans = %d", z >= y && y >= x ? 1 : 0 ) ;
        }

(12)    main( )
        {
            int x = 3, y = 4, z = 4 ;
            printf ( "ans = %d", ( z >= y >= x ? 100 : 200 ) ) ;
        }

(13)    main( )
        {
            float a = 12.25, b = 13.65 ;
            if ( a = b )
                printf ( "a and b are equal" ) ;
            else
                printf ( "a and b are not equal" ) ;
        }

(14)    main( )
        {
            if ( 'Z' < 'z' )
                printf ( "Pilots are on strike..." ) ;
```

```
         else
              printf ( "for absolutely outlandish demands" ) ;
    }

(15) main( )
    {
         int x = 10 ;
         if x >= 2
              printf ( "%d\n", x ) ;
    }

(16) main( )
    {
         int i = 10, j = 40 ;
         if ( ( j - i ) % 10 )
              printf ( "man sees your actions.." ) ;
         else
              printf ( "god sees your motives.." ) ;
    }

(17) main( )
    {
         int i = -4, j, num = 10 ;
         j = i % -3 ;
         j = ( j ? 0 : num * num ) ;
         printf ( "j = %d", j ) ;
    }

(18) main( )
    {
         float a = 0.7 ;
         if ( a < 0.7 )
              printf ( "Stoned" ) ;
         else
              printf ( "Avenged" ) ;
    }
```

```
(19)  main( )
      {
            int i = 400 * 400 / 400 ;
            if ( i == 400 )
                printf ( "Filibusters" ) ;
            else
                printf ( "Sea gherkins" ) ;
      }

(20)  main( )
      {
            int k = 12, n = 30 ;
            k = ( k > 5 && n = 4 ? 100 : 200 ) ;
            printf ( "k = %d", k ) ;
      }

(21)  main( )
      {
            int c = 0, d = 5, e = 10, a ;
            a = c > 1 ? d > 1 || e > 1 ? 100 : 200 : 300 ;
            printf ( "a = %d", a ) ;
      }

(22)  main( )
      {
            int a = 10, b = 10 ;
            printf ( "ans = %d", a > b ? a * a : b / b ) ;
      }

(23)  main( )
      {
            int x = 10, y = 20 ;
            x = !x ;
            y = !x && !y ;
            printf ( "x = %d y = %d", x, y ) ;
      }
```

```
(24)   main( )
       {
            int x = 10, y = 20 ;
            if ( ! ( !x ) && x )
                 printf ( "x = %d", x ) ;
            else
                 printf ( "y = %d", y ) ;
       }

(25)   main( )
       {
            float a = 0.5, b = 0.9 ;
            if ( a && b > 0.9 )
                 printf ( "Idleness is a virtue.." ) ;
            else
                 printf ( "..so is stupidity!" ) ;
       }

(26)   main( )
       {
            int x = 100 ;
            if ( !!x )
                 printf ( "x = %d", !x ) ;
            else
                 printf ( "x = %d", x ) ;
       }
```

[B]   Improve the following programs by reorganising the statements:

```
(1)    main( )
       {
            int i = 10 ;
            if ( i > 10 )
                 ;
            else
```

```
                printf ( "Hello Cocaine!" ) ;
        }

(2)     main( )
        {
            int i = 5, j = 30, k = 5 ;
            if ( i < 30 )
            {
                if ( j < 20 )
                {
                    if ( k == 40 )
                        printf ( "Hi Computerist!" ) ;
                    else
                        ;
                }
                else
                    ;
            }
            else
                ;
        }
```

[C] Attempt the following:

(1) A semiconductor manufacturer sells three types of microprocessors: 8-bit, 16-bit and 32-bit. It differentiates between three types of customers: industry, government, and university. It has the following discount policy that depends on the type of microprocessor, the amount of order, and the type of customer:

For 32-bit microprocessor, if the order is for less than Rs. 50,000, allow 5 % discount to industrial customers and 6.5 % discount to the government agencies. If the order is Rs. 50,000 or more, a discount of 7.5 % and 8.5 % respectively is given to the industrial customers and the government agencies. A discount of 10 % is given to both industrial customers and government agencies if the order is more than Rs. 1,00,000. Universities get a discount of 7.5 % irrespective of the amount of order.

For 16-bit microprocessors, no discount is given for orders less than Rs 10,000. For orders of Rs 10,000 or more, 5 % discount is given to the industrial customers and universities, and 6 % discount is given to the government agencies.

For 8-bit microprocessors, a flat discount of 10 % is given to all the three types of customers for any order.

Write a program that reads the type of the customer, the type of the product, the amount of the order, and prints the net amount payable by the customer.

(2)   The following rules enable an insurance company to determine the type of motor-insurance to issue, and the cost of the premium with any excesses to its clients.

If the age of the driver is 25 years or more, the car is manufactured in India and the accident record of the car is good, the premium charged is 6 % of the declared value of the car and a comprehensive policy is issued. If the accident record is not good, the premium is raised to 7 %, the policy holder pays the first 100 rupees of a claim and a comprehensive policy is issued.

If the age of the driver is 25 years or more, the car is not manufactured in India and the accident record of the car is good, the policy holder pays first 100 rupees of any claim and a comprehensive policy of 6 % premium is issued. If the above conditions apply except that the accident record is not good, the premium is raised to 7 % and a third party policy is issued.

If the age of the driver is less than 25 years, the car is manufactured in India and the accident record of the car is good, the premium charged is 6 % of the declared value of the car and a comprehensive policy is issued with the holder paying the first 100 rupees of a claim.

If the age of the driver is less than 25 years, the car is not manufactured in India and the accident record of the car is good, the premium charged is 8 % of the declared value of the car, the policy holder pays the first 100 rupees of any claim and a comprehensive policy is issued. If the accident record is not good and all other conditions apply, then considering the risk, no policy car be taken out.

Assume that if a person has not had an accident in the last three years then the condition of the car is considered good. Write a program to output the following:

(a) type of motor insurance policy
(b) the amount of the premium
(c) excess payable on any claim if applicable

(3) A number is entered through the keyboard. The number may contain 1, 2, 3, 4, or 5 digits. Write a program to find the number of digits in the number

Answers

Answers to [A]

(1)   *Output*

p = 1 q = 1

Explanation

Since **x** is greater than 9, the condition evaluates to true. In C, while checking a condition if it evaluates to true, the result of the test is treated as 1 otherwise it is treated as 0. Hence **p** contains value 1.

In the statement.

q = x > 3 && y != 3 ,

the first condition evaluates to true, hence is replaced by 1. Similarly, second condition also evaluates to true and is replaced by 1. Since the conditions are combined using **&&** and since both are true, the result of the entire expression becomes 1, which is assigned to **q**.

(2)   *Output*

x = 1

Explanation

a != 10 evaluates to true and is replaced by 1. **b = 50** uses an assignment operator (=), hence 50 is assigned to **b**. Therefore the condition becomes, x = 1 && 50

Since 1 and 50 both are truth values (any non-zero number is treated as truth in C), the result of the entire condition is truth, i.e. 1, which is assigned to **x**.

(3)   *Output*

c = 1

Explanation

Here the condition **a == 100** evaluates to true and is therefore replaced by 1. The two conditions **a == 100** and **b > 200** are combined using ‖ operator, and since the first condition evaluates to true, the second condition doesn't get tested at all. The truth value, 1, of the first condition is therefore assigned to **c**.

(4)   *Output*

z = 1

Explanation

The first condition **x == 5** fails since value of **x** is 11, and is therefore replaced by a 0. However, the second condition is true, and is replaced by 1. Therefore the statement gets reduced to,

z = 0 ‖ 1

Since the conditions are combined using ‖ operator and since one of them is true (second one), the whole thing is treated as true and hence 1 is assigned to **z**.

(5) *Output*

b = 300 c = 200

Explanation

The condition (**a >= 400**) evaluates to false since **a** is neither equal to nor greater than 400. The condition is therefore replaced by 0. But the NOT operator (**!**) negates the result of this condition. This means it reverses the result of the condition (0) to 1. Thus the **if** gets reduced to,

```
if ( 1 )
    b = 300 ;
```

Obviously, **b = 300** would get executed, followed by **c = 200**, hence the output.

(6) *Output*

b = 100 c = 200

Explanation

According to precedence of operators in C, out of **!** and **>=**, **!** enjoys a higher priority. Therefore **!500** is performed first which makes it 0, which is then compared with 400. Since 0 is neither greater than nor equal to 400, the condition fails and the control straightaway jumps to the statement **c = 200**, following which it prints the values of **b** and **c**.

(7) *Output*

x = 10 y = 10

Explanation

Contrary to usual belief, the statement **y = 100 % 90** is perfectly acceptable. It means while declaring a variable, not only can it be initialised to a particular value, but also to an expression which on evaluation gives a value. In this case **100 % 90** is evaluated and the remainder obtained, i.e. 10, is assigned to **y**.

Since the variables **x** and **y** both have the same value the condition (**x != y**) fails. Therefore the control jumps to the **printf( )** and prints out values of **x** and **y**. Note that there is a ; after the **if**. This is called a null statement. Due to the ; the condition becomes:

```
if ( x != y )
    ;
printf ( "x = %d y = %d", x, y ) ;
```

(8)   *Output*

x = 0 y = 0

Explanation

! operator reverses the truth value to falsity and false value to truth. Here, since **x** to begin with has a truth value (10), it is negated to 0 by **!x** and then stored in **x**. Thus a 0 is stored in **x**. Same thing happens for the next statement. **!y** yields a 0 and this 0 is stored in **y**. Note that ! when applied to a non-zero negative or a non-zero positive value results into a 0.

(9)   *Output*

x = 0 y = 1

Explanation

To begin with **x** is zero, therefore **!x** would give 1, which is stored in **y**. This value of **y** is then negated, yielding 0 in the process which is stored in **x**.

(10) *Output*

Until my evil purse was filled

Explanation

3.14, being a positive number, is a truth value, and on negating it using the ! operator it results into a 0. Thus the result of the condition is false, hence the second **printf( )** is executed.

(11) *Output*

ans = 1

Explanation

Let us isolate the condition for closer examination.

z >= y && y >= x

If we replace the variables with their values, the condition becomes,

4 >= 4 && 4 >= 3

Since both the conditions are true and they have been combined using **&&**, the whole thing evaluates to true. This is deduced from the fact that truth **&&** truth

yields truth.

Thus the **printf( )** is reduced to,

printf ("ans = %d", truth ? 1 : 0) ;

Hence **ans = 1** gets printed. Note that conditional, relational or logical operators, or for that matter any other operators can occur in **printf( )** without any problem.

(12) *Output*

ans = 200

Explanation

Look carefully at the condition:

(z >= y >= x ? 100 : 200)

Here, first **z** is compared to **y** and the result of this condition is then compared with **x**. Since **z** and **y** are equal, the first condition is satisfied and is hence replaced by 1. Thus the condition is now reduced to,

(1 >= x ? 100 : 200)

Since 1 is neither greater than nor equal to the value of **x**, the condition fails and the conditional operators now go into action and yield 200, which is printed by **printf( )**.

(13) *Output*

a and b are equal

Explanation

To begin with **a** and **b** are not equal. The catch here is the assignment operator used in the **if** statement. It simply assigns the value of **b** to **a**, and hence the condition becomes,

if (13.65)

The condition evaluates to true since 13.65 being a non-zero positive constant is a truth value and hence executes the first **printf( )**.

(14) *Output*

Pilots are on strike...

Explanation

Any character enclosed within a pair of quotes is replaced by the ascii value of the character. For example, the ascii value of **Z** is 90 whereas that of **z** is 122. Thus the condition becomes,

if (90 < 122)

Since the condition is satisfied, 'Pilots...strike' gets printed.

(15) *Output*

Error message: if statement missing (in function main

Explanation

You guessed it right! What is missing is a pair of parentheses surrounding the condition, which Dennis Ritchie says is a must. The cryptic error message says that the **if** statement used in function **main( )** has a missing parentheses.

(16) *Output*

god sees your motives..

Explanation

This is quite straight-forward. **(j - i) % 10**, on substituting the values of **j** and **i**, becomes **(40 - 10) % 10**. That is **30 % 10**, which gives the remainder as 0. Thus the condition would now become,

if (0)

Since 0 is treated as falsity in C, the control reaches the second **printf( )** which prints out the philosophical message.

(17) *Output*

j = 0

Explanation

Look at the statement **j = i % -4**. On substituting the value of **i**, it becomes,

j = -4 % -3

Usual arithmetic would have prompted us to cancel the minus signs from numerator and denominator and then perform the division. But not C. In C, first division is carried out assuming that there are no signs and then the sign of the numerator is assigned to the remainder obtained. Thus **j** is assigned a value

-1. Then comes the statement involving conditional operators. Here **j** is checked for truth or falsity. Since **j** is -1, it is treated as truth and hence 0 is assigned to **j**, which is printed out through **printf( )**.

(18) *Output*

Stoned

Explanation

The output is very surprising! 0.7 is never less than 0.7, so the condition should evaluate to false. But that doesn't happen. Reason is, when 0.7 stored in **a**, due to precision considerations, it is stored as something less than 0.7. Naturally, when value stored in **a** is compared with 0.7, the condition evaluates to true and 'stoned' gets printed.

To get rid of this problem there are two solutions:

(a)   Declare **a** as a **long double** as shown below:

long double a ;

(b)   Typecast 0.7 to a **float** while comparing as shown below:

if (a < (float) 0.7)

Typecasting means converting to the specified datatype. For example, in the above condition 0.7 is converted from **long double** to a **float** before comparison.

Moral of the story is: exercise utmost care while comparing floating point values in an **if** statement.

(19) *Output*

Sea gherkins

Explanation

Can a variable be initialised to an expression? The answer is
yes. Thus the statement **int i = 400 * 400 / 400** is quite alright.
But on evaluating the expression it doesn't turn out to be 400.
Reason is, when **400 * 400** is done we don't get 160000 because
160000 falls outside the integer range (-32768 to +32767).
Whenever a number exceeds 32767, it goes to the negative side
and picks up the appropriate number. For example, 32768
would become -32768. Similarly, 32769 would become -
32767. Likewise, 32770 would become -32766 and so on.

Thus in our program **400 * 400** would exceed the integer range
and hence some appropriate number would be picked after
going to the other side of the range. When this number is
divided by 400 it would not yield 400. Naturally, the condition
would fail, and therefore 'Sea gherkins' would get printed.

(20) *Output*

Error message: Lvalue required in function main

Explanation

First let us understand the meaning of the word lvalue. An
lvalue is any variable whose value can change (have a new
value assigned to it). As against this, an **rvalue** is a variable
whose value cannot change. The easiest way to differentiate
between the two is to remember that an rvalue goes to the right
of the assignment operator, and an lvalue to the left.

Back to the current problem:

k = (k > 5 && n = 4 ? 100 : 200) ;

Go to the precedence table. It will tell you that **&&** enjoys a higher priority compared to the assignment operator **=**. Hence the condition becomes something like this,

(k > 5 && n) = 4

Naturally, this cannot be evaluated since the compiler will not know to which variable 4 should be assigned. And it certainly cannot assign it to the expression (**k > 5 && n**). In other words, there is no lvalue to which 4 can be assigned. Hence the error message 'Lvalue required in function main'.

The problem can be eliminated by parenthesising the condition as shown below:

k = (k > 5 && (n = 4) ? 100 : 200) ;

Here assignment gets a preference over **&&**, hence the problem of lvalue is avoided.

(21) *Output*

a = 300

Explanation

c > 1 fails since value of **c** is 0, and the control reaches 300 which is assigned to **a**. It would become easier to understand the statement if we parenthesise the expression as shown below.

a = (c > 1 ? (d > 1 || e > 1 ? 100 : 200) : 300) ;

Moral is, the conditional operators can be nested.

(22) *Output*

ans = 1

Explanation

No, this doesn't give an error message. Conditional operators can very well be used within **printf( )** statement. In fact, any other operators can also be used within **printf( )**.

Since the condition **a > b** fails, the statement after the :, i.e. **b / b** is evaluated and its result is printed by **printf( )**.

(23) *Output*

x = 0 y = 0

Explanation

! reverses the value of its operand. Thus !x becomes !20 which is equal to 0. This 0 is assigned to **x**. Consider the next statement:

y = !x && !y

Substituting the values of **x** and **y**, the statement becomes,

y = !0 && !20

!0 is 1 and **!20** is 0. Thus the statement is now,

y = 1 && 0

which evaluates to falsity and hence 0 is assigned to **y**.

(24) *Output*

x = 10

Explanation

Firstly (**!x**) is evaluated. Since **x** has a truth value (a non-zero positive value), **!** negates this value and yields a 0. Thus the condition is reduced to,

if (!(0) && x)

!(0) yields a 1. Note that the value of **x** is still 10, hence the condition becomes,

if (1 && 10)

Since both conditions yield truth and they have been combined using **&&**, the whole thing is treated as true, and hence the first **printf( )** is executed, printing the value of **x** in the process.

(25) *Output*

..so is stupidity!

Explanation

Let us carefully go over the condition step by step. Since **a** is 0.5 which is a truth value, the first condition in the statement evaluates to true. Thus the **if** statement now becomes,

if (truth && b > 0.9)

The contents of variable **b** are something less than 0.9. This is because any real number is treated as a **long double** by C, and when this **long double** is stored in a **float,** due to precision considerations the value stored in the **float** variable is something less than the actual real number. Therefore the condition now becomes,

if (truth && (0.9 - small value) > 0.9)

Obviously, the second condition would evaluate to false and the **if** would now look like,

if (truth && falsity)

Naturally, the whole condition evaluates to false since the 2 conditions have been linked together using the **&&** operator. Thus the **if** fails and hence the second **printf( )** gets executed.

(26) *Output*

x = 0

Explanation

x to begin with is 100, and hence a truth value. **!x** negates this truth value and makes it false, i.e. 0. **!0** once again negates and yields a truth value, 1. Thus the condition is satisfied and the control reaches the first **printf( )**. Here, we print the value of **!x**. Remember the value of **x** is still 100, since while performing **!!x** no value was assigned to **x**; the value of **x** was simply used to evaluate **!!x** and hence **!x** gives 0 and **printf( )** prints it out.

Remember that **!x** will negate the value of **x** temporarily for checking the condition. Value of **x** will change only if we use a statement like,

x = !x ;

Solutions to **[B]**

```
(1)    main( )
       {
            int i = 10 ;
            if ( i <= 10 )
                 printf ( "Hello Cocaine!" ) ;
       }
```

Explanation

If the condition is satisfied, only the null statement (;) is to be executed. Therefore it is better to reverse the condition, so that the **else** block gets completely eliminated.

```
(2)    main( )
       {
            int i = 5, j = 30, k = 5 ;
            if ( i < 30 && j < 20 && k == 40 )
                 printf ( "Hi Computerist!" ) ;
       }
```

Explanation

Since after checking the three nested conditions only one **printf( )** is to be executed, it makes sense to combine the conditions using the logical operator **&&**. As there are no statements to be executed in the **else** block, the **else** block can as well be dropped.

Solutions to **[C]**

(1)   *Program*

```
       main( )
```

```
{
    char customer ;
    float order, discount = 0, amt ;
    int mptype ;

    printf ( "\nEnter microprocessor type, customer type \
and order amount\n" ) ;
    scanf ( "%d %c %f", &mptype, &customer, &order ) ;

    if ( mptype == 32 )
    {
        if ( customer == 'u' )
            discount = 7.5 ;

        if ( customer == 'i' )
        {
            if ( order < 50000 )
                discount = 5 ;
            else
                discount = 7.5 ;

            if ( order > 100000 )
                discount = 10 ;
        }

        if ( customer == 'g' )
        {
            if ( order < 50000 )
                discount = 6.5 ;
            else
                discount = 8.5 ;

            if ( order > 100000 )
                discount = 10 ;
        }
    }
```

```c
if ( mptype == 16 )
{
    if ( order > 10000 )
    {
        if ( customer == 'u' || customer == 'i' )
            discount = 5 ;
        else
            discount = 6 ;
    }
}

if ( mptype == 8 )
    discount = 10 ;

amt = order * ( 100 - discount ) / 100 ;

printf ( "\nCustomer = %c Order = %f", customer, order ) ;
printf ( "\nMp = %d bit Amount = %f", mptype, amt ) ;
}
```

Sample run

```
Enter microprocessor type, customer type and order amount
32 i 65000
Customer = i Order = 65000.000000
Mp = 32 bit Amount = 60125.000000
```

Explanation

The first few lines are straight-forward. Once the customer type, microprocessor type and the order amount have been scanned from the keyboard, the control reaches the cluster of **if** statements. Firstly the microprocessor type is checked, followed by the type of customer. And then depending on the order amount, **discount** is assigned an appropriate value.

Towards the end the actual amount to be paid is calculated and displayed on the screen.

(2) *Program*

```
main( )
{
    int age, acc, excess = 0 ;
    float cost, prper, amt ;
    char type, inout ;

    printf ( "\nEnter age of driver " ) ;
    scanf ( "%d", &age ) ;
    printf ( "\nEnter no. of accidents in last 3 years " ) ;
    scanf ( "%d", &acc ) ;
    printf ( "\nEnter cost of car " ) ;
    scanf ( "%f", &cost ) ;
    printf ( "\nCar mfd. in or outside India (i/o) " ) ;
    scanf ( "%c", &inout ) ;

    if ( age >= 25 )
    {
        if ( inout == 'i' )
        {
            if ( acc == 0 )
                prper = 6 ;
            else
            {
                prper = 7 ;
                excess = 100 ;
            }
            type = 'C' ;
        }
        else
        {
            if ( acc == 0 )
```

```
            {
                    prper = 6 ;
                    type = 'C'
                    excess = 100 ;
            }
            else
            {
                    prper = 7 ;
                    type = 'T' ;
            }
        }
    }
    else
    {
        if ( inout == 'i' )
        {
            if ( acc == 0 )
            {
                    prper = 6 ;
                    type = 'C' ;
                    excess = 100 ;
            }
        }
        else
        {
            if ( acc == 0 )
                    type = 'C' ;
            else
                    type = 'R' ;

            prper = 8 ;
            excess = 100 ;
        }
    }

    amt = cost * prper / 100 ;
```

```
        printf ( "\nC - Comprehensive T - Third party" ) ;
        printf ( "\nR - Risk, no policy" ) ;
        printf ( "\n\nType of policy = %c", type ) ;
        printf ( "\nAmount of premium = %f", amt ) ;

        if ( excess != 0 )
            printf ( "\nExcess amount on claim = %d", excess ) ;
}
```

Sample run

```
Enter age of the driver 30
Enter no. of accidents in last three years 0
Enter cost of car 100000
Car mfd. in or outside India (i/o) i
C - Comprehensive T - Third party
R - Risk, no policy
Type of policy = C
Amount of policy = 6000.000000
```

Explanation

The program opens with a group of **scanf( )**s which receive the inputs to the program. The conditions are plenty and you can understand them if you follow the guideline - first check for age, then where the car is manufactured and then the accident record. Once the premium percentage, type of policy and the excess amount, if any, have been determined, the amount of premium is calculated and then these details are printed.

(3)   *Program*

```
main( )
{
    int n, count = 1 ;
```

```
printf ( "\nEnter a number " ) ;
scanf ( "%d", &n ) ;

n = n / 10 ;
if ( n != 0 )
    count = count + 1 ;
n = n / 10 ;
if ( n != 0 )
    count = count + 1 ;
n = n / 10 ;
if ( n != 0 )
    count = count + 1 ;
n = n / 10 ;
if ( n != 0 )
    count = count + 1 ;

printf ( "\nNo. of digits = %d ", count ) ;
}
```

Sample run

```
Enter a number 1235
No. of digits = 4
```

Explanation

The program begins with a **scanf( )** which receives a number entered through the keyboard into the variable **n**. The number is then successively divided by 10 four times, and each time if the quotient obtained is non-zero then **count** is incremented to count the digit. At the end of all divisions **count** contains the number of digits in the number, which is then printed out.

3

Merry go Round

A loop involves repeating some portion of the program either a specified number of times, or until a particular condition is being satisfied. This repetitive operation (looping) is achieved in C through a **for** or a **while** or a **do-while**.

Examine Figure 3.1 carefully before reading any further. It explains the working of **while**, **for** and **do-while** by taking a simple example of printing numbers from 1 to 10.

Having understood the basic working of the loops, let's understand their finer points.

Any **while**, **for** and **do-while** loops would more or less take the form shown in Figure 3.1. The initialisation, testing and incrementation hold the key to the working of the loop. Before we complete our discussion of **loops** it would be worthwhile to imbibe the following details:

- The statements within the loop would keep getting executed till the condition being tested remains true. When the condition becomes false, the control passes to the first statement that follows the body of the loop.

- The condition being tested may use relational or logical operators.

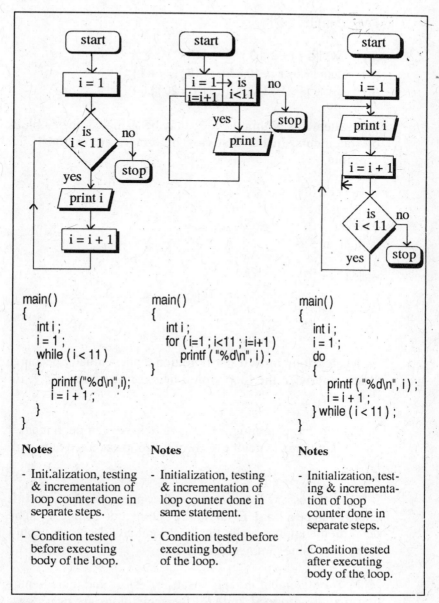

```
main()
{
    int i ;
    i = 1 ;
    while ( i < 11 )
    {
        printf ("%d\n",i);
        i = i + 1 ;
    }
}
```

Notes

- Initialization, testing
  & incrementation of
  loop counter done in
  separate steps.

- Condition tested
  before executing
  body of the loop.

```
main()
{
    int i ;
    for ( i=1 ; i<11 ; i=i+1 )
        printf ("%d\n", i) ;
}
```

Notes

- Initialization, testing
  & incrementation of
  loop counter done in
  same statement.

- Condition tested before
  executing body
  of the loop.

```
main()
{
    int i ;
    i = 1 ;
    do
    {
        printf ( "%d\n", i) ;
        i = i + 1 ;
    } while ( i < 11 ) ;
}
```

Notes

- Initialization, test-
  ing & incrementa-
  tion of loop
  counter done in
  separate steps.

- Condition tested
  after executing
  body of the loop.

Figure 3.1 Working of **while**, **for** and **do-while** loops

For example,

(a)   while (i <= 10)
(b)   for (i = 0 ; i <= 10 && j <= 15 ; i = i + 1)
(c)   while (j > 10 && (b < 15 || c < 20))

The statements within the loop may be a single line or a block of statements. In the first case the braces are optional. For example,

```
while ( i <= 10 )
    i = i + 1 ;
```

is the same as

```
while ( i <= 10 )
{
    i = i + 1 ;
}
```

-    As a rule a loop must test a condition that eventually becomes false, otherwise the loop would be executed forever, i.e. indefinitely.

-    Instead of incrementing a loop counter, we can decrement it and still manage to get the body of the loop executed repeatedly.

-    It is not necessary that a loop counter must only be an **int**. It could even be a **float**. Even floating point loop counters can be decremented. Once again the increment and decrement could be by any value, not necessarily 1.

-    In the **for** statement the initialisation, testing and incrementation may be dropped, but still the semicolons are necessary. For example,

```
main( )
{
    int i = 1 ;
    for ( ; ; )
    {
        printf ( "%d", i ) ;
        i = i + 1 ;
        if ( i > 10 )
            break ; /* takes control out of the loop */
    }
}
```

In the **for** loop, more than one variable can be initialised and incremented. While doing so the multiple initialisations (or the multiple incrementations) must be separated by the comma (,) operator. For example,

```
main( )
{
    int i, j ;
    for ( i = 1, j = 10 ; i + j < 25 ; i = i + 1 , j = j + 1 )
        printf ( "%d %d", i, j ) ;
}
```

The way **if** statements can be nested, similarly **while, for** and **do- while** statements can also be nested.

More Operators

Operators are C's forte. C is exceptionally rich in operators. These operators fall into distinct categories, as Figure 3.3 would confirm. To understand them thoroughly consider a problem wherein we want to display numbers from 1 to 10 on the screen. Figure 3.2 shows the various ways of writing this program, introducing new operators every time.

```
main()
{
    int i = 1 ;
    while ( i <= 10 )
    {
        printf ( "%d", i ) ;
        i++ ;
    }
}
```

```
main()
{
    int i = 1 ;
    while ( i <= 10 )
    {
        printf ( "%d", i ) ;
        i += 1 ;
    }
}
```

++ is an increment operator. It increments the value of **i** by 1.

-- is another such operator which decrements the value of a variable by 1.

, **//, **%%** operators do not exist.

+= is a compound assignment operator. It increments the value of **i** by 1.

Similarly, **j = j + 10** can also be written as **j += 10**.

Other compound assignment operators are **-=**, ***=**, **/=** and **%=**. **+++**, **---** operators do not exist.

```
main()
{
    int i = 0 ;
    while ( ++i <= 10 )
        printf ( "%d", i ) ;
}
```

```
main()
{
    int i = 0 ;
    while ( i++ < 10 )
        printf ( "%d", i ) ;
}
```

In the statement, **while (++ i <= 10)** first incrementation of **i** takes place, then the comparison of value of **i** with 10 is performed.

In the statement **while (i++ < 10)**, first the comparison of value of **i** with 10 is performed, and then the incrementation of value of **i** takes place.

Figure 3.2 **Incrementation**, **decrementation** & **compound assignment** operators

Precedence of Operators

Following figure shows the precedence of all the operators covered so far. Unary operators have the highest precedence, whereas the comma operator has the lowest precedence.

Description	Operator	Associativity
Increment/decrement	++ --	Right to left
Negation	!	Right to left
Unary minus	-	Right to left
Size in bytes	sizeof	Right to left
Multiplication	*	Left to right
Division	/	Left to right
Mod	%	Left to right
Addition	+	Left to right
Subtraction	-	Left to right
Less than	<	Left to right
Less than or equal to	<=	Left to right
Greater than	>	Left to right
Greater than or equal to	>=	Left to right
Equal to	==	Left to right
Not equal to	!=	Left to right
Logical AND	&&	Left to right
Logical OR	||	Left to right
Conditional	? :	Right to left
Assignment	= %= += -= *= /=	Right to left
Comma		Left to right

Figure 3.3 Precedence of operators

Use of break and continue

We often come across situations where we want to jump out of a loop instantly, without waiting to get back to the conditional test. The keyword **break** allows us to do this. When **break** is encountered inside a loop, control automatically passes to the first statement after the loop.

In some programming situations we want to take the control to the beginning of the loop, bypassing the statements inside the loop which have not yet been executed. The keyword **continue** allows us to do this. When **continue** is encountered inside any C loop, control automatically passes to the beginning of the loop.

A **break** and **continue** is usually associated with an **if**. The following figure shows **break** and **continue** at work.

```
main( )
{
    int i ;
    for ( i = 1 ; i <= 10 ; i++ )
    {
        if ( i == 5 )
            break ; ----------------+
        else                        | takes
            printf ( "%d\n", i ) ;  | control
    }                               | here
    printf ( "Hello" ) ; <----------+
}
```

```
main( )
{
    int i ;
    for ( i = 1 ; i <= 10 ; i++ )
    {                          ^
        if ( i == 5 )          |  takes con-
            continue ; --------+  trol here
        else
            printf ( "%d\n", i ) ;
    }
}
```

Figure 3.4a Working of **break** and **continue**

The working of the programs given in Figure 3.4a is straightforward. But if you still have any doubts, the following figure would take care of them.

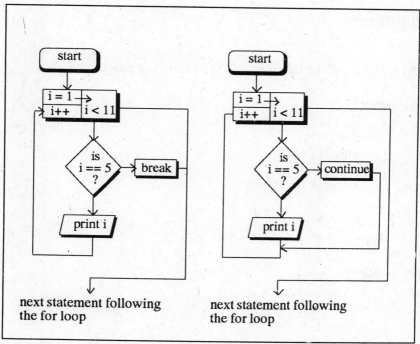

Figure 3.4b Working of **break** and **continue**

Exercise

[A]   What will be the output of the following programs:

```
(1)    main( )
       {
           char j = 1 ;
           while ( j <= 255 )
           {
               printf ( "%d\n", j ) ;
               j = j + 1 ;
           }
       }
```

```
(2)    main( )
       {
           int j = 1 ;
           while ( j <= 255 ) ;
           {
               printf ( "%c %d\n", j, j ) ;
               j++ ;
           }
       }
```

```
(3)    main( )
       {
           int j = 1 ;
           while ( j <= 255 )
               printf ( "%d\n", ++j ) ;
       }
```

```
(4)    main( )
       {
           int a ;
           for ( a = 1 ; a <= 32767 ; a++ )
```

```
                printf ( "%d ", a ) ;
        }

(5)    main( )
       {
            int i ;
            for ( i = 1 ; i++ <= 5 ; printf ( "%d ", i ) ) ;
       }

(6)    main( )
       {
            int i = 1, j = 1 ;
            for ( ; j ; printf ( "%d %d\n", i, j ) )
                 j = i++ <= 5 ;
       }

(7)    main( )
       {
            int i = 1 ;
            for ( ; i++ ; )
                 printf ( "%d ", i ) ;
       }

(8)    main( )
       {
            int a = 5 ;
            do
            {
                 printf ( "%d\n", a ) ;
                 a =- 1 ;
            } while ( a > 0 ) ;
       }

(9)    main( )
       {
            int a = 3, b = 4 ;
```

```
        b %= 3 + 4 ;
        a *= a + 5 ;
        printf( "b = %d a = %d", b, a ) ;
    }
```

(10)   main( )
```
    {
        int x = 3 ;
        x *= x + 4 ;
        printf ( "x = %d", x ) ;
    }
```

(11)   main( )
```
    {
        int x = 3, y, z ;
        z = y = x ;
        z *= y = x * x ;
        printf ( "x = %d y = %d z = %d", x, y, z ) ;
    }
```

(12)   main( )
```
    {
        int x = 3, y, z ;
        z = y = x ;
        z *= y /= x ;
        printf ( "x = %d y = %d z = %d", x, y, z ) ;
    }
```

(13)   main( )
```
    {
        int x = 1, y = 5 ;
        y *= x ;
        printf ( "x = %d y = %d", x, y ) ;
    }
```

```
(14)  main()
      {
          int x = 3, y, z ;
          z = y = x ;
          z = y += x =- z ;
          printf ( "x = %d y = %d z = %d", x, y, z ) ;
      }

(15)  main()
      {
          int x = 5 ;
          x++ ;
          printf ( "x = %d\n", x ) ;
          ++x ;
          printf ( "x = %d\n", x ) ;
      }

(16)  main()
      {
          int x = 3, z ;
          z = x++ + 10 ;
          printf ( "x = %d z = %d", x, z ) ;
      }

(17)  main()
      {
          int x = 3, z ;
          z = ++x + 10 ;
          printf ( "x = %d z = %d", x, z ) ;
      }

(18)  main()
      {
          int x = 3, z ;
          z = x---111 ;
          printf ( "x = %d z = %d", x, z ) ;
```

```
        }

(19)    main( )
        {
            int x = 3, z ;
            z = x--- -1 ;
            printf ( "x = %d z = %d", x, z ) ;
        }

(20)    main( )
        {
            int x = 3, z ;
            z = x++ + x++ ;
            printf ( "x = %d z = %d", x, z ) ;
        }

(21)    main( )
        {
            int x = 3, z ;
            z = x++ + ++x ;
            printf ( "x = %d z = %d", x, z ) ;
        }

(22)    main( )
        {
            int x = 3, z ;
            z = x----1 ;
            printf ( "x = %d z = %d", x, z ) ;
        }

(23)    main( )
        {
            int x = 3, z ;
            z = x / ++x ;
            printf ( "x = %d z = %d", x, z ) ;
        }
```

```
(24)  main( )
      {
          int i = 3, j ;
          j = ++i * ++i * ++i ;
          printf ( "%d", j ) ;
      }


(25)  main( )
      {
          int x = 3, y = 3, z = 3 ;
          z -= -x-- - --y ;
          printf ( "x = %d y = %d z =%d", x, y, z ) ;
      }


(26)  main( )
      {
          int x = 10, y = x, z = x ;
          y -= x ;
          z = -x ;
          t =- x ;
          printf ( "y = %d z = %d t = %d", y, z, t ) ;
      }


(27)  main( )
      {
          int x = 10, y, z ;
          z = y = x ;
          y -= x-- ;
          z -= --x ;
          x -= --x - x-- ;
          printf ( "y = %d z = %d x = %d", y, z, x ) ;
      }


(28)  main( )
      {
          int x = 4, y = 3, z ;
```

```
        z = x-- -y ;
        printf ( "x = %d y = %d z = %d", x, y, z ) ;
    }

(29)  main( )
    {
        int x, y, z ;
        x = y = z = 1 ;
        z = ++x || ++y && ++z ;
        printf ( "x = %d y = %d z = %d\n", x, y, z ) ;
    }

(30)  main( )
    {
        int x, y, z ;
        x = y = z = 1 ;
        z = ++x && ++y || ++z ;
        printf ( "x = %d y = %d z = %d\n", x, y, z ) ;
    }

(31)  main( )
    {
        int x, y, z ;
        x = y = z = 1 ;
        z = ++x && ++y && ++z ;
        printf ( "x = %d y = %d z = %d\n", x, y, z ) ;
    }

(32)  main( )
    {
        int x, y, z ;
        x = y = z = -1 ;
        z = ++x && ++y || ++z ;
        printf ( "x = %d y = %d z = %d\n", x, y, z ) ;
    }
```

```
(33)   main( )
       {
            int x, y, z ;
            x = y = z = -1 ;
            z = ++x || ++y && ++z :
            printf ( "x = %d y = %d z = %d\n", x, y, z ) :
       }

(34)   main( )
       {
            int x, y, z ;
            x = y = z = -1 ;
            z = ++x && ++y && ++z ;
            printf ( "x = %d y = %d z = %d\n", x, y, z ) ;
       }

(35)   main( )
       {
            int i ;
            for ( i = -1 ; i <= 10 ; i++ )
            {
                if ( i < 5 )
                    continue ;
                else
                    break ;
                printf ( "Gets printed only once!!" ) ;
            }
       }

(36)   main( )
       {
            int x = 10, y ;
            y = --x-- ;
            printf ( x = %d y = %d", x, y ) ;
       }
```

(37) ```
      main( )
      {
          int i = 2 ;
          printf ("i-- = %d", i--) ;
      }
      ```

[B]   Attempt the following:

(1)   Here is an ecological simulation of wolf and rabbit populations. Rabbits eat grass. Wolves eat rabbits. There is plenty of grass, so wolves are the only obstacle to the rabbit population increase. The wolf population increases with the population of rabbits. The day-by-day changes in the rabbit population R and the wolf population W can be expressed by the following formulae:

R(tomorrow) = (1 + a).R(today) - c.R(today).W(today)

W(tomorrow) = (1 - b).W(today) + c.d.R(today).W(today)

a = 0.01 = fractional increase in rabbit population without threat from wolves ( 0.01 means 1 % increase)

b = 0.005 = fractional decrease in wolf population without rabbit to eat

c = 0.00001 = likelihood that a wolf will encounter and eat a rabbit

d = 0.01 = fractional increase in wolf population attributed to a devoured rabbit.

Assume that initially there are 10,000 rabbits and 1000 wolves. Write a program to calculate populations of rabbits and wolves over a 1000-day period. Have the program print the populations every 25 days. See what happens when you start with 500 wolves instead of 1000. Try starting with 2000 wolves too.
      ```

(2)   Super-Duper Micros currently sells 100 Super-Dupers per month at a profit of Rs. 500/- per Super-Duper. They have a fixed operating cost of Rs 10,000/- that does not depend on the volume of sales. They currently spend Rs 1000/- per month on advertising. A marketing consultant advised them that if they double the amount spent on advertising, sales will increase by 20 %. Write a program that begins with the company's current status, and successively doubles the amount spent on advertising until the net profit begins to decline. Have the program print the number of Super-Duper sales, the advertising budget, and the net profit just before the profit begins to decline.

(3)   The equation $x^2 + y^2 = r^2$ represents a circle with centre at origin and radius **r**. Write a program that reads **r** from the keyboard and prints the number of points with integer coordinates that lie within the circle.

(4)   Write a program that, for all positive integers **i, j, k,** and **l** from 1 through 1000, finds and prints all combinations of **i, j, k,** and **l** such that $i + j + k = l$ and $i < j < k < l$.

(5)   Write a program which finds four digit perfect squares where the number represented by the first two digits and the number represented by the last two digits are also perfect squares.

(6)   Write a program which finds a four digit number AABB which is a perfect square. A and B represent different digits.

Answers

Answers to [A]

(1)   *Output*

1
2
3
..
..
127
-128
-127
-126
..
..
0
1
..
..

Explanation

Strange output at first glance, you would agree. In C, a **char** is always 1 byte long and hence can only hold values in the range -128 to +127. In this program, till value of **j** is less than or equal to 127 there is no problem. Its value gets printed through **printf**( ). But once **j** becomes 127, **j = j + 1** tries to make it 128, which it cannot become (being a **char**). Hence it goes to the otherside and picks up the value - 128. This goes on increasing through **j = j + 1** until it becomes 127, and then again goes to the negative side. This goes on indefinitely, hence the above output.

(2) *Output*

No output

Explanation

This is an indefinite loop and contrary to common expectations it doesn't print out the ascii table. The reason is the ; after the **while**. This semi-colon reduces the loop to...

```
while ( j <= 255 )
```

It means the null statement ';' keeps getting executed repeatedly. And since **j** doesn't get incremented, the condition **j <= 255** remains true forever.

(3) *Output*

2
3
..
..
256

Explanation

The **printf( )** statement is a little tricky. Would **j** be incremented first and then printed or vice versa? Since **++** precedes **j, j**'s value would be first incremented, and then this new value would be printed out. Therefore when **j** is 1, the condition is satisfied and the control reaches **printf( )**. Here firstly **j** becomes 2 and then it is printed. Thus the first output is 2, and not 1. Similarly, towards the end when **j** is 255, the condition in the **while** is once again satisfied and the control reaches

printf( ). Here it becomes 256 and is printed out. Now when the control reaches **while** with **j**'s value as 256, the condition fails and the execution is terminated.

(4)   *Output*

1 2 3 .... 32766 32767 -32768 -32767 .. 0 1 2 .. 32767 ..

Explanation

Here we have an indefinite **for** loop. The output from 1 to 32767 is as expected. When **a** is 32767, its value is printed and **a++** attempts to increment **a** to 32768. **a** cannot become 32768, since this falls outside the integer range. Hence it goes to the negative side of the range and becomes -32768. With this value of **a** the condition is tested, which is bound to get satisfied since -32768 is less than 32767. And from here onwards **a** keeps incrementing until it becomes 32767, and then once again the same process is repeated all over again. Thus, control never comes out of the **for** loop. Therefore it becomes an indefinte loop.

What if we want to print numbers from 1 to 32767 using a **for** loop? Write it in the following form·

```
for ( a = 0 ; a < 32767 ; a++ )
    printf ( "%d ", a + 1 ) ;
```

(5)   *Output*

2 3 4 5 6

Explanation

Let us isolate the condition in the **for** loop for closer examination:

i++ <= 5

In this expression value of **i** is first compared with 5, and then incremented. Thus when **i** is 1, the condition is satisfied, and **i** is incremented to 2. Then the control reaches the null statement, executes it, and then goes to **printf( )**, where **i** is printed out. Having printed out 2, control once again reaches the condition, where since 2 is less than 5, the condition is satisfied and **i** is incremented to 3. Once again control reaches the null statement, executes it , reaches **printf( )** and prints out 3. Last time through the loop when **i** is 5, the condition is once again satisfied, **i** is incremented to 6, null statement is executed, value of **i** (i.e. 6) is printed, and then the condition fails. On failure the control reaches the closing brace of **main( )** and the execution is terminated. Thus, the output isn't numbers from 1 to 5, but from 2 to 6.

(6) *Output*

```
2 1
3 1
4 1
5 1
6 1
7 0
```

Explanation

In the normal place of a condition in **for** loop, here we have just a **j**. This means the statements in the loop would keep getting executed till **j** is non-zero. To begin with **j** is non-zero, hence first time around the condition in the **for** loop is satisfied, and hence the control reaches the statement **j = i++ <= 5**. Here i is first tested against 5, the result of this test (1 or 0) is assigned to **j**, and then value of **i** is incremented. First time through the loop, with **i** as 1, the condition is satisfied, hence 1 is assigned to **j** and **i** is incremented to 2. With **i** as 2 and **j** as 1, the control then reaches the **printf( )** which prints out values of **i** and **j**. This whole operation is repeated, printing in the process the values 3 1, 4 1 and 5 1. With **i** as 5 and **j** as 1 when the control reaches **j = i++ <= 5**, the condition is satisfied, therefore 1 is assigned to **j** and **i** is incremented to 6. With these values the control reaches **printf( )**, which prints out 6 1 and then reaches the condition in **for**. Since **j** is 1, this condition is satisfied and the control once again reaches **j = i++ <= 5**. Here the condition fails, so 0 is assigned to **j** and **i** is incremented to 7. These values are then printed through **printf( )**, and then the control reaches the condition in **for** loop. Since **j** is 0, the condition fails and the loop is therefore terminated.

(7)   *Output*

2 3 ... 32767 ... -32768 -32767 ... -1 0

Explanation

Since **i++** is being used in the **for** loop, two operations are being carried out. Firstly **i** is tested for truth or falsity, and then it is incremented. To begin with, as **i** is equal to 1, the test results into a truth and then **i** is incremented to 2. This 2 is then printed through **printf( )**. Next time when the control reaches **i++**, since **i** is 2, the test once again results into truth, **i** is incremented to 3 and printed out. This goes on smoothly till **i** becomes 32767. When **i** is 32767, it evaluates to truth and **++** tries to make it 32768, which being an **int** it cannot become. Therefore the number from the negative side of the range (- 32768) is assigned to **i**, which is then printed out. This goes on and then sometime later **i** becomes -1. With **i** as -1 the test results into a truth and **i++** makes the value of **i** as 0. This value is printed out and once again the control reaches the test in the **for** loop. This time, however, the test fails since value of **i** is 0. Therefore the loop is terminated and the execution comes to an end.

(8)   *Output*

5

Explanation

A **do-while** allows the body of the loop to get executed before testing the condition. Therefore to begin with, value of **a**, i.e. 5, gets printed, and then the control reaches the statement **a =-1**. Be careful. This is different from **a -= 1**. **a =- 1** would simply assign -1 to **a**, whereas **a -= 1** would decrement the value of **a** by 1. In our case, -1 is assigned to **a** and then the control reaches the condition in the **while**. Since -1 is not greater than 0, the condition fails and the loop is terminated.

(9)   *Output*

b = 4 a = 24

Explanation

Get back to the precedence table. You would observe that **+** enjoys a higher priority as compared to **%=**. Hence the addition is carried out first and the statement therefore reduces to **b %= 7**, which evaluates to 4. This 4 is assigned to **b**. Similarly, the next statement first performs the addition and then ***=**, thereby resulting in 24.

(10)   *Output*

x = 21

Explanation

According to the precedence table, firstly + will be performed, followed by *=. Thus, first 3 + 4 results into 7, and on multiplication with 3 results into 21.

(11) *Output*

x = 3 y = 9 z = 27

Explanation

z = y = x is evaluated from right to left, assigning firstly 3 to y and then to z. The next statement is also evaluated from right to left. Therefore firstly 3 * 3, i.e. 9 is assigned to y and then z *= y is performed. z *= y evaluates to 27, which is assigned to z.

(12) *Output*

x = 3 y = 1 z = 3

Explanation

z = y = x is evaluated from right to left assigning the value 3 to the variables z and y. The next statement is also evaluated from right to left. Firstly y /= x is evaluated, which is same as y = y / x. Thus, 1 is assigned to the variable y. After this z *= y is evaluated, which is same as z = z * y. This assigns the value 3 to the variable z.

(13) *Output*

Error message: Expression syntax in function main

Explanation

While using the operator ***=**, a blank between ***** and **=** is never allowed. They must go together as ***=**. Hence the error message.

(14) *Output*

x = -3 y = 0 z = 0

Explanation

To begin with, **z** and **y** are assigned the value of **x**, i.e. 3. Look at the next statement closely. This expression is evaluated from right to left. Firstly the value **-z** is assigned to **x**. Hence **x** gets a value -3. Then **y += x** is evaluated. This is same as **y = y + x**, and **3 + -3**, i.e. 0, is assigned to **y**. The value of **y** is then assigned to **z**. Thus, **z** also turns out to be 0.

(15) *Output*

x = 6
x = 7

Explanation

x++ increments the value of **x** to 6 and the **printf( )** promptly prints it out. **++x** also increments the value of **x** to 7 which is then printed out by the **printf( )**. Note that **++**, as used here, won't make any difference whether the **++** occurs before or after the variable. However, when used in association with something else (like in **a = i++** or **a = ++i**, in which case each statement would store a different value in **a**), the position of **++** operator does matter. Thus, the following **printf( )**s are different.

```
printf ( "%d", ++x ) ;
printf ( "%d", x++ ) ;
```

(16) *Output*

x = 4 z ⇒ 13

Explanation

Here, since the incrementation operator **++** is present after the variable **x**, firstly the value of **x** is used in evaluation of the expression and is then incremented. Thus, firstly **x + 10** is performed which results into 13, 13 is assigned to **z**, then **x** is incremented to 4. Thus, finally the values of **z** and **x** are 13 and 4.

(17) *Output*

x = 4 z = 14

Explanation

Here, since the incrementation operator **++** is present before the variable **x**, firstly the value of **x** is incremented and is then used in evaluation of the expression. Thus, firstly **++x** is performed which increments **x** to 4 and then this 4 is added to 10 to yield 14, which is then assigned to **z**. Thus, finally the values of **z** and **x** are 14 and 4.

(18) *Output*

x = 2 z = -108

Explanation

Look at **x---111** as **x-- - 111** and the expression immediately becomes comprehensible. Since **--** follows the variable **x**, firstly 111 is subtracted from **x** (3 - 111, i.e -108), then -108 is assigned to **z**, and finally the decrementation operator reduces the value of **x** to 2.

(19) *Output*

   x = 2 z = 4

Explanation

The expression which assigns the value to **z** becomes simple to understand if we look at it as **z = x-- - -1**. Thus firstly -1 is subtracted from **x**, which gives 4, then 4 is assigned to **z**, and finally **x** is decremented to 2.

(20) *Output*

   x = 5 z = 6

Explanation

Since **++** occurs after the variable **x**, its value is first used to evaluate the expression, and then **x** is incremented twice. Thus **x + x** would result into 6, and the result would be assigned to **z**. After this, the first **x++** would increment the value of **x** to 4, followed by second **x++**, which would further increment **x** to 5.

(21) *Output*

   x = 5 z = 8

Explanation

This one is a bit tricky, follow it carefully. We might be led to believe that while evaluating **z** what would be added is 3 and 4. But this is definitely wrong. This is because while calculating **z**, the very first operation that is performed is **++x**, which increments the value of **x** to 4. So by the time the addition (**x + x**) is performed, **x** has already become 4. Thus 4 + 4 would be performed and not 3 + 4. After this the result of the addition (4 + 4) is assigned to the variable **z**, and then **x** is incremented to 5 (because of **x++**).

(22) *Output*

Error message: Lvalue required in function main

Explanation

What do we mean by lvalue? An lvalue is a variable whose value can change (can have a new value assigned to it). Contrary to this an rvalue represents a variable whose value cannot change. An easy way to differentiate the two is that an lvalue can occur on the left of assignment operator, whereas an rvalue can occur to its right.

x----1 is interpreted by the compiler as **x-- --1**. And since -- cannot be applied to constants (in this case **--1**), it flas¹ es the error message. Had the statement been written as **x-- - -1**, it would have worked.

(23) *Output*

x = 4 z = 1

Explanation

++ enjoys a higher priority than /. Therefore, firstly x is incremented to 4. So by the time the division is carried out, x has already become 4. During division 4 / 4 is performed and the result is assigned to z.

(24) *Output*

216

Explanation

i is initialised to 3 and then j is assigned the cube of ++i. Among the multiplication operator * and the increment operator ++, the ++ operator has the higher priority. Hence, first i gets incremented as many times as the ++ is encountered, so that i is now 6. After this j is evaluated as 6 * 6 * 6, giving the output 216.

(25) *Output*

x = 2 y = 2 z = 8

Explanation

While evaluating z, the highest priority is enjoyed by the unary minus, which attaches a minus sign to the value of x, making it -3. Note that on doing this the value of the variable x remains unchanged. Next operation performed is --y which decrements y to 2. Following this, the binary minus is performed (-3 - 2), which evaluates to -5, and then -= results into 8 (3 - -5), which is assigned to z. Lastly x is decremented to 2.

(26) *Output*

y = 0 z = -10 t = -10

Explanation

Is **y = x** acceptable in the declaration statement? Answer is yes. So long as **x** has been defined earlier, it can be assigned to **y** while declaring **y**. Same is true about **z = x**. The next statement is simple. It performs **y - x** and the result 0 is assigned to **y**. **z = -x** performs a unary minus operation on **x**, which results into -10. This is then assigned to **z**. Note that by using unary minus, the value stored in **x** remains unchanged. **t =- x** is similar to the previous statement and hence assigns -10 to **t**. It highlights the fact that while using the unary minus operator, the blank between the minus sign and the variable name is optional. Thus, **t =- x** is same as **t = -x**.

(27) *Output*

y = 0 z = 2 x = 6

Explanation

In the first arithmetic statement since -- occurs after the variable **x**, firstly value of **x** is used to calculate **y - x**, and then **x** is decremented. Thus **y - x** results into 0, which is assigned to **y**, and **x** is decremented to 9. In the next statement, firstly **x** is decremented and then this decremented value is used to calculate **z - x**. This results into **x** being decremented to 8 and **z - x** being evaluated to 2, which is then assigned to **z**.

The next statement deserves a careful look. Here, firstly **x** is decremented (through **--x**) to 7, and then this 7 is used to calculate the value of **x - x**. This evaluates to 7 - 7, which is 0. After this **x -= 0** is performed, which results in **x** being once again assigned a value 7. And finally **x--** is performed, which decrements **x** to 6.

(28) *Output*

x = 3 y = 3 z = 1

Explanation

While evaluating **z**, since -- operator occurs after the variable **x**, firstly value of **x** is used to calculate **x - y**, and then **x** is decremented. Thus **x - y** results into 1, which is assigned to **z**, and **x** is decremented to 3.

(29) *Output*

x = 2 y = 1 z = 1

Explanation

First let us bind the operators according to the precedence table. **&&** has higher priority over **||**. Therefore, binding the operators we get,

z = ++x || (++y && ++z) ;

Firstly **x** will be incremented to 2. This is a truth value (since it is non-zero), and the operator **||** requires only one of its conditions to be true for the entire statement to be true. Thus once 2 is checked for truth, and indeed it turns out to be true, the rest of the statement would be ignored. So **y** and **z** would both remain unchanged, i.e. at 1. The truth value of the test, 1, is then assigned to **z**.

(30) *Output*

x = 2 y = 2 z = 1

Explanation

Here **&&** enjoys a higher priority as compared to **||**. Hence the first condition (**++x && ++y**) would be evaluated first. If it turns out to be false only then the second condition (**++z**) would be evaluated. While evaluating the first condition **x** and **y** are both incremented to 2. Thus the first condition becomes,

(2 && 2)

&& requires a truth value to its left and right for the whole statement to evaluate to true. In this case since there are truth values on left and right of **&&** the statement is treated as true and hence 1 is assigned to **z**. Since the first condition has evaluated to true the second condition is not evaluated at all.

(31) *Output*

x = 2 y = 2 z = 1

Explanation

Since **++x**, **++y** and **++z** are all combined using **&&** operators, to check the truth or falsity of the statement **x**, **y** and **z** are first incremented, resulting in they taking a value 2 each. Thus the condition becomes,

z = 2 && 2 && 2

Since all three conditions are true, the whole condition is treated as true. The truth value of this condition (i.e 1) is then assigned to the variable **z**.

(32) *Output*

x = 0 y = -1 z = 0

Explanation

Since priority of **&&** is higher than that of **||**, the first condition to be evaluated is (**++x && ++y**). If this condition turns out to be true, then a truth value, 1, is assigned to **z**. If this turns out to be false, then the second condition is evaluated.

To evaluate the first condition, **x** is incremented from -1 to 0. So the condition becomes (**0 && ++y**). Since **++x** has evaluated to 0 and **++x** and **++y** are combined using the **&&** operator, irrespective of what is the result of **++y**, the condition is going to evaluate to false. Therefore, the condition is abandoned here itself without incrementing **y**. Since the first condition is evaluated to falsity, the second condition (**++z**)is evaluated now. On incrementing **z** the condition evaluates to (0), which is also false. Since neither of the two conditions are true, 0 is assigned to **z**. So in the final output **x** and **z** are 0 while **y** remains -1.

(33) *Output*

x = 0 y = 0 z = 0

Explanation

Taking into account the priorities of logical operators, the conditions to be evaluated are (**++x**) and (**++y && ++z**). Since the first and second conditions have been combined using **||** operator, the second condition would be evaluated only if first turns out to be false. And the first one indeed turns out to be false since incrementing **x** by 1 makes it 0, which is the falsity value in C. Therefore the second condition is evaluated. And the second condition too meets the same fate, since on incrementing **y** it becomes 0. Therefore the condition becomes (**0 && z++**), which turns out to be false. Here, **z** doesn't get a chance to get incremented, as the condition before **&&** is already 0. Now since both the conditions have evaluated to falsity, the false value 0 is assigned to **z**.

(34) *Output*

x = 0 y = -1 z = 0

Explanation

For the entire condition to evaluate to true, **++x**, **++y** and **++z** all must evaluate to true. So to test the condition, firstly **++x** is performed, which results into a 0. Now, since **++x** has evaluated to 0, irrespective of the results of **++y** and **++z**, the whole condition is going to evaluate to false. Therefore C doesn't bother to evaluate **++y** and **++z**, and assigns a falsity value, i.e. 0, to the variable **z**. Thus **x** has become 0 due to incrementation, **z** has become 0 due to evaluation of the whole condition to falsity, whereas **y** doesn't get a chance to change at all, and hence remains at -1.

(35) *Output*

No output

Explanation

The **for** loop begins with an initial value of **i** equal to -1. When **i** has a value -1, the condition (**i < 5**) is satisfied hence the **continue** statement gets executed. This sends the control to **i++** in the **for** statement. On incrementing **i** to 0, the condition in the **for** loop is tested which evaluates to true, and hence once again the control reaches inside the loop. Once inside, again the **if**'s condition is satisfied and **continue** takes the control to **i++**. This is repeated till value of **i** remains less than 5. The moment **i** equals 5, the condition **i < 5** fails, hence the control reaches the **else** block and executes the **break** statement. **break** takes the control outside the **for** loop. Here, since there are no statements, the execution is terminated. The **printf( )** inside the loop doesn't get a chance to get executed, hence there is no output in this program.

(36) *Output*

Error message: Lvalue required in function main

Explanation

Lvalue is a variable which can be assigned a new value in the program. Here, **--x**, if evaluated, would result into 9, which would be assigned to **y**. But the problem comes after this, when **9--** is to be evaluated. This can't be done because 9 is a constant and in that sense cannot be changed. Therefore, in place of 9 the compiler expects something which can change; in general an lvalue. Hence the error message.

(37) *Output*

i-- = 2

Explanation

Anything other than a format specification when enclosed in the format string of **printf( )** is printed as it is. Therfore i-- = is transferred to the screen as it is. Then **%d** prints the current value of **i**, i.e. 2 and the operation then proceeds to decrement **i** to 1. Since -- occurs after **i** in **printf( )**, firstly the value of **i** is printed and then decremented.

Solutions to **[B]**

(1)   *Program*

```
main( )
{
    float a = 0.01, b = 0.005, c = 0.00001, d = 0.01 ;
    int r1 = 10000, w1 = 2000, r2, w2 ;
    int i ;

    for ( i = 1 ; i <= 1000 ; i++ )
    {
        r2 = ( 1 + a ) * r1 - c * r1 * w1 ;
        w2 = ( 1 - b ) * w1 + c * d * r1 * w1 ;

        if ( i % 25 == 0 )
            printf ( "\nAfter %d days R = %d W = %d", i, r2, w2 ) ;

        r1 = r2 ;
        w1 = w2 ;
    }
}
```

Sample run

```
After 25 days R = 7958 W = 1800
After 50 days R = 6654 W = 1602
After 75 days R = 5832 W = 1427
After 100 days R = 5337 W = 1206
After 125 days R = 5070 W = 1116
......... ..... ......... .. .. ......... .  .. .......
......... ..... ......... .. .. ......... .  .. .......
```

Explanation

Here **r1** and **w1** represent today's populations of rabbits and wolves respectively, whereas **r2** and **w2** represent their tommorrow's populations. Beginning with 10000 and 2000 as rabbits' and wolves' populations, through the **for** loop their tomorrow's populations are calculated using the formulae. The populations calculated are printed after a gap of 25 days. Whether 25 days are over is checked through the **if** statement within the **for** loop. The same program can be run with different initial values of **r1** and **w1**.

(2)   *Program*

```
main( )
{
    float opercost = 10000, pps = 500, adv = 1000 ;
    float curprof, newprof ;
    int sale = 100 ;

    curprof = ( sale * pps ) - ( opercost + adv ) ;

    while ( 1 )
    {
        adv *= 2 ;
        sale = ( sale * 120 / 100 ) ;

        newprof = ( sale * pps ) - ( opercost + adv ) ;

        if ( newprof < curprof )
            break ;

        curprof = newprof ;
    }

    printf ( "Sale = %d\n", sale ) ;
    printf ( "Advertising expenses = %f\n", adv ) ;
    printf ( " Profit = %f", curprof ) ;
```

```
}
```

Sample run

```
Sale = 296
Advertising expenses = 64000
Profit = 81500
```

Explanation

To begin with, the current profit is calculated using the current sale, and current advertising expenses. Then within an indefinite **while** loop, the advertisement expenses are doubled with a corresponding rise (20 %) in the sales figure. On the basis of these new sales figures and advertising expenses, new profit is calculated. This value is stored in the variable **newprof**. The moment the **newprof** figure goes below the last **newprof** figure, the control breaks out of the loop and prints the sale, advertising expenses and the profit figures.

(3) *Program*

```
main( )
{
    float r ;
    int x, y, points = 0, i ;

    printf ( "\nEnter the radius of the circle " ) ;
    scanf ( "%f", &r ) ;

    for ( x = 0 ; x <= r ; x++ )
    {
        for ( y = 1 ; y <= r ; y++ )
        {
            if ( ( x * x + y * y ) <= ( r * r ) )
```

```
                    points++ ;
            }
    }

    points = points * 4 + 1 ;
    printf( "No. of points inside the circle = %d", points ) ;
}
```

Sample run

```
Enter the radius of the circle 4
No. of points inside the circle = 49
```

Explanation

Assume that the centre of the circle is at origin (0, 0). Now, if a point lies inside the circle, its distance from the centre of the circle must be less than the radius of the circle. If **x** and **y** are the coordinates of the point, then for this point to lie inside the circle, it must satisfy the condition given in the **if** statement in the program above. If this condition is satisfied, then the variable **points** is incremented, which keeps track of the number of such points encountered. The two **for** loops change the **x** and **y** coordinates of points from 0 to **r** and 1 to **r** respectively. This would count the points lying in the first quadrant of the circle, and those on the positive Y axis. This figure is multiplied by 4 to take care of the points lying inside the circle in the other three quadrants and remaining axes. Finally, as the coordinate (0, 0) never got included, we add 1 to **points** and obtain the total number of points with integer coordinates.

(4) *Program*

```
main( )
{
```

```
int i, j, k, l ;

for ( l = 1 ; l <= 1000 ; l++ )
{
    for ( k = 1 ; k < l ; k++ )
    {
      , for ( j = 1 ; j < k ; j++ )
        {
            for ( i = 1 ; i < j ; i++ )
            {
                if ( ( i + j + k ) == l )
                    printf ( "\n%d + %d + %d = %d", i, j, k, l ) ;
            }
        }
    }
}
```

Sample run

```
1 + 2 + 3 = 6
1 + 2 + 4 = 7
1 + 3 + 4 = 8
1 + 2 + 5 = 8
2 + 3 + 4 = 9
1 + 3 + 5 = 9
.. .. .. .. .. ..
.. .. .. .. .. ..
```

Explanation

Since **i, j, k,** and **l** all are to vary from 1 to 1000, should we not write each **for** loop to vary from 1 to 1000? This is not necessary, since there is no point in increasing the value of **k** beyond that of **l**, or value of **j** beyond that of **k**. This is because then the condition (**i < j < k < l**) would get violated. The for loops thus have been written such that the condition is met at all times. Within the innermost loop, if the other condition (**i + j + k == l**) is satisfied, the values of **i, j, k** and **l** get printed, otherwise the control loops around to try the condition for the next set of values.

(5) *Program*

```
#include "math.h"
main( )
{
    int i, a, num, d1, d2, d3, d4, nleft, nright, x, y ;

    for ( i = 1000 ; i <= 9999 ; i++ )
    {
        a = sqrt ( i ) ;

        if ( i == a * a )
        {
            num = i ;
            d4 = num % 10 ;
            num = num / 10 ;
            d3 = num % 10 ;
            num = num / 10 ;
            d2 = num % 10 ;
            num = num / 10 ;
            d1 = num % 10 ;

            nleft = d1 * 10 + d2 ;
            nright = d3 * 10 + d4 ;
            x = sqrt ( nleft ) ;
            y = sqrt ( nright ) ;

            if ( nleft == x * x && nright == y * y )
                printf ( "Desired number = %d\n", i ) ;
```

```
        }
    }
}
```

Sample run

```
Desired number = 1600
Desired number = 1681
Desired number = 2500
Desired number = 3600
Desired number = 4900
Desired number = 6400
Desired number = 8100
```

Explanation

Inside the **for** loop, first we get the square root of **i** and test whether **i** is a perfect square or not. If it is a perfect square, then we segregate the four digits of this number into variables **d1**, **d2**, **d3** and **d4**. Next we construct two numbers **nleft** and **nright** from the first two and the last two digits of the four digit number. Having done this, we test whether these two numbers are perfect squares or not. If they turn out to be perfect squares then we have met the number satisfying our requirements. Hence we print it out. It is necessary to include the file "math.h" for the **sqrt( )** function to work.

(6)   *Program*

```
#include "math.h"
main( )
{
    int a, i, d1, d2, d3, d4, num ;

    for ( i = 1100 ; i <= 9988 ; i++ )
```

```
    {
        num = i ;
        d4 = num % 10 ;
        num = num / 10 ;
        d3 = num % 10 ;
        num = num / 10 ;
        d2 = num % 10 ;
        num = num / 10 ;
        d1 = num % 10 ;

        if ( d1 == d2 && d3 == d4 && d1 != d3 )
        {
            a = sqrt ( i ) ;
            if ( i == a * a )
                printf ( "Desired number = %d\n", i ) ;
        }
    }
}
```

Sample run

Desired number = 7744

Explanation

The smallest 4 digit number of the form AABB is 1100, whereas the biggest 4 digit number of this form is 9988. So the number desired by us lies in the range 1100 to 9988. Hence these values have been used as the initial and final values in the **for** loop. Within the loop, firstly the digits of **i** are separated out into **d1**, **d2**, **d3** and **d4**. If these digits are of the form AABB, then it is tested whether **i** is a perfect square or not. If so, the value of **i** is printed out, otherwise the control loops back and begins all over again, this time for the next four digit number.

4

A Multi-point Switch

N ow let's switch over to **switch**. In serious C programming, the choice we have to make is more complicated than merely selecting between two alternatives. C provides a special control structure called **switch** that allows us to handle such cases effectively. The following figure demonstrates its usage.

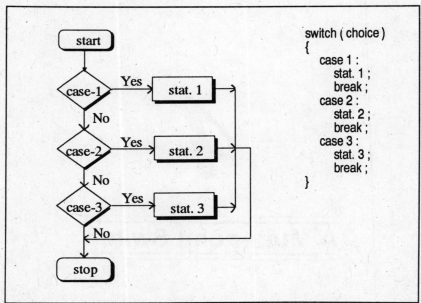

Figure 4.1 Operation of **switch**

As you would now agree, **switch** is impressive in style and elegant in presentation. If you have even a flicker of doubt then try writing the above program using **if - else** and we are sure at the end you would more than agree.

A few useful tips about the usage of **switch**:

(a)   The cases need not necessarily be arranged in ascending order, 1, 2, 3 and default.

(b)   Even if there are multiple statements to be executed in each case, there is no need to enclose them within a pair of braces (unlike **if** and **else**).

(c)   The **default** case is optional. If it is absent, and no case matches with the value of the expression, then the program simply falls through the entire **switch** and continues with the next instruction (if any) that follows the control structure.

(d)   The limitation of **switch** is that the logical operators cannot be used in cases. Thus, a case like,

case i <= 20 :

is unacceptable. All that we can have after the **case** is an **int** or a **char**. Even a **float** is not allowed.

(e)   In principle, a **switch** may occur within another, but in practice it is rarely done.

goto

This keyword is used when we want to transfer the control to some point in the program which is not in the normal, step by step sequence of the program. It takes control from one place to another unconditionally, so a different path for the execution of the program is set up. The following program illustrates the use of **goto**.

```
/* Use of goto */
main( )
{
    printf ( "Hope is hoping against hope..." ) ;
    goto hope ;
    printf ( "even if it seems hopeless." ) ;

    hope :
    exit ( 0 ) ;
}
```

On running this program, what would show up is:

```
Hope is hoping against hope...
```

The second part of the message will not get printed, as due to the **goto,** control skips to the label **hope** and execution is terminated due to the **exit(0)** present here. Had there been any executable statements after **hope,** those would have got executed.

Though **goto** seems to be handing over to us a magic wand for placing control where we please, we would do well to employ combinations of **if, for, while** and **switch** instead. This is because **goto** makes the program less readable and hard to debug. Besides, once the control is given to **goto,** there's no telling how the program would behave, as is illustrated in the exercises that follow.

Exercise

[A]   What will be the output of the following programs:

(1)
```c
main( )
{
    int i ;
    printf ( "Enter any number " ) ;
    scanf ( "%d", &i ) ;
    switch ( i )
    {
        case 1 :
            printf ( "Do" ) ;
        case 2 :
            printf ( "Re" ) ;
        case 3 :
            printf ( "Me" ) ;
        case default :
            printf ( "Fa So La Ti Do" ) ;
    }
}
```

(2)
```c
main( )
{
    int i = 3 ;
    switch ( i )
    {
        case 1 :
            printf ( "au revoir!" ) ;
        case 2 :
            printf ( "adieu!" ) ;
            break ;
        case 3 :
            continue ;
        default :
```

```
                    printf ( "plain simple goodbye!" ) ;
             }
       }

(3)    main( )
       {
             char s = 3 ;
             switch ( s )
             {
                   case '1' :
                         printf( "Seagherkins\n" ) ;
                   case '2' :
                         printf( "Baboons\n" ) ;
                   default :
                         printf( "Bucaneers\n" ) ;
             }
             printf( "Gallows fodder" ) ;
       }

(4)    main( )
       {
             int k = -2, j = 4 ;
             switch ( k /= j / k )
             {
                   default :
                         printf ( "All are same!\n" ) ;
                   case 0 :
                         printf ( "Happy birthday\n" ) ;
                   case 1 :
                         printf ( "A punch on the mouth\n" ) ;
                   case 2 :
                         printf ( "A kick in the back\n" ) ;
             } .
       }

(5)    main( )
```

```
    {
        int j, x = 0 ;
        for ( j = 0 ; j <= 5 ; j++ )
        {
            switch ( j - 1 )
            {
                case 0 :
                case -1 :
                    x += 1 ;
                    break ;
                case 1 :
                case 2 :
                case 3 :
                    x += 2 ;
                    break ;
                default :
                    x += 3 ;
            }
            printf ( "%d", x ) ;
        }
    }

(6)  main( )
    {
        int i ;
        for ( i = 2 ; i <= 10 ; i++ )
        {
            switch ( i )
            {
                case 2 :
                    printf ( "O" ) ;
                    continue ;
                case 3 :
                    break ;
                case 4 :
                case 5 :
                    printf ( "H" ) ;
```

```
                    break ;
                default :
                    printf ( "!" ) ;
            }
        }
    }

(7)    main( )
    {
        char ch = 'E' ;
        switch ( ch )
        {
            case ( ch >= 65 && ch <= 90 ) :
                printf ( "Capital Letter" ) ;
                break ;
            case ( ch >= 97 && ch <= 122 ) :
                printf ( "Small case Letter" ) ;
                break ;
            case ( ch >= 48 && ch <= 57 ) :
                printf ( "Digit" ) ;
                break ;
            default :
                printf ( "Any other character" ) ;
        }
    }

(8)    main( )
    {
        int i ;
        for ( i = 1 ; i <= 5 ; i++ )
        {
            if ( i * i >= 121 )
                goto there ;
            else
                printf ( "%d ", i ) ;
        }
        there :
```

```
                    printf ( "\nNo more murphy's laws" ) ;
        }

(9)    main( )
       {
            int i, j ;
            for ( j = 1 ; j <= 10 ; j++ )
            {
                for ( i = 1 ; i <= 10 ; i++ )
                {
                    if ( j < 10 )
                        goto out ;
                }
                printf ( "Murphy's first law\n" ) ;
                printf ( "If the price of the PC is a dream...\n" ) ;
                printf ( "then the service would be a nightmare" ) ;
            }
            out :
                printf ( "Dream about a nightmare" ) ;
       }

(10)   main( )
       {
            int i, j, k ;
            for ( j = 1 ; j <= 4 ; j++ )
            {
                if ( j * j == 16 )
                    goto secretplace ;
            }
            for ( i = 1 ; i <= 5 ; i++ )
            {
                k = i * i ;
                j = k + 2 ;

                secretplace :
                    printf ( "Murphy's second law\n" ) ;
                    printf ( "Good computers are always priced...\n" ) ;
```

```
                printf ( "just beyond your budget\n" ) ;
        }
    }

(11)  #include "stdio.h"
      main( )
      {
          int i ;
          char j ;
          printf ( "Enter any number ..." ) ;
          scanf ( "%d", &i ) ;

          switch ( i )
          {
              case 1 :
                  printf ( "\nEnter any alphabet ..." ) ;
                  fflush ( stdin ) ;
                  scanf ( "%c", &j ) ;

                  switch ( j )
                  {
                      case 'a' :
                          printf ( "\nIf you love something..." ) ;
                          goto out ;
                      case 'b' :
                          printf ( "\nSet it free..." ) ;
                          break ;
                  }
                  break ;
              case 2 :
                  printf ( "\nIf it returns, its yours...." ) ;
          }
          out :
              printf ( "\nElse it was never meant to be." ) ;
      }

(12)  main( )
```

```
        {
            int i, k = 1 ;
            here :
            if ( k > 2 )
                goto out ;

            there :

            for ( i = 1 ; i <= 5 ; i++ )
                printf ( "%d", i ) ;

            k++ ;
            goto there ;

            out : ;
        }
```

(13)   main( )
```
        {
            int i = 1 ;
            switch ( i )
            {
                case 1 :
                    goto label ;
                    label :
                case 2 :
                    printf ( "He looks like a Saint ..." ) ;
                    break ;
            }
            printf ( "\nA Saint Bernard!" ) ;
        }
```

[B]   Attempt the following:

(1)   If a number 972 is entered through the keyboard, your program
       should print "Nine Seven Two". Write the program such that
       it does this for any positive integer.

(2)   A positive integer is entered through the keyboard. Alongwith it the base of the numbering system in which you want to convert this number is entered. Write a program to display the number entered, the base, and the converted number.

For example, if the input is 64 2 then the output should be 64 2 1000000. Similarly, if the input is 64 16, then the output should be 64 16 40.

Answers

Answers to **[A]**

(1)   *Output*

    Error message: Expression syntax in function main

    Explanation

    In a **switch**, the default case must be specified simply as **default**, and not **case default**. Hence the error.

(2)   *Output*

    Error message: Misplaced continue in function main

    Explanation

    Observe **case 3**. Our program says, if **case 3** is satisfied then loop back to the **switch**. And there lies the error. **continue** cannot take the control back to **switch**. Unlike **break**, **continue** can work only with loops, never with **switch**.

(3)   *Output*

    Bucaneers
    Gallows fodder

    Explanation

    To begin with, 3 is stored in the variable s. In **switch**, this 3 is tested against '1' and '2'. Remember that 1 and '1' are different. Whenever we use '1', it is replaced by ascii value of 1 i.e. 49. Similarly '2' is replaced by 50. Naturally, value of **s** doesn't match with 49 or 50. Hence the control reaches the **default** clause of **switch** and prints 'Bucaneers'. Followed by this the control reaches outside **switch**, where the second **printf( )** gets executed.

(4)   *Output*

```
A punch on the mouth
A kick in the back
```

Explanation

Is an expression allowed in **switch**? Yes, provided the expression involves only **int**s or **char**s. Let us see how **k /= j / k** gets evaluated. / has a higher priority as compared to /= hence is evaluated first. Thus the expression would become,

k /= (4 / -2)

Here, 4 / -2 would give -2. Thus the expression reduces to:

k /= -2

which evaluates to 1.

Hence **case 1** in the **switch** is satisfied and the message 'A punch on the mouth' is printed. Since there is no **break** in **case 1** after the **printf( )**, the control just falls through till the end of **switch** and executes all statements that come in its path. In our example **printf ("And a kick in the back")** falls in its path and hence gets executed.

Note that in the **switch** the very first case is the **default** case. This is perfectly acceptable.

(5)   *Output*

X = 1
X = 2
X = 4
X = 6
X = 8
X = 11

Explanation

The following figure shows which case is selected and the corresponding value of **x** outputted for **j** varying from 0 to 5. Note that the absence of **break** causes the control to simply fall through the subsequent cases, until a **break** or the end of **switch** is encountered.

j	j - 1	case satisfied	Value of x outputted
0	-1	case -1	1
1	0	case 0	2
2	1	case 1	4
3	2	case 2	6
4	3	case 3	8
5	4	default	11

Figure 4.2

(6)   *Output*

OHH!!!!!

Explanation

The following figure lists out the values printed for each case.

i	case satisfied	output
2	case 2	0
3	case 3	No value is printed
4	case 4	H
5	case 5	H
6	default	!
7	default	!
8	default	!
9	default	!
10	default	!

Figure 4.3

(7) *Output*

Error message: Constant expression required in main

Explanation

switch has not been made intelligent enough to handle relational operators while testing cases. After a **case** there must always be a constant (either integer or character), hence the error message.

(8) *Output*

1 2 3 4 5

No more murphy's laws

Explanation

For no value of **i** is the condition (**i * i >= 121**) satisfied. Hence on testing the condition, every time the control reaches the **else** block and prints the current value of **i**. Thus when the loop is getting executed, the **goto** statement doesn't get a chance to get executed, and hence the control doesn't reach the lable **there**. However, once the control reaches outside the loop after normal termination of the **for**, it reaches **there** and hence the **printf( )** prints the message about murphy's laws.

(9)   *Output*

Dream about a nightmare

Explanation

Can we abruptly break out of the loop using **goto**? Yes. In fact **goto** can take the control anywhere in the program. Here, first time through the loop itself the condition is satisfied, and **goto** takes the control directly to the label **out**, where the **printf( )** gets executed.

(10)   *Output*

Murphy's second law
Good computers are always priced...
just beyond your budget

Explanation

Look at the first **for** loop. The moment **j * j** equals 16, the **goto** statement is executed, which takes the control to **secretplace** inside the second **for** loop. This is perfectly acceptable. **goto** can virtually take the control anywhere - even deep inside a **for** loop. Having reached the **secretplace**, Murphy's second law is printed out and then the control reaches the closing brace of the **for** loop. As a result, control jumps to the beginning of loop i.e. to **i++**, which increments **i** and then the condition **i <= 5** is tested. Whether the condition is satisfied or not depends upon the garbage value that was picked up for **i**. Why garbage value? Because we entered the loop directly at **secretplace** as a result of which **i = 1** couldn't get executed. Hence a garbage value of **i** is assumed. Thus after printing Murphy's law once, how many more times it would get printed entirely depends upon the garbage value that has been picked up for **i**.

(11) *Output*

```
Enter any number ...1 <ENTER>
Enter any alphabet ...a
If you love something...
Else it was never meant to be.
```

Explanation

We can use nested **switch**es. On entering number 1 and alphabet a, the **case 'a'** of **switch (j)** is executed. The **goto** takes control out, to the last **printf( )**, and hence the output. Had we entered number 2, control would have reached **case 2** of **switch (i)**, printing "If it returns ... ". Following this, the line "Else it was ... " would get printed this time also, as **out** happens to occur in the normal course of execution of the program.

Puzzled about the weighty looking **# include** and **fflush( )** statements? The file "stdio.h" is required for the function **fflush( )** to work. This function empties the keyboard buffer before the alphabet entered by us is scanned. The reason for this is that when **scanf( )** is used for reading an **int**, it collects everything till the the enter key is hit as the value of the **int**, and leaves the enter key itself unread. When a **char** is to be scanned next, the **scanf( )** accepts the enter key as the character entered, which certainly won't do if we were to exercise our choice in the **switch( )**. The **fflush( )** ensures that the Enter key pending in the keyboard buffer is flushed out before the alphabet entered by us is scanned.

(12)   *Output*

1234512345123451234512345.....

Explanation

Here's an example of how the **goto** statement can capture more control than we would like it to. Though we have not said **goto here**, it is executed anyway, since it lies in the normal execution path. To begin with **k** is 1, i.e. less than 2. Hence control skips the **if** and reaches the next statement in line, which is the label **there**. In the **for** loop, 1,2,3,4 and 5 get printed, and then **k** is incremented to 2. The following **goto** statement takes the control back up to **there**, and once again the **for** loop is executed. Next, **k** is incremented to 3, again control is taken to **there** and so on. Thus, the **for** loop is executed indefinitely, irrespective of the fact that **k** is no longer less than 2. The **if** condition can exercise no control now that the **goto** has taken over.

(13)   *Output*

He looks like a Saint ...
A Saint Bernard!

Explanation

Since **i** is 1, case 1 is executed, which takes control to **label**. Once the control is here, contrary to what one might expect, case 2 gets executed, as is clear from the output. Legally speaking, case 2 should have got executed only for value of **i** equal to 2. But **goto** overrules this, and whatever follows **goto**, is taken as the law. You'll agree that **goto** would rather be used sparingly, as it seems to have a mind of its own!

Solutions to **[B]**

(1)   *Program*

```
main( )
{
    unsigned int num, num2, no_dig = 0, p ;
    int i ;

    printf ( "\nEnter any positive integer " ) ;
    scanf ( "%d", &num ) ;

    num2 = num ;

    do
    {
        no_dig++ ;
        num2 = num2 / 10 ;
    } while ( num2 != 0 ) ;

    for ( ; no_dig > 0 ; no_dig--, num %= p )
    {
    .   p = 1 ;
        for ( i = no_dig - 1 ; i > 0 ; i-- )
            p = p * 10 ;
```

```
switch ( num / p )
{
    case 0 :
        printf ( "ZERO " ) ;
        break ;
    case 1 :
        printf ( "ONE " ) ;
        break ;
    case 2 :
        printf ( "TWO " ) ;
        break ;
    case 3 :
        printf ( "THREE " ) ;
        break ;
    case 4 :
        printf ( "FOUR " ) ;
        break ;
    case 5 :
        printf ( "FIVE " ) ;
        break ;
    case 6 :
        printf ( "SIX " ) ;
        break ;
    case 7 :
        printf ( "SEVEN " ) ;
        break ;
    case 8 :
        printf ( "EIGHT " ) ;
        break ;
    case 9 :
        printf ( "NINE " ) ;
        break ;
    }
  }
}
```

Sample run

Enter any positive integer 972
NINE SEVEN TWO

Explanation

The number is accepted from the keyboard and stored in **num**.
Using a **do-while,** the number of digits in the number are
counted, which is stored in **no_dig**. In the **for** loop, each digit
of the number is separated by dividing by an appropriate
multiple of 10 and assigning the remainder to **num** itself. Then
depending on what the number is, the **switch** causes the same
to be printed in words.

(2) *Program*

```
main( )
{
    unsigned int num, num2, no_dig = 0, p, base ;
    int i ;

    printf ( "\nEnter any positive integer & base " ) ;
    scanf ( "%d %d", &num, &base ) ;
    printf ( "\n%d %d ", num, base ) ;

    num2 = num ;

    do
    {
        no_dig++ ;
        num2 = num2 / base ;
    } while ( num2 != 0 ) ;

    for ( ; no_dig > 0 ; no_dig--, num %= p )
```

```
        {
            p = 1 ;
            for ( i = no_dig - 1 ; i > 0 ; i-- )
                p = p * base ;

            if ( base == 16 )
                printf ( "%X", num / p ) ;
            else
                printf ( "%d", num / p ) ;
        }
}
```

Sample run

```
Enter any positive integer and base 64 2
64 2 1000000
```

Explanation

The program uses the concept of successive divisions of the number by the base of the numbering system in which it is to be outputted. Assume that we want to convert 64 to its binary equivalent. Therefore, when 64 is entered, first the number of digits that the binary equivalent of 64 would have are determined using the **do-while**. 64 can be divided by 2 a maximum of 7 times, till a 0 is obtained. Thus, **no_dig** in this case turns out to be 7. The first time through the inner **for** loop, **i** is 6. Once outside the **for** loop, **p** would be 64, and **num** gets divided by 64, and hence 1 is printed out. Now the control reaches **num %= p**, where **num** is set to 0 since both **num** and **p** are 64. Next time through the loop **p** turns out to be 32, and **num** / **p**, i.e. 0 gets printed. This process continues till all the digits of the binary equivalent of 64 have been printed.

Note that if the base of the numbering system is 16, then the format specification **%X** is used to print hexadecimal digits.

5

Functioning
with Functions

A C program, except for the simplest one, cannot handle all the tasks by itself. Instead, it requests other program-like entities - 'functions' - to get its tasks done. Functions provide the mechanism for producing programs that are easy to write, read, understand, debug, modify and maintain.

A function is a self-contained block of code that performs a coherent task of some kind. Every C program is a collection of these functions. Following figure shows functions in action.

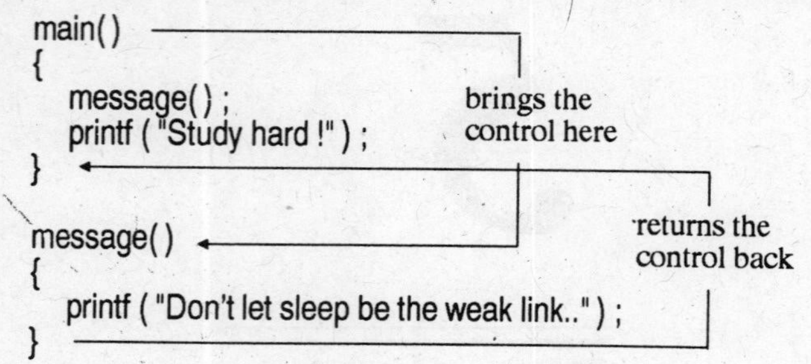

```
main( )
{
    message( ) ;                        brings the
    printf ( "Study hard !" ) ;          control here
}

message( )                               returns the
{                                        control back
    printf ( "Don't let sleep be the weak link.." ) ;
}
```

Notes

- A function gets called if the function name is followed by a semicolon.
- A function gets defined if the function name is not followed by a semi-colon.

Figure 5.1 Calling and defining functions

Let's now assimilate a few facts about functions and lay them out neat and clear.

(a)   Functions can be either library functions or user-defined functions. For example, **printf( )**, **scanf( )** are library functions whereas **message( )** is a user-defined function.

Library functions come alongwith the compiler and are present on the disk. The procedure of calling both types of functions is exactly same.

(b)   There can be any number of functions in a program and any function can call any other function any number of times. However, program execution always begins with **main( )**.

(c)   The order in which the functions get called and the order in which they are defined in a program need not necessarily be same.

(d)   The use of user-defined functions allows a large program to be broken down into a number of smaller self-contained components, each of which has a definite purpose. There are several advantages to this breaking up of program into functions. For one, writing functions avoids rewriting the same code over and over. For another, breaking down of logic into separate functions makes the entire process of program writing and debugging easier.

Communication between Functions

Not only can one function call another, if needed we can pass values to and fro between functions. Following figure shows this mechanism of passing and returning values between functions.

```
            main( )
            {
                int a, b, c, sum ;
                printf ( "Enter any three numbers " ) ;
                scanf ( "%d %d %d", &a, &b, &c ) ;

                sum = calsum ( a, b, c ) ;

                printf ( "Sum = %d", sum ) ;          values of a, b, c get
                                                      passed to x, y, z
    this        }
    value is
    returned  calsum ( x, y, z )
    and col-  int x, y, z ;
    lected    {
    in sum        int s ;
                  s = x + y + z ;
                  return ( s ) ;
              }
```

Figure 5.2 Passing values between functions.

Note the following points carefully.

(a)   There is no restriction on the number of **return** statements that may be present in a function. Also, the **return** statement need not always be present at the end of the called function.

(b)   Any C function by default returns an **int** value. More specifically, whenever a call is made to a function, the compiler assumes that this function would return a value of the type **int**. If we desire that a function should return a non-integer value, then it is necessary to explicitly mention so in the calling function as well as called function. This is shown in the following figure.

```
main()                      main()                      main()
{                           {                           {
  int a, b, c, p ;            float a, b, c, p ;          float a, b, c ;
                              float prod() ;              void prod() ;
  a = b = c = 5 ;             a = b = c = 1.5 ;
  p = prod ( a, b, c ) ;      p = prod ( a, b, c ) ;      a = b = c = 1.5 ;
  printf ( "p = %d", p ) ;    printf ( "p = %f", p ) ;    prod ( a, b, c ) ;
}                           }                           }

prod ( x, y, z )            float prod ( x, y, z )      void prod ( x, y, z )
int x, y, z ;               float x, y, z ;             float x, y, z ;
{                           {                           {
  int p ;                     float p ;                   float p ;
  p = x * y * z ;             p = x * y * z ;             p = x * y * z ;
  return ( p ) ;              return ( p ) ;              printf ( "p = %f", p ) ;
}                           }                           }
```

Notes

- An **int** value is being returned by function **prod( )**.
- No special provision is to be made for returning an **int** value.

Notes

- A **float** value is being returned by function **prod( )**.
- For returning a **float** value the declaration in **main( )** as well as while defining the function is necessary.

Notes

- No value is being returned by function **prod( )**.
- To ensure that no value is returned, **void** declaration is made in **main( )** and while defining the function.

Figure 5.3 Returning **int, float** and **void**

Pointers

Functions can be called either by value or by reference. We have so far used a call by value. To be able to understand a call by reference it is necessary to first understand the concept of pointers. Pointers is one concept which beginners find hard to digest. But once pointers are mastered there are many tricks that one can perform. Let's meet the concept head on. Look at the following program. It says it all.

```
main()
```

```
{
    int i = 30 ;
    int *j, **k ;
    j = &i ;  /* store address of i in j */
    k = &j ;  /* store address of j in k */
    printf ( "Address of i  = %d %d %d\n", &i, j, *k ) ;
    printf ( "Address of j  = %d %d\n", &j, k ) ;
    printf ( "Address of k = %d\n", &k ) ;
    printf ( "Value of i = %d %d %d %d", i, *(&i), *j, **k ) ;
}
```

And here is the output...

```
Address of i = 6484 6484 6484
Address of j  = 9006 9006
Address of k = 9888
Value of i = 30 30 30 30
```

Consider the declaration,

```
int i = 30 ;
```

This declaration reserves space in memory, associates the name **i** with it and stores the value 30 in it. The following figure gives the snapshot of this reserved space.

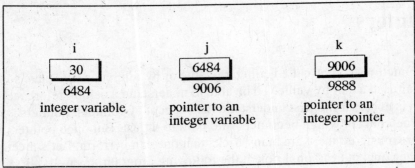

Figure 5.4 Pointers

We see that the compiler has selected location number (address) 6484 as the place to store the value 30. The location 6484 we took only for example, the compiler may choose any other location as well. The important point is, **i**'s address in memory is a number.

Next, the address of **i** is stored in **j** through the statement **j = &i**. Since **j** contains the address of **i** (an integer variable), **j** is called an integer pointer. Similarly, the address of **j** is stored in **k** through the statement **k = &j**. Since **k** contains the address of **j** (an integer pointer), **k** is called a pointer to an integer pointer. Here **&** is 'address of' operator. Since **j** and **k** contain addresses their declaration is different from that of **i**. In the declaration of **j** and **k**, * is being used. This is a pointer operator called 'value at address'. Thus the declaration **int *j** means the value at address contained in **j** is an **int**. Or in other words **j** is an integer pointer. Similarly, the declaration **int **k** means the value at address contained in ***k** is an **int**. Once this concept is clear, rest of the program is a breeze. Figure 5.4 would help you check the output as you step through the program.

Pointers throw open the gates of programmers' imagination. Can you imagine a pointer to a pointer's pointer? A three star phenomenon. Or how about a pointer to a pointer's pointer's pointer? There is no limit on how far can we stretch this definition. Possibly, till the point we can comprehend it. And that point of comprehension is usually a pointer to a pointer. Beyond this one rarely requires to extend the definition of a pointer.

Back to Function calls

Having had a tryst with the pointers now let us get back to where we had left off - the function calls. Functions can be called in two ways: either by passing values of arguments or by passing addresses of arguments. The former is called a 'Call by Value' and the latter a 'Call by Reference'. These calls are illustrated in the following figure.

```
/* Call by value */                          /* Call by reference */
main( )                                      main( )
{                                            {
    int a = 10, b = 20 ;                         int a = 10, b = 20 ;

    swapv ( a, b ) ;                             swapr ( &a, &b ) ;
    printf ( "a = %d b = %d\n", a, b ) ;         printf ( "a = %d b =%d\n", a, b ) ;
}                                            }
swapv (x, y )                                swapr (x, y )
int x, y ;                                   int *x, *y ;
{                                            {
    int t ;                                      int t ;
    t = x ;                                      t  = *x ;
    x = y ;                                      *x = *y ;
    y = t ;                                      *y = t ;
    printf ( "x = %d y = %d\n", x, y ) ;         printf ( "*x = %d *y = %d\n", *x, *y ) ;
}                                            }
```

Output   Output

x = 20 y = 10   *x = 20 *y = 10
a = 10 b = 20   a = 20 b = 10

Notes   **Notes**

- Changes made in **x** and **y** in   - Changes made in **swapr**( ) using
  swapv( ) are not reflected back   **x** and **y** are reflected back in **a**
  in **a** and **b**.   and **b**.

Figure 5.5 Call by value and call by reference

Recursion

When some statement in a function calls the same function it is in, we say that recursion has occurred. Such a function is called a recursive function. Taking the example of calculating the factorial of a number, let us see the working of a recursive function.

```
main( )
{
    int a, fact ;

    printf ( "Enter any number " ) ;
    scanf ( "%d", &a ) ;

    fact = rec ( a ) ;
    printf ( "Factorial value = %d", fact ) ;
}
rec ( x )
int x ;
{
    int f ;

    if ( x == 1 )
        return ( 1 ) ;
    else
        f = x * rec ( x - 1 ) ;

    return ( f ) ;
}
```

Assume that the number entered is 3. Using Figure 5.6, we try to visualise what exactly happens when the recursive function **rec( )** gets called.

Go through the figure carefully. The first time when **rec( )** is called from **main( )**, **x** collects 3. From here, since **x** is not equal to 1, the **if** block is skipped and **rec( )** is called again with argument (**x - 1**), i.e. 2. This is a recursive call. Since **x** is still not equal to 1, **rec( )** is called yet another time, with argument (2 - 1). This time as **x** is 1, control goes back to the previous **rec( )** with the value 1, and **f** is evaluated as 2. Similarly, each **rec( )** evaluates its **f** from the returned value, and finally 6 is returned to **main( )**. The sequence would be grasped better by following the arrows in Figure 5.6. Let it be clear that while executing the program there do not exist so many copies of the function **rec( )**. These have been shown in the figure just to help you keep track of how the control flows during successive recursive calls.

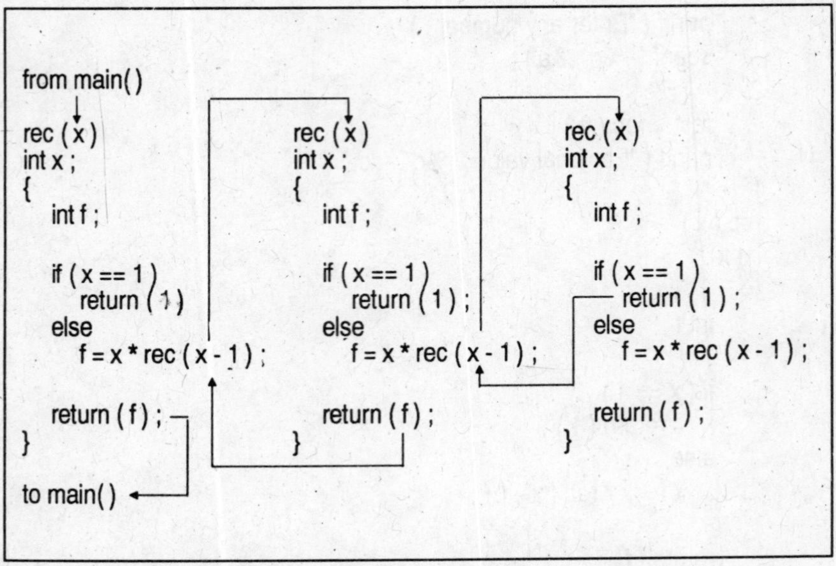

Figure 5.6 Recursion at work

Whatever a recursive program can do, a **for, while,** or **do-while** can do just as well. So don't feel daunted if you don't feel at home with recursion, as we can easily get by without it.

Exercise

[A]   What will be the output of the following programs:

(1)
```
main( )
{
    int i = 45 ;
    float c ;
    c = check ( i ) ;
    printf ( "c = %f", c ) ;
}
check ( ch )
int ch ;
{
    ch >= 45 ? return ( 3.14 ) : return ( 6.28 ) ;
}
```

(2)
```
main( )
{
    int area ;
    float radius = 2.0 ;
    area = areacircle ( radius ) ;
    printf ( "area = %f", area ) ;
}
areacircle ( r )
float r ;
{
    float a ;
    a = 3.14 * r * r ;
    printf ( "a = %f\n", a ) ;
    return ( a ) ;
}
```

```
(3)    main( )
       {
            int c ;
            printf ( "c before call = %d\n", c ) ;
            c = message( ) ;
            printf ( "c after call = %d\n", c ) ;
       }
       message( )
       {
            printf ( "Live and let live\n" ) ;
       }

(4)    main( )
       {
            C( )
            {
                c( )
                {
                    printf ( "C is a C...\n" ) ;
                }
                printf ( "..is a c...\n" ) ;
            }
            printf ( "..is a sea afterall!" ) ;
       }

(5)    main( )
       {
            int i = 3, k, l ;
            k = add ( ++i ) ;
            l = add ( i++ ) ;
            printf ( "i = %d k = %d l = %d", i, k, l ) ;
       }
       add ( ii )
       int ii ;
       {
            ++ii ;
```

```
                    return ( ii ) ;
            }

(6)     main( )
        {
                int i = 135, a = 135, k ;
                k = function ( !++i, !a++ ) ;
                printf ( "i = %d a = %d k = %d", i, a, k ) ;
        }
        function ( j, b )
        int j, b ;
        {
                int c ;
                c = j + b ;
                return ( c ) ;
        }

(7)     main( )
        {
                int k = 35, z ;
                k = func1 ( k = func1 ( k = func1 ( k ) ) ) ;
                printf ( "k = %d", k ) ;
        }
        func1 ( k )
        int k ;
        {
                k++ ;
                return ( k ) ;
        }

(8)     main( )
        {
                int k = 35, z ;
                z = func ( k ) ;
                printf ( "z = %d", z ) ;
        }
```

```
func ( m )
int m ;
{
    ++m ;
    return ( m = func1 ( ++m ) ) ;
}
func1 ( m )
int m ;
{
    m++ ;
    return ( m ) ;
}
```

(9)   ```
       main( )
       {
           void message( ) ;
           int c ;
           printf ("c before call = %d\n", c) ;
           c = message( ) ;
           printf ("c after call = %d", c) ;
       }
       void message( )
       {
           printf ("Only he will survive who is C-fit") ;
       }
       ```

(10)   ```
       main( )
       {
           int p = 23 , f = 24 ;
           packman ( p, f ) ;
           printf ( "p = %d f = %d", p, f ) ;
       }
       packman ( q, h )
       int q, h ;
       {
           q = q + a ;
           h = h + h ;
       ```

```
            return ( q ) ;
            return ( h ) ;
        }

(11)   main( )
       {
            int i = 3, j ;
            j = add ( ++i++ ) ;
            printf ( "i = %d j = %d\n", i, j ) ;
       }
       add ( ii )
       int ii ;
       {
            ii++ ;
            printf ( "ii = %d\n", ii ) ;
       }

(12)   main( )
       {
            int i = 10, j = 20, k ;
            k = addsub ( i, j ) ;
            printf ( "k = %d", k ) ;
       }
       addsub ( c, d )
       int c, d ;
       {
            int x, y ;
            x = c - d ;
            y = c + d ;
            return ( x, y ) ;
       }

(13)   main( )
       {
            int i = 10, j = 20 , k ;
            display ( i ) ;
```

```
            show ( i, j ) ;
    }
    display ( c, d )
    int c, d ;
    {
            printf ( "%d %d ", c, d ) ;
    }
    show ( c )
    int c ;
    {
            printf ( "%d", c ) ;
    }


(14)    main( )
    {
            char a = 65, ch = 'C' ;
            printit ( a, ch ) ;
    }
    printit ( a, ch )
    {
            printf ( "a = %d ch = %c", a, ch ) ;
    }


(15)    main( )
    {
            float a = 3.14 ;
            int i = 99 ;
            pri ( i, a ) ;
            printit ( a, i ) ;
    }
    pri ( i, a )
    {
            printf ( "i = %d a = %f\n", i, a ) ;
            printf ( "a = %f i = %d\n\n", a , i ) ;
    }
    printit ( a, i )
    float a ;
```

```
        {
            printf ( "a = %f i = %d\n", a, i ) ;
            printf ( "i = %d a = %f\n\n", i, a ) ;
        }

(16)   main( )
        {
            int k = 35, z ;
            z = check ( k ) ;
            printf ( "z = %d", z ) ;
        }
        check ( m )
        {
            int m ;
            if ( m > 40 )
                return ( !m++ ) ;
            else
                return ( !++m ) ;
        }

(17)   main( )
        {
            int k = 35, *z, *y ;
            z = &k ;  /* suppose address of k is 1008 */
            y = z ;
            *z++ = *y++ ;
            k++ ;
            printf ( "k = %d z = %d y = %d", k, z, y ) ;
        }

(18)   main( )
        {
            int a = 100, *b, **c, ***d ;
            b = &a ;
            c = &b ;
            d = &c ;
```

```
              printf ( "%d %d %d %d", a, *b, **c, ***d ) ;
       }

(19)   main( )
       {
              int z = 4 ;
              printf ( "%d", printf ( "%d %d", z, z ) ) ;
       }

(20)   main( )
       {
              int i = -5, j = -2 ;
              junk ( i, &j ) ;
              printf ( "i = %d j = %d", i, j ) ;
       }
       junk ( i, j )
       int i, *j ;
       {
              i = i * i ;
              *j = *j * *j ;
       }

(21)   main( )
       {
              float a = 7.999999 ;
              float *b, *c ;
              b = &a ;
              c = b ;
              printf ( "%d %d %d\n", &a, b, c ) ;
              printf ( "%d %d %d %d\n", a, *(&a), *b, *c ) ;
       }

(22)   main( )
       {
              int *c ;
              c = check ( 10, 20 ) ;
```

```
            printf ( "c = %d", c ) ;
        }
        check ( i, j )
        int i, j ;
        {
            int *p , *q ;
            p = &i ;
            q = &j ;
            i >= 45 ? return ( p ) : return ( q ) ;
        }
```

(23)   main( )
```
        {
            float *jamboree( ) ;
            float p = 23.5, *q ;
            q = &p ;
            printf ( "q before call = %d\n", q ) ;
            q = jamboree ( &p ) ;
            printf ( "q after call = %d\n", q ) ;
        }
        float *jamboree ( r )
        float *r ;
        {
            r = r + 1 ;
            return ( r ) ;
        }
```

(24)   main( )
```
        {
            int i ;
            printf ( "In the year of lord\n" ) ;
            for ( i = 1 ; i <= 10 ; i++ )
                main( ) ;
        }
```

(25)   main( )

```
      {
          int i ;
          for ( i = 1 ; i <= 10 ; i++ )
              main( ) ;
          printf ( "In the year of lord\n" ) ;
      }

(26)  main( )
      {
          if ( printf ( "C for yourself how it works\n" ) )
              main( ) ;
      }

(27)  main( )
      {
          message( ) ;
          printf ( "..selling cocaine in Xolombo" ) ;
      }
      message( )
      {
          printf ( "making a fast buck..\n" ) ,
          main( ) ;
      }

(28)  main( )
      {
          int i = 1 ;
          if ( ! i )
              printf ( "Recursive calls are real pain!" ) ;
          else
          {
              i = 0 ;
              printf ( "Recursive calls are challenging\n" ) ;
              main( ) ;
          }
      }
```

[B]   Attempt the following:

(1)   Consider a currency system in which there are notes of seven denominations, namely,

Re. 1, Rs. 2, Rs. 5, Rs. 10, Rs. 50, Rs. 100

If a sum of Rs. N is entered through the keyboard, write a program to compute the smallest number of notes that will combine to give Rs. N.

(2)   There are three pegs labelled A, B and C. Four disks are placed on peg A. The bottom-most disk is largest, and disks go on decreasing in size with the topmost disk being smallest. The objective of the game is to move the disks from peg A to peg C, using peg B as an auxiliary peg. The rules of the game are as follows:

(a)   Only one disk may be moved at a time, and it must be the top disk on one of the pegs.
(b)   A larger disk should never be placed on the top of a smaller disk.

Write a program to print out the sequence in which the disks should be moved such that all disks on peg A are finally transferred to peg C.

(3)   Write a program to obtain the sum of the first ten terms of the following series using recursion.

$$x - \frac{x^3}{3!} + \frac{x^5}{5!} - \frac{x^7}{7!} + \frac{x^9}{9!} - \cdots$$

(4)   Two dates are entered through the keyboard in dd,mm,yy format. Write a program to find out the difference in these two dates in terms of number of days.

Answers

Answers to **[A]**

(1)   *Output*

c = 3.000000

Explanation

When the function **check( )** is called 45 gets collected in the variable **ch**. In **check( )** the condition **ch >= 45** is satisfied hence 3.14 gets returned. Does it really? No, because by default any function is capable of returning only an **int**. Hence 3.14 gets truncated to 3 while returning the value.

What if we really want to return 3.14. Just make the declaration **float check( )** in **main( )**, as well as while defining the function.

(2)   *Output*

a = 12.560000
area = 12.000000

Explanation

On calling the function **areacircle( )** value of **a** (**3.14 * 2.0 * 2.0**) gets calculated, which is printed out as 12.560000. But when this value is returned to **main( )** it is truncated to 12 and then returned. This happens because the function **areacirle( )** is not capable of returning a **float** value. This 12 when assigned to the variable **area** gets promoted to 12.000000, since **area** has been declared as **float**. Moral is - just by declaring **area** as

float won't ensure that a **float** value would be returned from the function.

(3)   *Output*

```
c before call = 34
Live and let live
c after call = 457
```

Explanation

Since **c** has not been initialised in **main( )** it contains a garbage value. When we ran the program this garbage value was 34. When you execute the program this might as well turn out to be something else. After this **message( )** gets called, which ouputs the message on the screen. And having printed the message the control returns back to **main( )** alongwith some garbage integer value which gets collected in **c** and is then printed out.

Thus it is important to remember that whether we want or whether we don't, any time a function is called and the control comes back from the function, a value always gets returned. This value could be the value that you are specifically returning using the **return** statement, or some garbage integer value if a specific value is not being returned.

(4)   *Output*

Error message: Statement missing ; in function main

Explanation

The compiler reports an error saying there is a missing semi-colon. But where is it missing? After **C( )**. But suppose we only want to define the function **C( )**, logically we shouldn't be required to give a semi-colon after **C( )**. That's the point. At the most you can call a function from within the body of another function. You are not allowed to define another function within the body of another function. And that is what the above program is attempting to do. It is trying to define **C( )** and **c( )** in **main( )**, which is not acceptable, hence the error message.

(5) *Output*

i = 5 k = 5 l = 5

Explanation

Whenever the **++** operator precedes the variable, first the variable's value is incremented and then used. As against this, whenever the **++** operator succeeds the variable, its value is first used and then incremented. According to this rule the first call **add (++i)** would first increment **i** to 4 and then pass its value to function **add( )**. In **add( )** 4 is collected in **ii**, incremented to 5, returned to **main( )** and finally stored in **k**. Hence **k**'s value is printed as 5. In the next call, **add (i++)**, the current value of **i** (i.e. 4) is first sent to **add( )** and then **i**'s value is incremented to 5. In **add( )** **ii** is incremented to 5, which is returned and collected in **l**.

(6) *Output*

i = 136 a = 136 k = 0

Explanation

Observe the function call in **main( )**. Since **++** precedes **i** its value is incremented to 136, and then the **!** operator negates it to give 0. This 0 is however not stored in **i** but is passed to **function( )**. As against this while evaluating the expression **!a++**, since **++** follows **a**, firstly **a** is negated to 0, this 0 is passed to **function( )** and **a** is incremented to 136. Thus what get passed to **function( )** are 0 and 0, which are collected in **j** and **b**, added to give another 0 and finally returned to **main( )**, where it is collected in **k** and then printed out.

(7)   *Output*

    k = 38

Explanation

While evaluating **k** in **main( )** three calls to function **func1( )** are being made. These calls are evaluated inside out. That is, the innermost call is made first, followed by the next outer call and so on. So when first time the call is made with value of **k** as 35, it is incremented in **func1( )** to 36 and returned back to **main( )**. This 36 is then collected in **main( )** in **k**. This new value of **k** (i.e. 36) becomes the argument for the next call to **func1( )**, which proceeds exactly in the same manner as the previous call. One more such call and the value of **k** would finally become 38.

(8)   *Output*

    z = 38

Explanation

When **func( )** is called from **main( )**, 35 gets collected in the variable **m**. In **func( )** this value is incremented to 36 and then the **return** statement is executed. But the **return** cannot be immediately executed, since within the arguments of **return** there is another function call, this time to the function named **func1( )**. While sending a call to **func1( )** first the value of **m** is incremented to 37, and then this 37 is passed on to **func1( )**. In **func1( )**, **m** is further incremented to 38 and it is returned to **func( )**, where it gets collected once again in variable **m**. And now this 38 gets returned to **main( )**, where it is collected in **z** and then printed out.

(9)   *Output*

Error message: Not an allowed type in function main

Explanation

The error meassage comes because we are going back on our promise. First we are telling the compiler that **message( )** will not return any value. This is being achieved through the declaration **void message( )**. And then we are trying to collect in the variable **c**, the value returned by **message( )**. Conclusion - better stick to your word!

(10)   *Output*

p = 23 f = 24

Explanation

A call to **packman( )** from **main( )** sends 23 and 24 to variables **q** and **h**. In **packman( )** **q** and **h** are doubled and then the **return (q)** is executed, which sends the control back to **main( )** alongwith the value of **q**. But since this value is not collected in any variable in **main( )** it just gets ignored. As a result **p** and **f** stand unchanged at 23 and 24 respectively. Note that the statement **return (h)** never gets executed, since the previous **return** statement will not allow the control to reach there.

(11) *Output*

Error message: Lvalue required in function main

Explanation

'Lvalue' means a variable whose value can change. Or in other words, a variable which can occur on the left hand side of the assignment operator. Now look at the expression **++i++**. Here firstly **i** would be incremented to 4 (due to the **++** operator before **i**) and the expression would become **4++**. As a result 4 would be passed to **add( )** and then would attempt to get incremented owing to the operator that occurs after **i**. But 4 cannot be incremented because it is not a variable. Possibly if you consider the expression **i++** as **i = i + 1** then you would be able to appreciate the mistake in the program better. An attempt would be made to evaluate **4++** as **4 = 4 + 1**. And since 4 is not a variable it cannot occur on left hand side of **=**. In other words, on left hand side of assignment operator a variable (lvalue) should occur.

(12) *Output*

k = 30

Explanation

Values of **i** and **j** (10 and 20) are passed to **addsub( )** and collected in variables **c** and **d**. In function **addsub( )**, **x** evaluates to -10, whereas **y** evaluates to 30. Then the **return** statement attempts to return the values of **x** and **y**. Whenever we attempt to return more than one value through the **return** statement, the last value gets returned. Thus, in this case the value of **y**, i.e. 30 gets returned. Had the **return** statement been **return (y, x)** then value of **x** would have been returned.

(13) *Output*

10 457 10

Explanation

When **display( )** is called one argument is passed to it, whereas while defining **display( )** two arguments are used. Would it result into an error? No, since the compiler accepts a mismatch in the number of arguments being passed and collected. If this is so, which of the two variables would collect the value being passed to **display( )**? **c** collects the value being passed, hence the **printf( )** prints out the value of **c** as 10, whereas **d** is printed as garbage value.

What if we pass two arguments and collect them in one variable? This is what is being done in the call to function **show( )**. Here the first value gets collected in the variable **c**, whereas the second value gets ignored. The value collected in **c**, i.e. 10 then gets printed.

(14) *Output*

a = 65 ch = C

Explanation

First glance at the function **printit( )** would lead you to believe that the compiler should have flashed an error message since the variables **a** and **ch** have not been defined in **printit( )**. But then the Turbo C compiler is a fatherly old chap who knows the pulls and pressures a C programmer has to bear and therefore makes such concessions. While defining the function if the type of formal arguments (**a** and **ch** in this case) is not mentioned then they are treated as integer arguments. Thus **a** and **ch** are treated as integers, and hence printed out without any hitch by the **printf( )**.

(15) *Output*

```
i = 99 a = 0.000000
a = 0.000000 i = 99
a = 3.14 i = 99
i = 99 a = 3.14
```

Explanation

When **pri( )** is called the values passed to it are collected in the variables **i** and **a**. However, the type of these variables have not been declared. Therefore, they are assumed to be **int**s. The first **printf( )** in **pri( )** prints out the value of **i** correctly, but value of **a** gets messed up because we are trying to print an integer value collected in **a** using the specification **%f**. The second **printf( )** messes up both the values since the first specification itself in this **printf( )** is wrong. Remember that once the output of one variable goes awry the **printf( )** messes up the output of the rest of the variables too.

When **printit( )** is called **a** has been declared as **float** whereas **i** has not been declared, hence is assumed to be an **int**. Therefore both the **printf( )**s output the values as expected.

(16) *Output*

Error message: Redeclaration of 'm' in function check

Explanation

Observe the **check( )** function carefully. The variable **m** used in **check( )** has not been defined before the opening brace.

Therefore it is assumed to be an integer variable. And then after the opening brace we once again declare **m**, thereby causing the redefinition of the variable **m**. Hence the error message.

17) *Output*

k = 36 z = 1010 y = 1010

Explanation

In **main( )** the address of **k** is stored in **z** and the same address is then assigned to **y**. Since **y** and **z** contain addresses of an integer (35), they have been quite appropriately declared as integer pointers. The next statement is the most important statement in this program. What is done here is, the **z** and **y** pointers are incremented to point to the next integer location (which would be 1010, assuming that **z** and **y** contain 1008 before incrementation). But before the incrementation what is done is assignment. This is beacuse **++** is occurring after the variable names **y** and **z**. During assignment, value at the address contained in **z** is replaced by value at the address contained in **y** (i.e. 35). After that the value of **k** is incremented to 36 and then printed out.

(18) *Output*

100 100 100 100

Explanation

b contains the address of an integer **a**, hence **b** is an integer pointer. **c** contains the address of an integer pointer, hence **c** is a pointer to an integer pointer. Similarly, since **d** contains the address of a pointer to an integer pointer, **d** can be called a pointer to a pointer to an integer pointer. Foxed? Look at the following figure to sort it out.

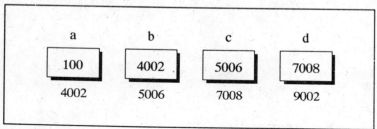

Figure 5.7

In **printf( )**, **a** would print out the value 100 which is straight-forward. ***b** would print the value at the address contained in **b**. Since the address contained in **b** is 4002, and the value at this address is 100, once again 100 would get printed. ****c** can be explained similarly. **c** would give 5006, ***c** means value at address contained in **c**, i.e. value at address 5006, i.e. 4002. Thus ***c** gives 4002, therefore ****c** would give value at address 4002, i.e. 100. I hope you would be able to extend the similar logic to understand the output of *****d**, which would also be 100.

(19) *Output*

   4 4 3

Explanation

Can a **printf( )** occur within another **printf( )**? Yes, by all means. Here the inner **printf( )** is executed first, and it prints out a 4, a space and another 4. Thus it totally prints out 3 characters. Whenever the **printf( )** function is called it returns the number of characters it has successfully managed to print. In this program the inner **printf( )** has printed out 3 characters, therefore it sends back 3 to the calling function, which is promptly printed out by the outer **printf( )**. Moral of the story is whenever a function is called, be it a user-defined or a standard library function, it always returns a value.

(20) *Output*

i = -5 j = 4

Explanation

Refer to the following figure first.

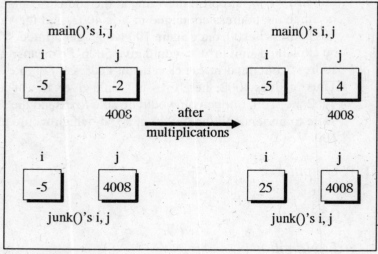

Figure 5.8

One doubt immediately comes to the mind - can we use same variable names in different functions? Yes, by all means, without absolutely any conflict. Thus, the two sets of **i** and **j** are two totally different sets of variables. While calling the function **junk( )** the value of **i** and the address of **j** are passed to it. Naturally, in **junk( )** **i** is declared as an ordinary **int**, whereas **j** is declared as a pointer to an **int**.

Even though the value of **i** is changed to 25 in **junk( )**, this change will not be reflected back in **main( )**. As against this, since **j**'s address is being passed to **junk( )**, any change in **junk( )** gets reflected back in **main( )**. Hence ***j * *j**, which evaluates to 4 is reflected back in **main( )**. Figure 5.8 would make the whole logic a little more palatable.

(21) *Output*

```
4200 4200 4200
0 24576 -3 16415
```

Explanation

b contains the address of variable **a**. Since **a** is a **float**, **b** must be a **float** pointer. The same address is then assigned to **c**. Therefore **c** has also been declared as a **float** pointer. The first **printf( )** prints the address of **a** in three different ways. No problem there. What is surprising is the output of the second **printf( )**. Through this **printf( )** we are attempting to print 7.999999 by applying pointer operators on **a**, **b** and **c**. **a**, ***(&a)**, ***b**, ***c** all yield 7.999999 but when they are printed using %d, **printf( )** blows it up as the output above would justify.

So always remember to use **%f** to print floating point values. Don't rely on **printf( )** to truncate a **float** value to an integer while printing by using a **%d**. Vice versa also its true. The following statements would not print 7.000000. Don't be surprised if you get some odd value. In that sense **%d** and **%f** are a little unreliable.

```
int i = 7 ;
printf ( "%f", i ) ;
```

(22) *Output*

Error message: Non portable pointer assignment in main

Explanation

The reason for the error is simple. The integers being passed to **check( )** are collected in **i** and **j**, and then their addresses are assigned to **p** and **q**. Then in the next statement the conditional operators test the value of **i** against 45, and return either the address stored in **p** or the address stored in **q**. It appears that this address would be collected in **c** in **main( )**, and then would be printed out. And there lies the error. The function **check( )** is not capable of returning an integer pointer. All that it can return is an ordinary integer. Thus just declaring **c** as an integer pointer is not sufficient. We must make the following modifications in the program to make it work properly.

```
main( )
{
    int *c ;
    int *check( ) ;
    c = check ( 10, 20 ) ;
    printf ( "c = %d", c ) ;
}
int *check ( i, j )
int i, j ;
{
    .....
    .....
}
```

(23) *Output*

```
q before call = 5498
q after call = 5502
```

Explanation

In **main( )**, **q** has been declared as a **float** pointer. It means **q** is a variable capable of holding the address of a **float**. Through **q = &p** the address of **p**, a **float**, is stored in **q** and then printed out through the **printf( )**. This is the value of **q** before **jamboree( )** is called. When **jamboree( )** is called the address of **p** is sent to it and is collected in **r**. At this juncture **r** contains 5498 (when we ran the program it was 5498; when you execute the program this may turn out to be some other address). When **r** is incremented it would become 5502. Why a step of 4? Because **r** is a **float** pointer and on incrementing it by 1 it would point to the next **float** which would be present 4 bytes hence, since every **float** is 4 bytes long. The **return** statement then returns this address 5502 back to **main( )**.

Since a **float** pointer is being returned, a declaration **float *jamboree( )** is necessary in **main( )**, which tells the compiler that down the line there exists a function called **jamboree( )**, which will return a **float** pointer.

(24) *Output*

```
In the year of lord
In the year of lord
In the year of lord
In the year of lord
.. .... ........ ... .....
.. .... ........ ... .....
```

Explanation

When the control enters **main( )** it meets the **printf( )** and promptly prints the message. Then comes the **for** loop. First time through the **for** loop the function **main( )** is called again.

This is nothing but recursion - a function calling itself. So control once again reaches the **printf( )**, and hence the second message. Once again the control reaches the **for** loop and with **i** equal to 1 once again **main( )** gets called. This results into another message printed on the screen followed by another call to **main( )** for value of **i** equal to 1. This goes on and on until either you abort the execution by pressing ctrl C or ctrl scroll-lock or when the internal stack overflows.

(25) *Output*

No output   .

Explanation

First time the control reaches the **for** loop **main( )** gets called once again. The control again reaches the **for** loop and for value of **i** equal to 1, **main( )** is called yet another time, so on and so forth. This continues until the stack becomes full or until the user aborts the program through ctrl scroll-lock.

(26) *Output*

```
C for yourself how it works
C for yourself how it works
C for yourself how it works
C for yourself how it works

.  .... ............. ....... .. .........
.  .... ............. ....... .. .........
```

Explanation

On execution, **printf( )** always returns the number of characters it has printed succesfully. In our case this value will be 27. Since the value returned is a non-zero value the **if** evaluates to true, hence **main( )** gets called. Next time around exactly the same thing happens. This goes on and on till either the user interrupts through ctrl scroll-lock or a stack overflow occurs.

(27) *Output*

making a fast buck
making a fast buck
making a fast buck
....
....

Explanation

From **main( )** firstly the function **message( )** gets called. In **message( )** 'making a fast buck' gets printed and once again **main( )** gets called, through which once again **message( )** gets called. This goes on and on. Thus, the control never reaches the **printf( )** statement in **main( )**, and therefore '..selling cocaine in Xolombo' doesn't appear in the output.

(28) *Output*

Recursive calls are challenging
Recursive calls are challenging
Recursive calls are challenging
....
....

Explanation

Since **i** is 1, **!i** results into a 0. Therefore the **if** fails and the control reaches the **else** block, where **i** is assigned a value 0, the **printf( )** is executed, and once again **main( )** is called. What is important is when **main( )** is called now, the variable **i** is reset to 1. Thus, **!i** would be 0, and again the control would reach the **else** block and the same process would be repeated all over again. No provision has been made to break out of these horrowing circles, hence this goes on indefinitely. The only way to break out of the loop is to press ctrl scroll-lock. I hope you too agree that 'Recursive calls are challenging'!

Solutions to [B]

(1)   *Program*

```
main( )
{
    int sum, notes = 0 ;

    printf ( "\nEnter the sum of rupees " ) ;
    scanf ( "%d", &sum ) ;

    denom ( &sum, &notes, 100 );
    denom ( &sum, &notes, 50 ) ;
    denom ( &sum, &notes, 10 ) ;
    denom ( &sum, &notes, 5 ) ;
    denom ( &sum, &notes, 2 ) ;
    notes += sum ;
    printf ( "\nSmallest number of notes = %d ", notes ) ;
}
denom ( s, n, c )
int *s, *n, c ;
{
    *n += ( (*s) / c ) ;
    *s %= c ;
}
```

Sample run

Enter the sum of rupees 159

Smallest number of notes = 5

Explanation

The function **denom( )** is passed the address of the variables **sum** and **notes**, and one of the 7 denominations of notes. First time when the function is called, the sum of rupees is divided by 100 to find out the maximum number of 100 rupee notes. The remainder is then assigned to the address of **sum**. Next time around, the value at **sum** is used to find the number of 50 rupee notes, and so on, till **sum** is reduced to 1. Corresponding to a 1 rupee note, **sum** itself is added to **notes**, yielding the total number of notes required.

(2)   *Program*

```
main( )
{
    int n = 4 ;
    move ( n, 'A', 'B', 'C' ) ;
}
move ( n, sp, ap, ep )
int n ;
char sp, ap, ep ;
{
    if ( n == 1 )
        printf ("\n Move from %c to %c ", sp, ep ) ;
    else
    {
        move ( n - 1, sp, ep, ap ) ;
        move ( 1, sp, ' ', ep ) ;
        move ( n - 1, ap, sp, ep ) ;
    }
}
```

Sample run

```
Move from A to B
Move from A to C
Move from B to C
Move from A to B
Move from C to A
Move from C to B
Move from A to B
Move from A to C
Move from B to C
Move from B to A
Move from C to A
Move from B to C
Move from A to B
Move from A to C
Move from B to C
```

Explanation

This problem is the famous Towers of Hanoi problem, wherein three pegs are to be employed for transferring the disks with the given criteria. Here's how we go about it. We have three pegs: the starting peg, **sp**, the auxiliary peg **ap**, and the ending peg, **ep**, where the disks must finally be. First, using the ending peg as an auxiliary or supporting peg, we transfer all but the last disk to **ap**. Next the last disk is moved from **sp** to **ep**. Now, using **sp** as the supporting peg, all the disks are moved from **ap** to **ep**.

The three pegs are denoted by 'A', 'B' and 'C'. The recursive function **move( )** is called with different combinations of these pegs as starting, auxiliary and ending pegs. Going through the following figure would be the best way to sort out how the control flows through the program.

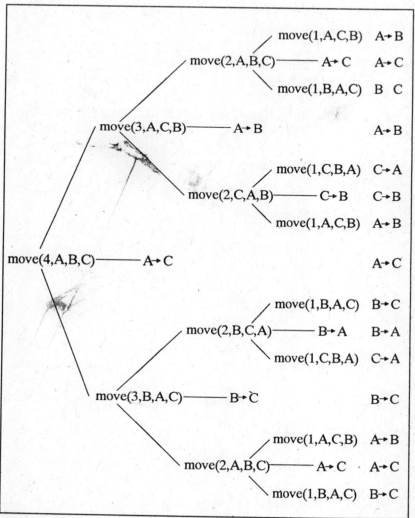

Figure 5.9

(3) *Program*

```
main( )
{
```

```
        float x ;
        float sum_series( ) ;

        printf ( "\nEnter value of x " ) ;
        scanf ( "%f", &x ) ;

        printf ( "Sum of first 10 terms = %f", sum_series ( x ) ) ;
}

float sum_series ( x )
float x ;
{
    static int i, sign = 1 ;
    float p, f ;
    static float sum ;
    int j, k ;

    if ( i < 10 )
    {
        j = 1 + 2 * i ;

        p = f = 1 ;

        for ( k = 1 ; k <= j ; k++ )
        {
            p *= x ;
            f *= k ;
        }

        sum += ( ( p / f ) * sign ) ;
        i++ ;
        sign *= -1 ;
        sum_series ( x ) ;
    }
    return ( sum ) ;
}
```

Sample run

```
Enter value of x 1.57
Sum of first 10 terms is = 1.000000
```

Explanation

The variable **j** is set up so that it stores values 1, 3, 5, 7, 9 etc. one after the other, corresponding to the degree of **x** in the series. Using a **for** loop, **p** is assigned the value of **x** raised to **j**, and **f** is made to store the factorial value of **j**. The series starts with a positive **x**, so **sign** is initialised to 1, and then made to toggle for the consecutive terms of the series.

To start with, **sum** is declared as **static float**, ensuring that it stores a zero. The first time **x**, i.e. 1.57 gets stored into **sum**, as for **i** equal to zero (**i** has been declared **static**), **p** evaluates to 1.57 itself and **f** to 1. Now **i** is incremented to 1, and **sum_series( )** is called recursively. Since **sum** and **i** both have a **static** storage class, their values, 1.57 and 1 respectively are retained in the second call. This call adds on to **sum** the value of the second term of the series. Following this **i** is again incremented and once again **sum_series( )** is called, and so on, till all the 10 terms are evaluated, and then control returns to **main( )**, wherein the value of the series is printed out.

(4)   *Program*

```
main( )
{
    int d1, m1, y1, d2, m2, y2, days, dm ;

    days = 1 ;
    dm = 0 ;
```

```
        printf ( "Input first date (dd,mm,yy) " ) ;
        scanf ( "%d %d %d", &d1, &m1, &y1 ) ;

        printf ( "Input second date (dd,mm,yy) " ) ;
        scanf ( "%d %d %d", &d2, &m2, &y2 ) ;

        dm = daysinmonth ( m1, y1 ) ;

        while ( 1 )
        {
            days = days + 1 ;
            d1 = d1 + 1 ;

            if ( d1 > dm )
            {
                m1 = m1 + 1 ;
                d1 = 1 ;

                if ( m1 > 12 )
                {
                    m1 = 1 ;
                    y1 = y1 + 1 ;
                }

                dm = daysinmonth ( m1, y1 ) ;
            }

            if ( d1 == d2 && m1 == m2 && y1 == y2 )
                break ;
        }

        printf ( "\n\nDifference in Dates = %d", days ) ;
}

daysinmonth ( m, y )
int m, y ;
{
```

```
    int dm ;

    if ( m == 1 || m == 3 || m == 5 || m == 7 || m == 8 || m == 10 || m == 12 )
        dm = 31 ;

    if ( m == 4 || m == 6 || m == 9 || m == 11 )
        dm = 30 ;

    if ( m == 2 )
    {
        dm = 28 ;
        if ( ( y % 400 == 0 ) || ( y % 100 != 0 && y % 4 == 0 ) )
            dm = 29 ;
    }
    return ( dm ) ;
}
```

Sample run

```
Input first date ( dd, mm, yy ) 01 01 1993
Input second date ( dd, mm, yy ) 31 12 1993

Difference in Dates = 365 days
```

Explanation

Firstly the two dates are received in dd,mm,yy format. Then the function **daysinmonth( )** is called to find out number of days in the month **m1** of year **y1**. Nextly, through the indefinite **while** loop the variable **days** is continuously incremented. It counts the number of days. If **d1** exceeds the days in a month, then we go to the next month by incrementing **m1**, and if **m1** exceeds 12 then we go to the next year's first month. This counting goes on till we reach the second date. This happens when **d1** equals **d2**, **m1** equals **m2** and **y1** equals **y2**. When this happens the control comes out of the loop by executing **break** and prints out the difference in dates stored in the variable **days.**

6

Datatypes

The Building blocks

I n all the earlier chapters we used the primary data types **char**, **int** and **float**. These primary datatypes themselves could be of several types. For example, a **char** could be a **signed char** or an **unsigned char**, an **int** could be a **short int** or a **long int**, or a real could be a **float**, a **double** or a **long double**. While storing **chars** and **ints**, the highest bit is always used for storing the sign of the number. What if we know that the value stored in an integer or a character variable is never going to be negative (for example the age of a person)? In such cases there is no point in wasting the sign bit. This wastage can be avoided by declaring the integer or the character variable in question as **unsigned**. By doing this the range of the variable is almost doubled, since the sign bit is no longer used for storing the sign. The fact that the ranges of different datatypes are different means that the memory occupied by each would also be different. Figure 6.1 shows the ranges, bytes occupied and the format specifications used for each datatype when they are used in **printf( )** and **scanf( )** statements.

While defining the various variables, C allows the abbreviation of a **short int** to **int**, and of **long int** to **long**. Thus a declaration **short int j** is same as **int j**. Similarly a **long int k** is same as **long k**. Sometimes we come across situations where the constant is small enough to be an **int**, but still we want to give it as much storage as a **long**. In such cases we add the suffix 'L' or 'l' at the end of the number.

Datatype	Range	Bytes	Format
signed char	-128 to +127	1	%c
unsigned char	0 to 255	1	%c
short signed int	-32768 to +32767	2	%d
short unsigned int	0 to 65535	2	%u
long signed int	-2147483648 to +2147483647	4	%ld
long unsigned int	0 to 4294967295	4	%lu
float	-3.4e38 to +3.4e38	4	%f
double	-1.7e308 to +1.7e308	8	%lf
long double	-1.7e4932 to +1.7e4932	10	%Lf

Figure 6.1 Datatypes in C

Storage Classes in C

Done with constants, we move on to C variables. Variables are nothing but a fixed number of locations reserved under a specific name. The mode in which a variable is assigned memory space is determined by its storage class. The computer allows access to two types of locations:

(a)   Memory
(b)   CPU registers

Besides the location of the stored variable, a storage class determines:

(a)   What is the default initial value, i.e. the value assumed when a variable has not been initialised
(b)   What is the scope of the variable, i.e. in which functions the value of the variable is available
(c)   What is the scope of the variable

(d)   What is the life of the variable

A C variable can have any of the following storage classes:

(a)   Automatic storage class
(b)   Register storage class
(c)   Static storage class
(d)   External storage class

The features of all the storage classes have been given in the following figure.

Storage class	Location	Default initial value	Scope	Life
Automatic	Memory	Unpredictable or garbage value	Local to block	Till control is within that block
Register	CPU Registers	garbage value	Local to block	Till control is within that block
Static	Memory	Zero	Local to block	Persists between various function calls

Figure 6.2 Types of storage classes

In the declaration of storage class for a variable, we mention the keyword for that particular class. For instance, for assigning **automatic, register, static** and **external** storage classes to variables **a, b, c** and **d** respectively we should say:

```
auto float a ;
register int b ;
static int c ;
```

extern double d ;

Tips on storage classes

Here are a few things that you must keep in mind about storage classes.

By default, **automatic** storage class is assumed for variables declared within a function, and an external storage class for those declared outside. This is why we could afford to drop the mention of storage classes in the variables used as yet.

static storage class should be used only when a program requires the value of a variable to persist between different function calls, like in recursive calls.

As there are only 14 CPU registers present, of which even less may be at our disposal due to the microprocessor itself using some, we must use them sparingly. Since the computer accesses them faster than it accesses memory, their best utility would be as loop counters which have to be used a number of times. However, if no registers are free at the time, **auto** storage class is assumed by the compiler and execution is carried on.

CPU registers are 2 bytes long. So their maximum range is equal to that of an **int. float**s cannot be stored in **register** storage. Even if we say **register float** x or the like, **auto** is assumed for **x**.

extern storage class should be used for only those variables which are being used by almost all the functions in the program. By doing so you are spared the botherence of passing and collecting them as function arguments. At the same time, declaring all the variables as **extern**s is not advisable, since they would remain active throughout the life of the program, wasting a lot of memory unnecessarily.

When you don't have any of the express needs mentioned above, use **auto** storage class. These variables are lost once they are used in a function, which is perfectly fine, as we no longer need them.

In case of a conflict between a global (**extern**) and a local variable of the same name, it is always the local variable that is given the higher priority.

Exercise

[A]   What will be the output of the following programs:

(1)
```
main( )
{
    int i ;
    for ( i = 1 ; 100 ; i++ )
        printf ( "%d\n", i ) ;
}
```

(2)
```
main( )
{
    char ch ;
    for ( ch = 65 ; ch <= 255 ; ch++ )
        printf ( "%d %c\n", ch, ch ) ;
}
```

(3)
```
main( )
{
    unsigned char ch ;
    for ( ch = 65 ; ch <= 255 ; ch++ )
        printf ( "%d %c\n", ch, ch ) ;
}
```

(4)
```
main( )
{
    unsigned int ch = 0 ;
    for ( ch = 65 ; ch <= 255 ; )
        printf ( "%d %c\n", ch, ch++ ) ;
}
```

(5)
```
main( )
{
    float a = 0.7 ;
```

```
            douwe b = 0.7 ;
            long double c = 0.7 ;
            if ( a == b || b == c )
                  printf ( "Condition satisfied" ) ;
            else
                  printf ( "Condition not satisfied" ) ;
            printf( "a = %f b = %lf c = %Lf", a, b, c ) ;
      }
```

(6)   ```
       main( )
       {
            float y = 0.9 ;
            long double z = 0.9 ;
            if (y == z)
                  printf ("Diamonds are forever...") ;
            else
                  printf ("forever... forever... forever") ;
       }
```

(7)    ```
       main( )
       {
            int i ;
            float f ;
            double d ;
            long l ;
            i = l = f = d = 100 / 3 ;
            printf ( "%d %ld %f %lf\n", i, l, f, d ) ;
            f = i = d = l = 100 / 3 ;
            printf ( "%f %d %lf %ld\n", f, i, d, l ) ;
            l = i = d = f = 100 / 3 ;
            printf ( "%ld %d %lf %f\n", l, i, d, f ) ;
            d = l = f = i = 100 / 3 ;
            printf ( "%lf %ld %f %d\n", d, l, f, i ) ;
       }
```

```
(8)    main( )
       {
           auto int i = 10 ;
           register int j = 20 ;
           printf ( "main's i and j are %d %d\n", i, j ) ;
           change( ) ;
           printf ( "main's i and j are %d %d\n", i, j ) ;
       }
       change( )
       {
           auto int i = 100 ;
           register int j = 200 ;
           printf ( "change's i and j are %d %d\n", i, j ) ;
       }

(9)    int i = 10, j = 20, k = 30 ;
       main( )
       {
           int i = 1, j = 2, k = 3 ;
           printf ( "i = %d j = %d k = %d\n", i, j, k ) ;
           val( ) ;
       }
       val( )
       {
           printf ( "i = %d j = %d k = %d", i, j, k ) ;
       }

(10)   int num ;
       main( )
       {
           int i, j ;
           for ( i = 1 ; i <= 3 ; i++ )
           {
               j = increment( ) ;
               printf ( "j = %d\n", j ) ;
           }
```

```
            printf ( "num = %d", num ) ;
        }
        increment( )
        {
            num++ ;
            return ( num ) ;
        }
```

(11)   ```
        main( )
        {
            int z, y ;
            z = recsum (1) ;
            y = recsum (1) ;
            printf ("z = %d\ny = %d", z, y) ;
        }
        recsum (i)
        int i ;
        {
            static int sum = 0 ;
            if (i == 3)
                return (sum) ;
            else
            {
                sum = sum + 10 ;
                i++ ;
                recsum (i) ;
            }
        }
        ```

(12)    ```
        int i = 0 ;
        main( )
        {
            printf ( "main's i = %d\n", i ) ;
            i++ ;
            val( ) ;
            printf ( "main's i = %d\n", i ) ;
            val( ) ;
        ```

```
        }
        val( )
        {
            i = 100 ;
            printf ( "val's i = %d\n", i ) ;
            i++ ;
        }
```

(13)   main( )
```
        {
            int y, s = 2, t = 5 ;
            y = fun ( s + t ) ;
            printf ( "s = %d t = %d y = %d", s, t, y ) ;
        }
        int t = 8 ;
        fun ( s )
        int s ;
        {
            s++ ;
            t++ ;
            return ( s + t ) ;
        }
```

(14)   main( )
```
        {
            double x, d = 4.4 ;
            int i = 2, y ;
            x = ( y = d / i ) * 2 ;
            printf ( "x = %lf y = %d\n", x, y ) ;
            y = ( x = d / i ) * 2 ;
            printf ( "x = %lf y = %d\n", x, y ) ;.
        }
```

(15)   main( )
```
        {
            double x, d = 5.0 ;
```

```
        int y ;
        x = d * ( x = 2.5 / d ) ;
        printf ( "x = %lf\n", x ) ;
        x = d * ( y = ( int ) 2.5 + 1.5 ) ;
        printf ( "x = %lf y = %d\n", x, y ) ;
    }


(16)  main( )
    {
        static int c = 5 ;
        printf ( "c = %d\n", c-- ) ;
        if ( c )
            main( ) ;
    }


(17)  main( )
    {
        int c = 5 ;
        printf ( "c = %d\n", c-- ) ;
        if ( c )
            main( ) ;
    }


(18)  int i ;
    main( )
    {
        int j ;
        for ( ; ; )
        {
            if ( j = function ( i ) )
                printf ( "j = %d\n", j ) ;
            else
                break ;
        }
    }
    function ( x )
```

```
        int x ;
        {
            static int v = 2 ;
            v-- ;
            return ( v - x ) ;
        }
```

(19)   main( )
```
        {
            long num = 2 ;
            short n = 2 ;
            signed no = 2 ;
            printf ( "num = %ld n = %d no = %d", num, n, no ) ;
        }
```

(20)   main( )
```
        {
            char ch = 122, ch1 = 'z' ;
            printf ( "ch = %c ", ch ) ;
            printf ( "ch1 = %d", ch1 ) ;
        }
```

(21)   main( )
```
        {
            unsigned int a = 25 ;
            unsigned b = 25 ;
            long unsigned c = 345L ;
            long signed d = 345L ;
            printf ( "a = %u b = %u", a, b ) ;
            printf ( "c = %lu d = %ld", c, d ) ;
        }
```

(22)   main( )
```
        {
            printf ( "in main i = %d\n", i ) ;
            func1( ) ;
```

```
        }
        int i = 5 ;
        func1( )
        {
            printf ( "In func1 i = %d\n", i ) ;
        }
```

(23)   ```
        main( )
        {
            register float r = 3.14 ;
            register double y = 3.4 ;
            printf ("r = %f y = %lf", r, y) ;
        }
        ```

(24)    ```
        main( )
        {
            auto int i = 100 ;
            printf ( "i = %d\n", i ) ;
            {
                int i = 1 ;
                printf ( "i = %d\n", i ) ;
                {
                    i += 1 ;
                    printf ( "i = %d\n", i ) ;
                }
                printf ( "i = %d\n", i ) ;
            }
            printf ( "i = %d\n", i ) ;
        }
        ```

(25)   ```
        i = 0 ;
        main( )
        {
            printf ("in main i = %d\n", i) ;
            i++ ;
            val( ) ;
        ```
        ```

```
            printf ( "in main i = %d\n", i ) ;
    }
    val( )
    {
        int i = 100 ;
        printf ( "in val i = %d\n", i ) ;
        i++ ;
    }
```

(26) Which of the following would work faster?

(a)
```
    main( )
    {
        register int i ;
        for ( i = 1 ; i <= 100 ; i++ )
        printf ( "%d\n", i ) ;
    }
```

(b)
```
    main( )
    {
        auto int i ;
        for ( i = 1 ; i <= 100 ; i++ )
        printf ( "%d\n", i ) ;
    }
```

[B] Attempt the following:

(1) For every non-zero odd number there exist two consecutive numbers which form a pythagorian triplet. For example, 3, 4, 5 form a pythagorian triplet where 3 is an odd number, whereas 4 and 5 are consecutive numbers. Another example is 9, 40, 41. Write a program to find all such pythagorian triplets for all odd numbers in the range 1 to 10.

(2) Square of 12 is 144. 21, which is a reverse of 12 has a square 441, which is same as 144 reversed. There are few numbers

which have this property. Write a program to find out whether any more such numbers exist in the range 10 to 100.

Answers

Answers to **[A]**

(1)   *Output*

```
1
2
..
...
32767
-32768
-32767
.:........
..........
```

Explanation

The usual form of **for** loop is as under:

for (initialisation ; condition ; increment)

Observe the **for** loop in our program carefully. Instead of a condition, there is 100, a truth value. To begin with **i** takes a value 1. After this the condition is tested. Due to the presence of a truth value, the execution proceeds to **printf( )**, which prints out the value of **i**, i.e. 1. Then the control reaches **i++**, which increments **i** to 2 and then proceeds to test the condition where it finds 100, the truth value. Therefore, the control reaches **printf( )** and prints out 2. Once again the increment and test is performed and then the new value of **i** i.e. 3 gets printed. This goes on indefinitely since the condition part is always going to be true, irrespective of the value of **i**. Once **i** exceeds the integer range of +32767, the values from the other side of the range (the negative side) are picked up.

(2)   *Output*

```
65 A
66 B
... ..
... ..
125 }
126 ~
..... ..
-128 Ç
..... ..
-126 ~
-125 }
..... ..
..... ..
-2
-1
... ..
65 A
66 B
... ..
```

Explanation

What does the declaration **char ch** do? It reserves one byte in memory and associates a name **ch** with it. Its a wrong notion that a character variable stores a character constant. This is because when we store an 'A' in a character variable, what gets stored is the ascii value of 'A', i.e. 01000001. Decimal equivalent of this ascii code is 65. Thus, storing 'A' in a character variable is as good as storing 65 in it.

Now look at the **for** loop and you would not be surprised to find that **ch** is being assigned a value 65, even though it has been declared as a **char**. Since 65 is less than 255, the condition is satisfied and the control reaches the **printf( )**. **%d** prints the value stored in **ch** (i.e. 65) as an integer, whereas **%c** prints the character corresponding to this value (i.e. 'A'). Then the control proceeds to **ch++** where **ch** is incremented to 66 and since the condition is satisfied, the **printf( )** once again goes to work, this time printing out 66 and 'B'. This goes on till **ch** reaches 127. After printing 127 and its corresponding character, when **ch++** attempts to increment it to 128, it falters. Why? Because a **char** (i.e. 1 byte) can store numbers in the range -128 to +127. Therefore **ch** cannot take a value 128, hence the value from the other side of the range i.e. -128 is picked up, and tested against 255. Since the test is satisified the **printf( )** gets executed. This goes on and on, indefinitely, because the value of **ch** would keep oscillating betwen -128 to +127 and hence would never exceed 255.

(3)   *Output*

65 A
66 B
... ..
... ..
125 }
126 ~
....
....
255
.. .
.. .
65 A
66 B
.. .

Explanation

Like an ordinary **char**, an **unsigned char** is also 1 byte long. But it has a bigger range (0 to 255), since unlike a **char**, it doesn't sacrifice 1 bit in storing the sign of the number. Through the loop the ascii values and their corresponding characters get printed from 65 to 255. Once **ch** has become 255, and **printf( )** has been executed, the control reaches **ch++** and attempts to increment **ch** to 256. **ch** being an **unsigned char** cannot become 256 since its range is only 0 to 255, and therefore becomes 0, and the whole procedure is repeated all over again. Thus, **ch** keeps oscillating between 0 to 255 and never becomes 256. So the condition is always satisfied and hence this is an indefinite loop.

(4) *Output*

```
65 A
66 B
... ..
... ..
125 }
126 ~
..... ..
..... ..
255
```

Explanation

The **for** loop begins with 65 and goes uptil 255, printing each of these numbers alongwith their corresponding characters. The incrementation of **ch** is being done in **printf( )**. Since **++** comes after **ch**, firstly its value would be used to carry out the printing, and then it would be incremented. Since **ch** has been declared as an **unsigned int** there is no question of exceeding the range, as the range of an **unsigned int** is 0 to 65535.

(5) *Output*

Condition not satisfied

a = 0.700000 b = 0.700000 c = 0.700000

Explanation

0.7 has NOT been stored in **a**, **b** and **c**, though apparently it appears so. What actually gets stored in **a**, **b** and **c** is 0.699999988, 0.699999999 and 0.7 respectively. This is because a real number by default is always represented as a **long double**, which occupies 10 bytes in memory. Thus 0.7 is represented as a 10 byte number in memory. Now, when this 10 byte number gets stored in a 4 byte **float** variable, or an 8 byte **double** variable, the precision considerations force this 10 byte 0.7 to get stored as 0.699999988 and 0.699999999 respectively. Thus, when it is tested whether **a** and **b** are equal, or whether **b** and **c** are equal, the condition fails and 'Condition not satisfied' gets printed. However, when the control reaches **printf( )**, the output is once again 0.700000. This is because the format specification **%f** converts 0.699999988 to 0.700000, and **%lf** converts 0.699999999 to 0.700000.

(6)   *Output*

forever... forever... forever

Explanation

On first glance you would be surprised by the output obtained. The reason lies in the fact that in the variable **y**, 0.9 doesn't get stored. What is stored is 0.899999976. This is because in C, any floating point number is represented as a **long double** and a **long double** is 10 bytes long. Now, when this 10 byte long 0.9 gets stored in a 4 byte **float** variable **y**, due to precision considerations what gets stored is only 0.899999976. As against this, in **z** exactly 0.9 gets stored. Naturally, the condi tion would fail since contents of **y** and **z** are different. Hence the none too surprising output.

(7)   *Output*

```
33 33 33.000000 33.000000
33.000000 33 33.000000 33
33 33 33.000000 33.000000
33.000000 33 33.000000 33
```

Explanation

As seen in the output, the answer 33.333333 is never obtained. This is because we are operating on two integers, 100 and 3. The result of dividing (for that matter multiplying, adding or subtracting) integers is always another integer. In keeping with this rule, **100 / 3** is evaluated as 33.333333, but the decimal part is truncated before it is stored in any variable, be it an **int** or a **float**.

In the first part, when **100 / 3** is assigned to **d**, 33.000000 gets stored. This remains as it is when the value in **d** is stored in **f**, a **float**. When this **float** value is assigned to **l**, it is stored after demoting it to 33, a **long** integer. Lastly, 33 is again stored in **i**, an **int**. The first output displays these values.

The second part stores the result in **l**, **d**, **i** and **f**, in that order. **l** collects 33, which is interpreted as 33.000000 by the **double** variable **d**. When 33.000000 is assigned to **int** variable **i**, it is demoted to 33 and then stored. Finally, 33 is promoted to a real number 33.000000 when assigned to **f**.

The third and fourth parts of the program can easily be evaluated similarly, keeping track of what type of variable is being used.

(8) *Output*

```
main's i and j are 10 20
change's i and j are 100 200
main's i and j are 10 20
```

Explanation

i and **j** are declared in **main( )** to have an **auto** and **register** storage classes respectively. The first **printf( )** outputs their values as 10 and 20, and then the function **change( )** is called. In **change( )**, **i** and **j** are again initialised to 100 and 200. But this pair of **i** and **j** has got nothing to do with the pair used in **main( )**. Initialising this pair to 100 and 200 doesn't change the values of the pair used in **main( )**. This is evident from the output of the second **printf( )** in **main( )**. In other words, the **auto** and **register** storage class variables are local to the function in which they are defined, and are not known to any other function. Hence, they cannot be modified by any other function.

(9) *Output*

```
i = 1 j = 2 k = 3
i = 10 j = 20 k = 30
```

Explanation

If **i, j** and **k** have been defined once on top of **main( )**, is redefining them again inside **main( )** allowed? Yes, because the two sets of **i, j** and **k** are two totally different sets of variables. The ones defined outside **main( )** are global variables, whereas those defined inside **main( )** are local variables. Global (**extern**) variables are available to all functions. So this leads to a conflict as to which variables' values should be printed in **main( )**. This conflict is resolved by giving preference to local variables over the global variables. Therefore, the **printf( )** in **main( )** would print out 1, 2 and 3 whereas the one in **val( )** prints out 10, 20 and 30.

(10) *Output*

```
j = 1
j = 2
j = 3
num = 3
```

Explanation

Since **num** has been declared outside all functions, its storage class is assumed to be **extern**, and its initial value is assumed to be 0. Through the **for** loop, when **increment( )** is called for the first time, **num** is incremented to 1 and this value is returned, to be collected in **j**. This value is then printed out through the **printf( )**. Subsequent calls to **increment( )** through the **for** loop would increment **num** every time and return this incremented value, only to be printed through the **printf( )**. Finally, the value of **num** is printed in **main( )**. Note that **num** is available to both the functions: **main( )** as well as **increment( )**.

(11) *Output*

```
z = 20
y = 40
```

Explanation

When **recsum( )** is called from **main( )** for the first time, a value 1 gets collected in variable **i** in the function **recsum( )**.

In **recsum**( ), the variable **sum** has been declared as **static**, therefore it is initialised during the first call to **recsum**( ) to a value 0. First time around, the condition (**i == 3**) fails, therefore **sum** is incremented to 10, **i** is incremented to 2 and once again **recsum**( ) is called with **i** equal to 2 - this time recursively. Once again the condition fails and **sum** is incremented to 20, **i** to 3 and again a recursive call is made, this time with **i** equal to 3. Now the condition in **if** is satisfied, therefore the latest value of **sum**, i.e. 20 is returned to **main**( ), where it is collected in the variable **z**.

Note that even though **recsum**( ) is called several times, only during the first call **sum** is initiated to 0. During all subsequent calls the declaration of **sum** is ignored, and the value of **sum** last time around is used in calculations. This is because **sum**'s storage class has been defined as **static**. This is once again proved when **recsum**( ) is called from **main**( ) the second time (**y = recsum (1)**). The last value of **sum**, i.e 20 is used in further calcualtions involving **sum**, resulting in **y** printing out as 40.

(12) *Output*

```
main's i = 0
val's i = 100
main's i = 101
val's i = 100
```

Explanation

To begin with, **i** is assumed as an **extern** storage class variable, as it is defined outside all functions. When the first **printf**( ) in **main**( ) is executed, **i** is 0. Next, **i** is incremented to 1 and the function **val**( ) is called. In **val**( ), **i** is reinitialised to 100. This value is printed out and **i** is incremented to 101. When the control goes back to **main**( ), the second **printf**( ) prints out the latest value of **i**, i.e. 101. After this once again **val( )** gets called, where **i** is reinitialised to 100 and then printed out.

All this goes to highlight one fact - once a variable is declared as **extern** it is available to all the functions in the program and hence can be easily manipulated in any of the functions.

(13) *Output*

s = 2 t = 5 y = 17

Explanation

When **fun( )** is called, 7 (i.e. **s + t**) is passed to it and is collected in the variable s. In **fun( )**, s is incremented to 8 whereas **t,** which is an external variable with an initial value 8, is incremented to 9. The **return** statement then returns the sum of **s** and **t**, i.e. 17, which is collected in **main( )** in the variable **y.** Note that since **s** and **t** have been declared inside **main( )** they are local variables. As a result, changing the value of **s** in the function **fun( )** does not have any effect on the value of **s** in **main( )**. What about the effect of changing the value of **t** in **fun( )?** This also will not have any effect on the value of **t** in **main( )**. This is because here we have two variables with the same name **t**. Therefore in **main( )** when we use **t**, it is always the local **t** which gets a priority above the global **t**. Hence, even though **t** is incremented to 9 in **fun( )**, in **main( )** while printing out the value of **t**, its the local **t** with a value 5 that is used.

(14) *Output*

x = 4.000000 y = 2
x = 2.200000 y = 4

Explanation

Let us analyse the first expression step by step after replacing the values of the variables in the expression.

```
x = ( y = 4.4 / 2 ) * 2
x = ( y = 2.2 ) * 2
x = 2 * 2
x = 4
```

Note that 2.2 is demoted to 2 while storing it in **y**, since **y** is an integer variable and hence can store only an integer constant.

Onto the second expression now.

```
y = ( x = d / i ) * 2
y = ( x = 2.2 ) * 2
y = 2.2 * 2
y = 4.4
```

While storing 4.4 in **y**, it is demoted to 4, since **y** is an integer variable.

(15) *Output*

```
x = 2.500000
x = 15.000000 y = 3
```

Explanation

What follows is a step by step evaluation of the expressions with the variables being replaced by the values stored in them.

```
x = d * ( x = 2.5 / d )
x = 5.0 * ( x = 2.5 / 5.0 )
x = 5.0 * ( x = 0.5 )
x = 2.5
```

Let us similarly evaluate the second expression:

x = d * (y = (int) 2.5 + 1.5)
x = 5.0 * (y = (int) 2.5 + 1.5)
x = 5.0 * (y = 2 + 1.5)
x = 5.0 * (y = 3.5)
x = 5.0 * 3
x = 15.0

What does the expression (**int**) **2.5** do? It casts the value 2.5 as an integer. This process is often called typecasting and it can be applied to any datatype. For example, (**long**) **123** would cast 123 as a **long** integer.

(16) *Output*

c = 5
c = 4
c = 3
c = 2
c = 1

Explanation

When **printf( )** is executed for the first time, firstly value of **c** (i.e.5) is printed and then **c** is decremented to 4. The condition in **if** evaluates to true since 4 is a truth value (recall that any non zero value is a truth value), hence **main( )** is called once again. But this time **c** is not reinitialised to 5, since its storage class has been declared as **static**. Thus the control jumps straightaway to **printf( )**, where the current value of **c**, i.e. 4 gets printed, **c** gets decremented to 3 and once again the condition is tested. Since this time also the condition evaluates to true, and **main( )** gets called yet again. This process is repeated till **c** becomes 0, wherein the condition fails and hence **main( )** doesn't get called.

What is to be understood from this program is that the value of the **static** storage class variable is initialised only once and thereafter the latest value of the variable persists between different function calls.

(17) *Output*

```
c = 5
c = 5
c = 5
.. . ..
.. . ..
```

Explanation

Unlike the previous program, here variable **c** has not been defined as **static**, and hence it is initialised to 5 every time **main( )** gets called. Thus when **printf( )** is executed for the first time, as **c** has been initiated to 5, it gets printed out and then -- reduces it to 4. Now, the condition is satisfied (since **c** is non-zero), therefore **main( )** gets called again. But the moment control reaches **int c = 5**, this statement gets executed and **c** is reset to 5. Once again 5 gets printed, **c** gets decremented, condition gets satisfied and **main( )** gets called. Thus **c** never becomes 0 and hence the condition never becomes false. In other words, the control falls in an indefinite loop.

(18) *Output*

```
j = 1
```

Explanation

In this program, having declared **i** as an **extern** variable, the control enters the **for** loop in **main( )**. Here **function( )** is called with a value 0. In **function( )** this value is collected in the variable **x**. Next **v** is initiated to 2, decremented to 1 and then the difference (**v - x**), i.e. 1, is returned to **main( )**, where it is collected in the variable **j**. Since **j** is 1, the condition is satisfied and **j**'s value gets printed. Since the **for** loop is an indefinite loop, once again the control reaches the **if** statement. From here, again a call to **function( )** is made, with **i** equal to 0. In **function( )** the latest value of **v**, i.e. 1 is decremented to 0 and the difference (**0 - 0**) is returned to **main( )**, where it is collected in **j**. Now the condition fails, since **j** is 0, and the control reaches the **else** block. Here the **break** takes the control outside the **for** loop and since there are no statements outside the loop, the execution is terminated.

(19) *Output*

num = 2 n = 2 no = 2

Explanation

Each of the variables **num, n** and **no** have been assigned a value 2, which is getting printed out through the **printf( )**. That's hardly a surprise. What is to be appreciated here is the compactness C offers in the variable declarations. Instead of declaring **signed long int num** we can get away with **long num**. Similarly, instead of **short signed int n** we are allowed to use **short n**. Likewise, we can use **signed no** instead of **short signed int no**.

(20) *Output*

ch = z ch1 = 122

Explanation

Does **ch1 = 'z'** really store the character 'z' in **ch1**? Not really. What is stored in **ch1** is the ascii value of 'z', which is 122. Understand that a **char** variable never holds characters. It can hold only values in the range -128 to +127. Once this fact sinks in, the output of the program can be easily understood. The first **printf( )** prints out a character corresponding to the value stored in **ch**, whereas the second **printf( )** prints the value stored in **ch1**.

(21) *Output*

a = 25 b = 25 c = 345 d = 345

Explanation

The first two declarations make one fact very clear - while declaring a variable to be of the type **unsigned int**, the **int** can as well be dropped from the declaration. Observe that in the next two declarations too the word **int** has been dropped. In these declarations a capital L occurs after 345. This ensures that 345 is treated as a **long int**. In place of a capital L a lower case l is also acceptable. Also observe the format specifications used in **printf( )**: %**u** for an **unsigned int**, %**lu** for an **unsgined long int** and %**ld** for a **long signed int**.

(22) *Output*

Error message: Undefined symbol 'i' in function main

Explanation

Note that here **i** has been declared in between the functions **main( )** and **func1( )**. Since this declaration falls outside both the functions its storage class is assumed to be **extern**. Thus **i** should be available to both the functions. However, since **i** physically occurs after **main( )**, it is not available to **main( )**. Hence the error message. What if we don't want to shift the declaration to top of **main( )** and yet want to make **i** available to **main( )**? To achieve this, the declaration **extern int i ;** should be made inside **main( )**. This tells the compiler that down the line somewhere **i** has been declared outside all functions. If you run the program with this change both **printf( )**s would output 5.

(23) *Output*

r = 3.140000 y = 3.400000

Explanation

The **register** storage class variables are stored in CPU registers. Since CPU registers are 2 bytes long, how can a **float** or a **double** variable be declared to have a **register** storage class? Should the compiler not flash an error message? It doesn't, because it doesn't expect you to know the details about what are CPU registers, how many bytes long are they, etc. Hence it makes this concession. However, internally it assumes **auto** storage class for these variables and proceeds with the execution.

(24) *Output*

i = 100
i = 1
i = 2
i = 2
i = 100

Explanation

In the outermost block (a block is statements within a pair of braces) the variable **i** has been declared as an **auto** storage class variable, with an initial value 100. This value gets printed through the first **printf( )**. Then the control reaches inside the next block, where again **i** is declared to have a value 1. This **i** is different, since it has been defined inside another block. The value of this **i** is then printed out through the second **printf( )**. Inside the next block, this **i** is incremented to 2 and then printed out. Then the control reaches outside this block where another **printf( )** is encountered. This **printf( )** is within the same block in which the second **i** has been defined. Hence it prints out the value of this **i**, which is still 2. And now the control reaches outside the block in which the second **i** has been defined. Therefore the second **i** dies. The first **i** is however still active, since the control has not gone out of the block in which it has been defined. Hence the last **printf( )** prints out the value of this **i**, which is 100.

(25) *Output*

Error mesage: Declaration needs type or storage class

Explanation

We get the error message because we have neither mentioned the type nor the storage class of the variable **i**. Saying **int i = 0** would make the program work.

(26) *Output*

Same output for both:

1
2
3
..

...
...
99
100

Explanation

Which of the two programs works faster depends on the status of the CPU registers at the time of program execution. If the CPU happens to be using all the 14 registers, **i** will not be allotted a **register** storage class, and its storage class will be assumed to be **auto**. In this case, both the programs will take the same time to run. However, if we are lucky, and the CPU does allow a register at our disposal, the first program will decidedly run faster. This is so because registers, being CPU's internal memory, are accessed faster than normal memory locations.

Solutions to **[B]**

(1) *Program*

```
main( )
{
    unsigned int i, j, k ;

    for ( i = 1 ; i <= 9 ; i = i + 2 )
    {
        for ( j = 1 ; ; j++ )
        {
            k = j + 1 ;

            if ( i * i + j * j == k * k )
            {
                printf ( "\n%u %u %u", i, j, k ) ;
                break ;
```

```
            }
          }
        }
    }
```

Sample run

```
1 32768 32769
3 4 5
5 12 13
7 24 25
9 40 41
```

Explanation

Here **i** is being used for the odd number whereas **j** and **k** signify the consecutive numbers. Since **i** represents the odd number, it varies from 1 to 9 in steps of 2. If sum of squares of **i** and **j** equals the square of **k**, then **i, j, k** forms a pythagorian triplet. The moment such a triplet is encountered it is printed out. Note that **i, j** and **k** have been declared as **unsigned int**s. This is because the range of such integers is 0 to 65535. In this program we do need a range bigger than -32768 to +32767.

(2) *Program*

```
main( )
{
    unsigned long num, rnum, square, rsquare, n2, num2 ;
    int d1, d2, d3, d4, d5 ;

    for ( num = 10 ; num <= 100 ; num++ )
    {
        num2 = num ;
        d1 = num2 % 10 ;
```

```
num2 = num2 / 10 ;
d2 = num2 % 10 ;
num2 = num2 / 10 ;
d3 = num2 % 10 ;
num2 = num2 / 10 ;
d4 = num2 % 10 ;
num2 = num2 / 10 ;
d5 = num2 ;

rnum = d5 + d4 * 10 + d3 * 100 + d2 * 1000L + d1 * 10000L ;

while ( rnum % 10 == 0 )
    rnum = rnum / 10 ;


square = num * num ;
rsquare = rnum * rnum ;

d1 = square % 10 ;
square = square / 10 ;
d2 = square % 10 ;
square = square / 10 ;
d3 = square % 10 ;
square = square / 10 ;
d4 = square % 10 ;
square = square / 10 ;
d5 = square ;
n2 = d5 + d4 * 10 + d3 * 100 + d2 * 1000L + d1 * 10000L ;

while ( n2 % 10 == 0 )
    n2 = n2 / 10 ;

if ( rsquare == n2 )
    printf ( "\n%lu", num ) ;
    }
}
```

Sample run

```
10
11
12
13
20
21
22
30
31
100
.....
.....
.....
```

Explanation

Within the **for** loop, firstly the digits of the number (say, 12) are separated out into variables **d1** through **d5**, and then using these, the reversed number (say 21) is constructed and stored in the variable **rnum**. The **while** loop that follows trims any trailing zeroes from this reversed number. Then squares of the original number (12) and the reversed number (21) are calculated. The set of statements that follow segregate the digits of the square of the original number (144) and then using these segregated digits, it constructs the reverse of the square (441). The **while** loop then trims out any trailing zeroes that might be present in this reverse of square of original number. Now if this number is same as **rsquare** calculated earlier, then the number in question satisfies the property and hence is printed out.

Note that some of the variables have been declared as **unsigned long int**s. This is just to ensure that the range is not exceeded while constructing the reversed numbers.

7

The C Preprocessor

T he facility of Preprocessing is something which you do not have with many other high level languages. As the name suggests, the Preprocessor is a program that processes our source program before passing it on for compilation. Though the facility is not an indispensable one, it is popular with C programmers as it helps in better coding of a program. The commonly used preprocessor directives are:

(a)   Macro Expansion
(b)   File Inclusion
(c)   Conditional Compilation

Let us now understand these preprocessor directives one by one.

Macro Expansion

Here's a simple example illustrating the use of macro expansions.

```
#define NUM 100
#define SQUARE(x) (x * x)
main( )
{
    int i = 5;
```

```
if ( SQUARE(i) <= NUM )
        printf ( "Eat, drink and be merry..." ) ;
else
        printf ( "for tomorrow you may have to diet!" ) ;
```

The above program would output:

    Eat, drink and be merry...

The first two statements in the program are called macro definitions. They comprise of 'macro templates' NUM and SQUARE(x) and their corresponding 'macro expansions', 100 and (**x * x**). During preprocessing, the macro templates are replaced by their corresponding macro expansions. The first macro expansion is a simple macro, whereas the second one is said to be taking an argument **x**. (Note that there is no space between SQUARE and (x)). In our program, we have chosen the argument to be **i**, so the preprocessor expands the macro in terms of **i**.

Thus, before the program is sent to the compiler, the preprocessor replaces NUM by 100, and SQUARE(i) by (**i * i**). The **if** statement having been rewritten as **if((i * i) <= 100**), compilation proceeds just as usual.

File Inclusion

This directive causes one file to be included in another. The presence of a **#include** statement in a program causes the entire contents of the said file to be inserted at that point in the program. A typical use of this feature would be to store frequently used functions and macro definitions in a single file and **#include** it in whichever file we want.

The file inclusion directive can be written in two ways:

#include "a.c"   This commands the preprocessor to look for the file
                  a.c in the current directory as well as the specified
                  list of directories mentioned in the search path that
                  might have been set up.

#include <a.c>   The file **a.c** is looked up only in the specified list of
                  directories.

Conditional Compilation

The last on our list is conditional compilation using the preprocessor
commands **#ifdef** and **#endif**. Saying

```
#ifdef LABEL
    statement 1 ;
    statement 2 ;
#endif
```

will ensure that statements 1 and 2 will get compiled only if LABEL
has been **#define**d. If LABEL has not been defined as a macro, the
two statements won't be sent for compilation at all. Conditional
compilation can be used to make a program portable. For two
different makes of computers, we can write a single program and
conditionally compile only the code pertaining to either of the two
machines. The program would look like:

```
main( )
{
    #ifdef PCAT
        code for a PC/AT
    #else
        code for a PC/XT
    #endif
    code common to both the computers
}
```

Our program would run smoothly on a PC/AT as well as a PC/XT, depending on whether PCAT has been defined or not.

Exercise

[A]   What will be the output of the following programs:

(1)
```c
#define DEF
main( )
{
    int i = 2 ;
    #ifdef DEF
        printf ( "square of i = %d", i * i ) ;
    #else
        printf ( "i = %d", i ) ;
    #endif
}
```

(2)
```c
#define NO
#define YES
main( )
{
    int i = 5, j ;
    if ( i > 5 )
        j = YES ;
    else
        j = NO ;
    printf ( "%d", j ) ;
}
```

(3)
```c
#define MESS( m ) printf ( "m" )
main( )
{
    MESS( "But somewhere in my wicked miserable past.." ) ;
    MESS( "there must have been a moment of truth!" ) ;
}
```

(4)   `#define GOTONEXTLINE printf( "\n" )`

```
        main( )
        {
            printf ( "It's better to keep your mouth shut.." ) ;
            GOTONEXTLINE ;
            printf ( ".. and have people think you are a fool.." ) ;
            GOTONEXTLINE ;
            printf ( ".. than to open it and remove all doubt!" ) ;
        }

(5)     #define MESS( m ) printf( "m" )
        #define GOTONEXTLINE printf( "\n" )
        main( )
        {
            MESS( "A galaxy of persons were born on this day.." ) ;
            GOTONEXTLINE ;
            MESS( "But somehow you seem to be the best!!" ) ;
        }

(6)     #define ISUPPER( x ) ( x >= 65 && x <= 90 )
        #define ISLOWER( x ) ( x >= 97 && x <= 122 )
        #define ISALPHA( x ) ( ISUPPER( x ) || ISLOWER( x ) )
        main( )
        {
            char ch = '+' ;
            if ( ISALPHA( ch ) )
                printf ( "ch contains an alphabet" ) ;
            else
                printf ( "ch doesn't contain an alphabet" ) ;
        }

(7)     #define THIS
        #define THAT
        main( )
        {
            #ifdef THIS
                #ifdef THAT
```

```
                        printf ( "Definitions are hard to digest" ) ;
            #else
                        printf ( "But once mugged up, hard to forget" ) ;
        #endif
    }
```

(8)   ```
        #define THIS
        #define THAT
        main( )
        {
            #ifdef THIS && THAT
                printf ("Defintions are hard to digest") ;
            #else
                printf ("But once mugged up, hard to forget") ;
            #endif
        }
        ```

(9)     ```
        #define MEAN( a, b, c, d, e ) ( a + b + c + d + e ) / 5
        main( )
        {
            int a, b, c, d, e, m ;
            a = 1 ;
            b = 2 ;
            c = 3 ;
            d = 4 ;
            e = 5 ;
            m = MEAN( a, b, c, d, e ) ;
            printf ( "Mean of the five numbers is = %d" ) ;
        }
        ```

(10)   ```
        #define CUBE(X) (X * X * X)
        main( )
        {
            int a ;
            a = 27 / CUBE(3) ;
            printf ("%d", a) ;
        ```
        ```

```
        }

(11)    #define CUBE(X) (X * X * X)
        main( )
        {
            int a, b ;
            b = 3 ;
            a = CUBE(b++) / b++ ;
            printf ( "a = %d b = %d", a, b ) ;
        }


(12)

        #define CUBE(X) (X * X * X)
        main( )
        {
            int a, b = 3 ;
            a = CUBE(++b) / ++b ;
            printf ( "a = %d b = %d", a, b ) ;
        }

(13)    #define COND ( a >= 65 && a <= 90 )
        main( )
        {
            char a = 'R' ;
            if ( COND )
                printf ( "UPPER CASE" ) ;
            else
                printf ( "LOWER CASE" ) ;
        }

(14)    #define COND(a) a >= 65 && a <= 90
        main( )
        {
            char ch = 'R' ;
            if ( COND(ch) )
```

```
                    printf ( "ch is in upper case" ) ;
        else
                    printf ( "ch is in lower case" ) ;
        }
```

(15)   `#define COND(a) if ( a >= 65 && a <= 90 )`
```
        main( )
        {
            char ch = 'R' ;
            COND(ch)
                printf ( "Upper case" ) ;
            else
                printf ( "Lower case" ) ;
        }
```

(16)   `#define print(int) printf( "int = %d\n", int )`
```
        main( )
        {
            int x = 3 ;
            print(x) ;
        }
```

(17)   `#define P( format, var ) printf ( "var = %format\n", var )`
```
        main( )
        {
            int i = 3 ;
            float a = 3.14 ;
            P( d, i ) ;
            P( f, a ) ;
        }
```

(18)   `#define INTEGER int`
```
        main( )
        {
            INTEGER a = 10, b = 20 ;
            printf ( "a = %d b = %d", a, b ) ;
```

```
        }

(19)    #define DATATYPE char far *
        main( )
        {
            DATATYPE s ;
            s = 0xb8000000 ;
            *s = 'A' ;
        }

(20)    #define AND &&
        #define OR ||
        #define LE <=
        #define GE >=
        main( )
        {
            char ch = 'D' ;
            if ( ( ch GE 65 AND ch LE 90 ) OR ( ch GE 97 AND ch LE 122 ) )
                printf ( "Alphabet " ) ;
            else
                printf ( "Not an alphabet " ) ;
        }

(21)    #define ISLP(y) ( ( y % 400 == 0 ) || ( y % 100 != 0 && y % 4 == 0 ) )
        main( )
        {
            int y = 1992 ;
            if ( ISLP(y) )
                printf ( "Leap year" ) ;
            else
                printf ( "Not a Leap year" ) ;
        }

(22)    #define MAX( a, b ) ( (a) > (b) ? (a) : (b) )
        main( )
        {
```

```
        int m, x = 5, y = 6 ;
        m = MAX ( x + y, 10 ) ;
        printf ( "%d", m ) ;
        m = MAX ( x, y ) * 100 ;
        printf ( "\n%d", m ) ;
    }
```

(23)   ```
        #define ISLOWER(a) (a >= 97 && a <= 127)
        #define TOUPPER(a) (a - 32)
        main( )
        {
            char ch = 'c' ;
            if (ISLOWER(ch))
                ch = TOUPPER(ch) ;
            printf ("%c", ch) ;
        }
        ```

(24)    ```
        #define E exit(0)
        main( )
        {
            int i = 4 ;
            if ( i <= 5 )
                E ;
            else
                printf ( "Get out anyway!" ) ;
            printf ( "WELL!" ) ;
        }
        ```

(25)   ```
        #define exit exit(0)
        main( )
        {
            printf ("To be or not to be...") ;
            exit ;
            printf ("is the question.") ;
        }
        ```
        ```

(26)
```
#define IT 0.1
#define HRA 0.2
#define DA 0.3
main( )
{
    float bas_sal, net_sal ;
    bas_sal = 1000 ;
    net_sal = bas_sal * ( 1 + HRA + DA - IT ) ;
    printf ( "Gross salary = %f", net_sal ) ;
}
```

(27)
```
#define MYFILE "conio.h"
#include MYFILE
main( )
{
    window ( 10, 10, 40, 20 ) ;
    cprintf ( "A pinch of probably is much better than ..." ) ;
    cprintf ( "A pound of perhaps!" ) ;
}
```

(28)
```
main( )
{
    window ( 20, 10, 40, 15 ) ;
    #include "conio.h"
    cprintf ( "The love in your heart was not put to stay..." ) ;
    cprintf ( "Love is not love till you give it away." ) ;
}
```

Answers

(1)   *Output*

square of i = 4

Explanation

Since **DEF** has been defined, **#ifdef DEF** evaluates to true, hence square of **i** is calculated and printed through **printf( )**. Is it not necessary while defining **DEF** to use a macro expansion following **DEF**? No, since we don't intend to use the value of the macro expansion anywhere in the program. All that we want is to conditionally compile the program subject to the condition whether **DEF** has been defined or not.

(2)   *Output*

Error Message: Expression syntax in function main

Explanation

We have assigned values of **YES** and **NO** to **j** in the **if-else**, but what are the values of **YES** and **NO**? They have only been defined as macros without being given any expansions. Hence the error message.

(3)   *Output*

mm

Explanation

During preprocessing **MESS("But .... past..")** gets replaced by **printf ("m")**. Naturally, on execution this **printf( )** prints out **m**. The same thing happens to the next statement, which also prints out an **m**.

(4)   *Output*

It's better to keep your mouth shut..
.. and have people think you are a fool..
.. than to open it and remove all doubt!

Explanation

During preprocessing the preprocessor replaces all occurrences of **GOTONEXTLINE** in **main( )** with **printf("\n")**. Hence during execution, the three messages are output on different lines.

(5)   *Output*

m
m

Explanation

The preprocessor replaces both the occurrences of **MESS** with **printf("m")**. Similarly, **GOTONEXTLINE** is replaced by **printf("\n")**. Thus, when the program is sent for execution, it has been converted to the following form:

```
main( )
{
    printf( "m" ) ;
    printf("\n") ;
    printf( "m" ) ;
```

}

This would output two **m**s on different lines.

(6)   *Output*

ch doesn't contain an alphabet

Explanation

The first and second macros have the criteria for checking whether their argument **x** is an upper or a lower case alphabet. These two criteria have been combined in the third macro, **ISALPHA**. Thus when the program goes for compilation, the **if** statement has been converted to the form:

if (ch >= 65 && ch <= 90 || ch ₋ 97 && ch <= 122)

As **ch** has been initialised to character **+**, the conditions in the **if** fail and the control rightly passes to the **else** block, from where the output is obtained.

(7)   *Output*

Unexpected end of file in conditional

Explanation

The macros **THIS** and **THAT** have been correctly defined. The error lies in the imbalance of **#ifdef** and **#endif** statements in the program. Inserting another **#endif** would guarantee the output "Definitions are hard to digest". This also goes to show that the **#ifdef**s can be nested the same way the ordinary **if** statements can be.

(8)   *Output*

Definitions are hard to digest

Explanation

Logical operators are perfectly acceptable in **#ifdef** statements. Since both **THIS** and **THAT** are defined, the preprocessor allows only the first **printf( )** to go for compilation, which gets executed and we get our output.

(9)   *Output*

Mean of the five numbers is = 3

Explanation

The preprocessor substitutes the macro **MEAN** with its expansion. This expansion is the formula to calculate the average of 5 numbers. With the values of 5 numbers in this program, the result turns out to be 3, which then gets printed out through **printf( )**.

(10) *Output*

1

Explanation

The macro **CUBE(X)** is defined to give the cube of its argument. In the program, the preprocessor replaces **CUBE(3)** by (3 * 3 * 3) and then sends the program for compilation. Thus, **a** is calculated as,

$$a = 27 / (3 * 3 * 3)$$
$$a = 27 / 27$$
$$a = 1$$

Hence the result.

(11) *Output*

a = 9 b = 7

Explanation

Here, the argument of the macro **CUBE(X)** is made to be **b++**. The preprocessor puts the macro expansions in place of the macro templates used in the program, so that what reaches the compiler is:

a = (b++ * b++ * b++) / b++

As **++** succeeds **b**, first the value of **a** is derived using the initial value of **b** (i.e. 3), after which, the **++** does its job on **b**. Hence (3 * 3 * 3) / 3, i.e. 9 gets stored in **a**. Since **b++** is encountered four times in the program, **b** is incremented four times, resulting in the final value of **b** as 7. Thus, **a** stores 9 and **b**, 7 as the output would vouch for.

(12) *Output*

a = 49 b = 7

Explanation

Once again, **CUBE(X)** is expanded to give the cube of its argument. In the program, the argument is taken to be (**++b**), having initialised **b** to 3 at the outset. The preprocessor, before sending the program for compilation, converts the statement containing the macro to:

a = (++b * ++b * ++b) / ++b

The unary operator **++** has a higher priority than that of the binary operators ***** and **/**. Therefore, first the multiple incrementations of **b** take place. As **++b** occurs four times in the statement, **b** is incremented four times. Thus, **b** now has a value 7. This value is used to calculate the result as:

a = (7 * 7 * 7) / 7
a = 343 / 7
a = 49

(13) *Output*

UPPER CASE

Explanation

When 'R' is stored in the variable **a**, what gets stored is the ascii value of the letter 'R', which is 82. The criteria for the character in **a** being an upper case alphabet is defined in the macro **COND**. During preprocessing, in the **if** statement, the **COND** is replaced by (**a >= 65 && a <= 90**). Since **a** contains 82 the condition is satisfied and we get the output as UPPER CASE.

What we must bring to your notice is that this macro is without any argument. Hence it will work only for a variable called **a**. If we replace the variable **a** with any other variable, say **b** in the declaration statement, we would get an error message: 'variable a not defined'.

(14) *Output*

ch is in upper case

Explanation

We have taken care to provide an argument to the macro **COND(a)**. So, during preprocessing the **if** statement becomes:

if (ch >= 65 && ch <= 90)

Since **ch** is stated to be capital 'R' in the program, we rightly get the output as 'ch is in upper case'

(15) *Output*

Upper case

Explanation

During preprocessing **COND(ch)** gets replaced by **if (ch <= 65 && ch <= 90)**. Since **ch** has been initiated to 'R', naturally during execution, the condition is satisfied and 'Upper case' gets printed.

What if we define the macro as shown below:

#define COND(a) (if (a >= 65 && a <= 90))

Do you still expect the program to work as it did before? It doesn't. We get an error message because here the keyword **if** too has been placed within parentheses in the macro definition. As a result, after preprocessing the program takes the following form:

```
( if ( ch >= 65 && ch <= 90 ) )
    printf ( "Upper case" ) ;
else
    printf ( "Lower case" ) ;
```

Obviously, when this form is sent to the compiler, it flashes an a syntax error in the **if** statement due to the pair of parentheses surrounding it.

(16) *Output*

```
int = 3
```

Explanation

The output is not **x = 3** but **int = 3**. When the preprocessor replaced the macro with its corresponding expansion, it substituted only the **int** outside the double quotes, and left the one within the quotes untouched. Thus after preprocessing, the **print(x)** became **printf ("int = %d", x)**. During execution the function **printf( )** prints everything within its quotes as it is, except for the format specifications. Hence the result.

(17) *Output*

```
var = 49.920013ormat
var = 3.140000ormat
```

Explanation

During preprocessing, the **format** in the **printf( )** statement does not get replaced by the argument **d**. Thus the **printf( )** statements, after preprocessing, look like this:

```
printf ( "var = %format \n", i ) ;
```

printf ("var = %format\n", a) ;

This is only in keeping with what the previous example illustrated, that the macro template within the quotes doesn't get replaced by the macro expansion. When these **printf( )**s are executed, the material within quotes gets dumped on to the screen as it is, except when a format specification or an escape sequence (like '\n') is encountered.

Look at the first output. Where did 'f' go? And why were the numbers printed at all? This has the simple explanation that our argument **format** happened to have as its first letter, an 'f'. The **printf( )** interpreted %f as the format specification, and 'ormat' as something we wanted to write on the screen literally.

Note that we got the expected value for **a**, a **float**, but an absurd one for **int i**, since the **printf( )** attempted to print out an **int** using %f.

(18) *Output*

a = 10 b = 20

Explanation

We **#define** the keyword **int** as **INTEGER**, and use this macro in the declaration of variables inside **main( )**. By the time the compiler sees it, the preprocessor has substituted the macro **INTEGER** with **int** in the declaration statement. Hence our program works without a hitch.

(19) *Output*

A

Explanation

Normal pointers contain an address which is 16-bit long. These pointers are called **near** pointers. To access the address of top left corner of the screen we need a 32-bit pointer. Such pointers are called **far** pointers. These pointers are declared by qualifying them with the keyword **far** while declaring them. 0xb8000000 is an address that refers to the first element on the screen, i.e. the top left corner of your monitor. This address is a 32-bit address, so requires the keyword **far** to be associated with it. The declaration **char far *s** signifies that s will contain a 32-bit address.

The preprocessor replaces the macro **DATATYPE** with **char far *** in the program, and the character 'A' gets printed at the top left corner on the screen. What should be noted is that we have been able to print a character on the screen without using a **printf( )**. That is the power of pointers for you!

(20) *Output*

Alphabet

Explanation

Before **main( )** macro definitions have been given for logical operators **&&** and **||**, as also for relational operators **<=** and **>=**. These are then used to build a criteria for checking whether **ch** contains an alphabet or not. All macros are substituted by their expansions prior to compilation, and since 'D' satisfies the **if** condition, 'Alphabet' is printed out.

(21) *Output*

Leap year

Explanation

The macro **ISLP(y)** takes as its argument any year **y**, and tests if the year is a leap year or not. For a year to be leap, either it should be an integral multiple of 400, or if the year is not divisible by 100, an integral multiple of 4. Why is this so and why we are not told this in school, I leave for you to figure out. The year 1992 is not divisible by 400, hence the first condition fails, but the second part of the condition holds good. Hence the output that the year is indeed a leap year is obtained.

(22) *Output*

```
11
600
```

Explanation

The macro **MAX(a, b)** is defined using the conditional operators **?** and **:**. The preprocessor converts the first assignment statement for **m** to the following form:

$$m = (((x + y) > (10)) ? (x + y) : (10)) ;$$

In place of **a**, the argument is taken as **x + y**, and in place of **b**, the number 10. If you haven't recognised the conditional operators, think back to the decision control instructions. The statement is interpreted as:

If **x + y** is greater than **10**, **m** is to be assigned value **x + y**, otherwise the value **10**.

As **x** and **y** have been initialised as 5 and 6 respectively, their sum is 11, which is greater than 10. Hence **m** is assigned a value 11, which is printed out.

The second assignment statement after preprocessing becomes:

$$m = (((x) > (y)) ? (x) : (y)) * 100 ;$$

Since value of **y**, i.e. 6, is greater than **x**, which is 5, value of **y** is multiplied with 100, and the result is printed out as 600.

(23) *Output*

C

Explanation

The macro **ISUPPER** is used to check whether its argument is an upper case alphabet or not. If the argument is a lower case alphabet, the macro **TOUPPER** changes it to the upper case. The difference in the ascii values of lower case and upper case letters is 32, so this number is subtracted from the ascii value of the lower case letter to give the corresponding upper case letter. Thus, in this case 'c' gets converted to 'C'.

(24) *Output*

No output

Explanation

E is defined as a macro for the function **exit(0)**, which unconditionally terminates the execution of the program. Since **i** has been assigned a value less than 5, the control enters the **if** block, where the compiler finds the **exit(0)**. Control is immediately taken out of the program, leaving no chance for the 'WELL!' to get printed.

(25) *Output*

To be or not to be...

Explanation

From the above program we can gather that macros need not necessarily be defined in capital letters. Capital letters are used only to facilitate our comprehension of the program; i.e. to make out which is a variable and which is a macro. After executing the first **printf( )**, the compiler finds the **exit(0)**, as substituted by the preprocessor, and hence terminates the execution.

(26) *Output*

Gross salary = 1400.000000

Explanation

When the preprocessor sends the program for compilation, **IT**, **HRA** and **DA** have been replaced by 0.1, 0.2 and 0.3 respectively. With **bas_sal** set to 1000, the net salary is calculated as:

net_sal = bas_sal * (1 + 0.2 + 0.3 - 0.1) ;

Next the result is printed out.

(27) *Output*

A pinch of probably is much better than
...A pound of perhaps!

Explanation

The name of a file can be used as an expansion for a macro definition. Saying **#include MYFILE** is same as saying **#include "conio.h"**, as this is what the preprocessor sends for compilation after replacing the macro **MYFILE**.

The file "conio.h" is a header file which is required by the function **window( )**. This function defines an active text mode window. Here, the area on the console from the 10th column, 10th row to the 40th column, 20th row is made active. The function **cprintf( )** sees to it that the output of our program goes only to this particular area on the screen. (**printf( )**, on the other hand simply sends the formatted output to the portion of the screen where the cursor is currently located.) We can appreciate the point better when we take note of the fact that we have our output in two different lines, without having inserted a newline '\n'. As the message gets printed, when the cursor comes to the right edge of the window, it automatically goes to the left edge on the next line and prints the remaining message there.

(28) *Output*

Error message: Expression syntax in function main

Explanation

The above scheme would never work, as the **#include** must be specified outside the function **main( )**. That is why we get an error message.

8

A Tryst with Arrays

C provides a facility called array that enables the user to combine similar datatypes into a single entity. Ordinary variables are capable of holding only one value at a time. If there is a large amount of similar data to be handled, then using a different variable for each data item would make the job unwieldy, tedious and confusing. Instead, on combining all this similar data into an array, the whole task of organising and manipulating data would become easier and more efficient. The following figure shows the use of an array in a program.

```
main( )
{
    float avg, sum = 0 ;
    int i, n[5] ;

    printf ( "Enter 5 numbers " ) ;
    for ( i = 0 ; i <= 4 ; i++ )
        scanf ( "%d", &n[i] ) ;

    for ( i = 0 ; i <= 4 ; i++ )
        sum = sum + n[i] ;

    avg = sum / 5 ;
    printf ( "%f  %f", sum, avg ) ;
}
```

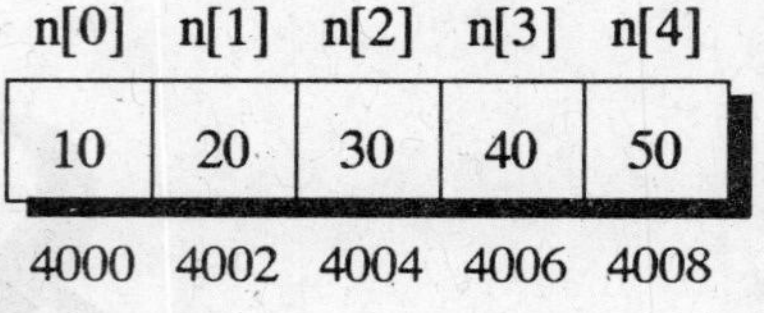

n[0]	n[1]	n[2]	n[3]	n[4]
10	20	30	40	50
4000	4002	4004	4006	4008

Notes
- Array elements are stored in contiguous memory locations.
- The size of the array should be mentioned while declaring it. e.g. **n[5]**.
- Array elements are always counted from 0 onwards.
- Array elements can be accessed using the position of the element in the array. e.g. **n[i]** refers to **i**th element.

Figure 8.1 Array at work

With the basics of arrays under our belt, let's delve into a few smaller issues.

(a)   Like ordinary variables, arrays too can be initialised during declaration. For example:

```
int num[6] = { 2, 4, 12, 5, 45, 5 } ;
int n[ ] = { 2, 4, 12, 5, 45, 5 } ;
float press[ ] = { 12.3, 34.2 -23.4, -11.3 } ;
```

If the array is initialised where it is declared, mentioning the dimension of the array is optional, as in the 2nd and 3rd examples above.

(b)   In C, there is no check to see if the subscript used for an array exceeds the size of the array. Data entered with a subscript exceeding the array size will simply be placed in memory outside the array; probably on top of other data, or on the program itself. This will lead to unpredictable results, to say the least, and there will be no error message to warn you that you are going beyond the array size. In some cases the computer may just hang.

The moral to be derived is: to keep your program fit and fighting, see to it that you never attempt to reach beyond the legal array size. The point is, the onus of doing so lies on the programmer's shoulders and not on the compiler's.

Arrays and Functions

Let's venture further and see how arrays and functions interact with one another. How do we pass array elements to a function? Naturally, by value and/or by reference. The following figure shows both these calls at work.

```
main()
{
    int i ;
    int m[] = { 55, 65, 75, 85, 95 } ;

    for ( i = 0 ; i <= 4 ; i++ )
    {
        d ( m[i] ) ; /* call by value */
        s ( &m[i] ) ; /* call by ref. */
    }
}

d ( n )
int n ;
{
    printf ( "%d", n ) ;
}

s ( k )
int *k ;
{
    printf ( "%d", *k ) ;
}
```

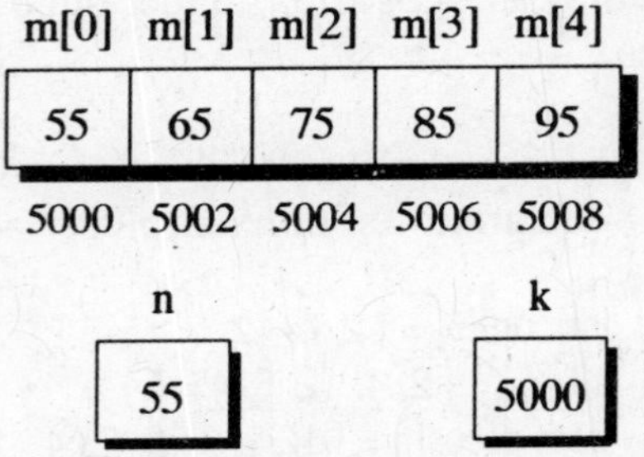

m[0]	m[1]	m[2]	m[3]	m[4]
55	65	75	85	95
5000	5002	5004	5006	5008

n

| 55 |

k

| 5000 |

Contents of **n** and **k** when first call to d() and s() is made.

Figure 8.2 Call by value/reference

Let us now digress a bit and see what lies below the outer garb of pointers. Having explored that, we would once again get back to arrays, better equipped.

Pointers: A second look

We had our first tryst with pointers in Chapter 5. We may recall that a pointer is a variable which stores the address of other variables. If a pointer variable stores the address of a **char** variable, we call it a **char** pointer. Same logic applies to an **int** pointer or a **float** pointer. With this much knowledge under our belt, its time to have a closer look at pointers and how they relate to arrays.

On incrementing a pointer, it points to the immediately next location of its type. The way a pointer can be incremented, it can be decremented as well, to point to earlier locations. This is illustrated in the following figure.

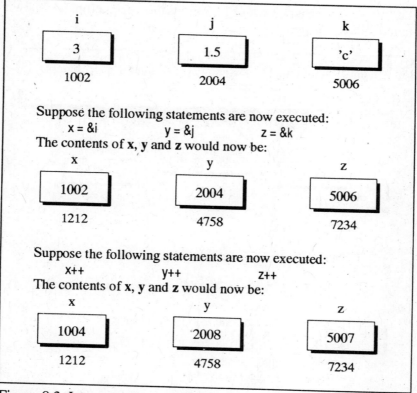

Figure 8.3 Incrementation of pointers

Pointers and Arrays

Pointers and arrays go hand in hand. In fact, use of pointers presents another way of accessing array elements. This derives from two facts:

(a) Array elements are always stored in contiguous memory locations.

(b) A pointer when incremented always points to the immediately next location of its type.

Let's concoct a program which highlights this correlation. It is shown in the following figure.

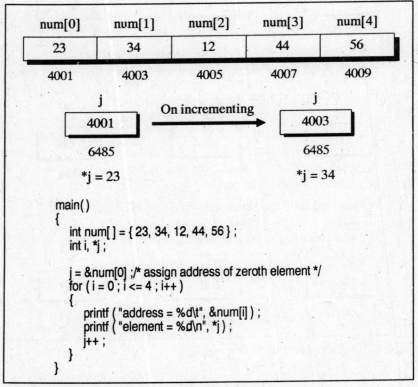

```
main( )
{
    int num[ ] = { 23, 34, 12, 44, 56 } ;
    int i, *j ;

    j = &num[0] ;/* assign address of zeroth element */
    for ( i = 0 ; i <= 4 ; i++ )
    {
        printf ( "address = %d\t", &num[i] ) ;
        printf ( "element = %d\n", *j ) ;
        j++ ;
    }
}
```

Figure 8.4 Interaction of array and pointer

Two Dimensional Arrays

It is also possible for arrays to have two or more dimensions. The two-dimensional array is also called a matrix. The following program shows a two-dimensional array at work.

```
main( )
{
    int s[4][2], i ;

    for ( i = 0 ; i <= 3 ; i++ )
    {
        printf ( "\nEnter roll no. and marks " ) ;
        scanf ( "%d %d", &s[i][0], &s[i][1] ) ;
    }

    for ( i = 0 ; i <= 3 ; i++ )
        printf ( "%d %d\n", s[i][0], s[i][1] ) ;
}
```

The program is fairly simple. Through the first **for** loop, we read the values of roll no. and marks into the two-dimensional array **s[4][2]** and through the second **for** loop we print out these values.

A few tips about the program are in order.

(a)   Before using the 2-D array its dimension must be mentioned. This has been done in our program by the statement **int s[4][2]**.

(b)   The elements of the 2-D array **s[ ][ ]** can be accessed using the subscript notation **s[i][j]**, where **i** represents the row number and **j** represents the column number in which the element is present.

(c)   The arrangement of array elements into rows and columns is only conceptually true, since in memory there are no rows and columns. Hence even 2-D array elements are arranged linearly in memory. This arrangement is shown below.

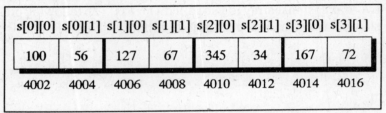

Figure 8.5   Arrangement of 2-D array in memory

(d)   A 2-D array can be declared and initialised at the same place. When this is done, mentioning the row dimension is optional. Such a declaration would look like:

```
static int s[4][ ] =  {
                        100, 56,
                        127, 67,
                        345, 34,
                        167, 72
                    } ;
```

(e)   A 2-D array can be considered as an array of a number of 1-D arrays. Since all that the compiler remembers about a 1-D array is its base address, to remember a 2-D array it obviously must be remembering a series of base addresses of the 1-D arrays present in it. Thus, if we consider the 2-D array **s[4][2]**, the base addresses of the four 1-D arrays would be stored in **s[0]**, **s[1]**, **s[2]**, **s[3]**. Naturally, the expression **s[2] + 1** would give the address of the first element in the second 1-D array. The value at this address can be obtained by the expression ***(s[2] + 1)**. But as we learnt in 1-D arrays, **s[2]** can be expressed in pointer notation as ***(s + 2)**. Therefore ***(s[2] + 1)** can be expressed as ***(*(s + 2) + 1)**. Thus, it can be deduced that the expressions s[2][1] and *(*(s + 2) + 1) both refer to the same element present in the first column of the second row.

Array of Pointers

The way there can be an array of **int**s or an array of **floats**, similarly there can be an array of pointers. Since a pointer variable always contains an address, an array of pointers would be nothing but a collection of addresses. The addresses present in the array of pointers could be addresses of isolated variables or addresses of array elements or any other addresses. All rules that apply to an ordinary array apply in toto to the array of pointers as well. The following figure shows the contents and arrangements of an array of pointers called **arr**. As you can observe, **arr** contains addresses of isolated **int** variables **i, j, k** and **l** .

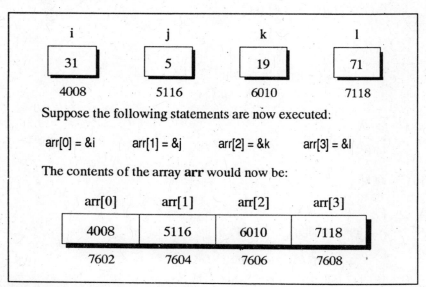

Figure 8.6 Array of pointers

Exercise

[A]   What will be the output of the following programs:

(1)
```c
main( )
{
    int a[5], i ;
    static int b[5] ;
    for ( i = 0 ; i < 5 ; i++ )
        printf ( "%d %d %d\n", i, a[i], b[i] ) ;
}
```

(2)
```c
main( )
{
    static int sub[5] = { 10, 20, 30, 40, 50 } ;
    int i ;
    for ( i = 0 ; i <= 4 ; i++ ) ;
    {
        if ( i <= 4 )
        {
            sub[i] = i * i ;
            printf ( "%d\n", sub[i] ) ;
        }
    }
}
```

(3)
```c
int b[5] ;
main( )
{
    static int a[5] ;
    int i ;
    for ( i = 0 ; i <= 4 ; i++ )
        printf ( "%d %d\n", b[i], a[i] ) ;
}
```

```
(4)    main( )
       {
            static float arr[ ] = { 1.2, 12, 2.4, 24, 3.5, 35 } ;
            int i ;
            for ( i = 0 ; i <= 5 ; i++ )
                printf ( "%f ", arr[i] ) ;
       }

(5)    main( )
       {
            int size = 10 ;
            int arr[size] ;
            for ( i = 1 ; i <= size ; i++ )
            {
                scanf ( "%d", &arr[i] ) ;
                printf ( "\n%d", arr[i] ) ;
            }
       }

(6)    main( )
       {
            int i, j = 10, arrsize ;
            int arr[arrsize] ;
            if ( j == 10 )
                arrsize = 20 ;
            else
                arrsize = 40 ;
            for ( i = 0 ; i < arrsize ; i++ )
                arr[i] = 100 ;
       }

(7)    main( )
       {
            int arr1[10], arr2[10], i ;
            for ( i = 0 ; i <= 9 ; i++ )
            {
```

```
                    arr1[i] = 'A' + i ;
                    arr2[i] = 'a' + i ;
                    printf ( "%d ", arr2[i] - arr1[i] ) ;
                }
        }
```

(8)   ```
       main( )
       {
            static int b[ ] = { 10, 20, 30, 40, 50 } ;
            int i ;
            for (i = 0 ; i <= 4 ; i++)
                printf ("%d ", i[b]) ;
       }
       ```

(9)    ```
       main( )
       {
            static int array[10] = { 1, 2, 3, 4, 5, 6 } ;
            int i ;
            for ( i = 0 ; i <= 9 ; i++ )
                printf ( "%d ", array[i] ) ;
       }
       ```

(10)   ```
       main( )
       {
            static int a[ ] = { 2, 3, 4, 5, 6 } ;
            int i ;
            for (i = 5 ; i > 0 ;)
                printf ("%d ", a[--i]) ;
       }
       ```

(11)   ```
       main( )
       {
            static int a[5] = { 5, 10, 15, 20, 25 } ;
            int i, j, m, n ;
            i = ++a[1] ;
            j = a[1]++ ;
       ```

```
            printf ( "i = %d j = %d a[1] = %d\n", i, j, a[1] ) ;

            i = 1 ;
            m = a[i++] ;
            printf ( "i = %d m = %d\n", i, m ) ;

            i = 2 ;
            n = a[++i] ;
            printf ( "i = %d n = %d", i, n ) ;
     }
```

(12)   main( )
```
       {
            int arr(25), i ;
            for ( i = 0 ; i <= 100 ; i++ )
            {
                arr(i) = 100 ;
                printf ( "%d ", arr(i) ) ;
            }
       }
```

(13)   main( )
```
       {
            static int a[ ] = { 10, 20, 30, 40, 50 } ;
            int j ;
            for ( j = 0 ; j < 5 ; j++ )
            {
                printf ( "%d", *a ) ;
                a++ ;
            }
       }
```

(14)   main( )
```
       {
            static float a[ ] = { 13.24, 1.5, 1.5, 5.4, 3.5 } ;
            float *j, *k ;
```

```
        j = a ;
        k = a + 4 ;
        j = j * 2 ;
        k = k / 2 ;
        printf ( "%f %f", *j, *k ) ;
    }


(15)  main( )
    {
        int n[25] ;
        n[0] = 100 ;
        n[24] = 200 ;
        printf ( "%d %d", *n, *( n + 24 ) + *( n + 0 ) ) ;
    }


(16)  main( )
    {
        static int b[ ] = { 10, 20, 30, 40, 50 } ;
        int i, *k ;
        k = &b[4] - 4 ;
        for ( i = 0 ; i <= 4 ; i++ )
        {
            printf ( "%d ", *k ) ;
            k++ ;
        }
    }


(17)  main( )
    {
        static int a[ ] = { 2, 4, 6, 8, 10 } ;
        int i ;
        for ( i = 0 ; i <= 4 ; i++ )
        {
            *( a + i ) = a[i] + i[a] ;
            printf ( "%d ", *( i + a ) ) ;
        }
```

```
        }

(18)  main( )
      {
            static int a[5] = { 2, 4, 6, 8, 10 } ;
            int i, b = 5 ;
            for ( i = 0 ; i < 5 ; i++ )
            {
                  f ( a[i], &b ) ;
                  printf ( "%d %d\n", a[i], b ) ;
            }
      }

      f ( x, y )
      int x, *y ;
      {
            x = *( y ) += 2 ;
      }

(19)  main( )
      {
            static int a[5] = { 2, 3, 4, 5, 6 } ;
            int i ;
            change ( a ) ;
            for ( i = 4 ; i = 0 ; i-- )
                  printf( "%d ", a[i] ) ;
      }

      change ( b )
      int *b ;
      {
            int i ;
            for ( i = 0 ; i <= 4 ; i++ )
            {
                  *b = *b + 1 ;
                  b++ ;
            }
```

```
        }

(20)   main( )
       {
           int arr[ ] = { 0, 1, 2, 3, 4 } ;
           int i, *ptr ;
           for ( ptr = &arr[0] ; ptr <= &arr[4] ; ptr++ )
               printf ( "%d ", *ptr ) ;
       }


(21)   main( )
       {
           int arr[ ] = { 0, 1, 2, 3, 4 } ;
           int i, *ptr ;
           for ( ptr = &arr[0], i = 0 ; i <= 4 ; i++ )
               printf ( "%d ", ptr[i] ) ;
       }


(22)   main( )
       {
           int arr[ ] = { 0, 1, 2, 3, 4 } ;
           int i, *p ;
           for ( p = arr, i = 0 ; p + i <= arr + 4 ; p++, i++ )
               printf ( "%d ", *( p + i ) ) ;
       }


(23)   main( )
       {
           int arr[ ] = { 0, 1, 2, 3, 4 } ;
           int i, *ptr ;
           for ( ptr = arr + 4 ; ptr = arr ; ptr-- )
               printf ( "%d ", *ptr ) ;
       }


(24)   main( )
       {
```

```
            int arr[ ] = { 0, 1, 2, 3, 4 } ;
            int i, *ptr ;
            for ( ptr = arr + 4, i = 0 ; i <= 4 ; i++ )
                printf ( "%d ", ptr[-i] ) ;
     }
```

(25) main( )
```
     {
            int arr[ ] = { 0, 1, 2, 3, 4 } ;
            int *ptr, i ;
            for ( ptr = arr + 4 ; ptr >= arr ; ptr-- )
                printf ( "%d ", arr [ ptr - arr ] ) ;
     }
```

(26) main( )
```
     {
            static int a[ ] = { 0, 1, 2, 3, 4 } ;
            static int *p[ ] = { a, a + 1, a + 2, a + 3, a + 4 } ;
            int **ptr = p ;
            printf ( "%d %d\n", a, *a ) ;
            printf ( "%d %d %d\n", p, *p, **p ) ;
            printf ( "%d %d %d\n", ptr, *ptr, **ptr ) ;
     }
```

(27) main( )
```
     {
            static int a[ ] = { 0, 1, 2, 3, 4 } ;
            static int *p[ ] = { a, a + 1, a + 2, a + 3, a + 4 } ;
            int   **ptr = p ;
            ptr++ ;
            printf ( "%d %d %d\n", ptr - p, *ptr - a, **ptr )

            *ptr++ ;
            printf ( "%d %d %d\n", ptr - p, *ptr - a, **ptr ) ;

            *++ptr ;
```

```
                printf ( "%d %d %d\n", ptr - p, *ptr - a, **ptr ) ;

                ++*ptr ;
                printf ( "%d %d %d\n", ptr - p, *ptr - a, **ptr ) ;
        }

(28)    main( )
        {
                static int a[ ] = { 0, 1, 2, 3, 4 } ;
                static int *p[ ] = { a, a + 1, a + 2, a + 3, a + 4 } ;
                int **ptr ;
                ptr = p ;

                **ptr++ ;
                printf ( "%d %d %d\n", ptr - p, *ptr - a, **ptr ) ;
                *++*ptr ;
                printf ( "%d %d %d\r:", ptr - p, *ptr - a, **ptr ) ;
                ++**ptr ;
                printf ( "%d %d %d\n", ptr - p, *ptr - a, **ptr ) ;
        }

(29)    main( )
        {
                static int n[3][3] = {
                                        2, 4, 3,
                                        6, 8, 5,
                                        3, 5, 1
                                } ;

                /* Assume that array begins at address 404 */
                printf ( "%d %d %d", n, n[2], n[2][2] ) ;
        }

(30)    main( )
        {
                static int n[3][3] = {
```

```
                                    2, 4, 3,
                                    6, 8, 5,
                                    3, 5, 1
                                } ;
        int i, *ptr ;
        ptr = n ;
        printf ( "%d ", n[2] ) ;
        printf ( "%d ", ptr[2] ) ;
        printf ( "%d ", *( ptr + 2 ) ) ;
    }
```

(31)
```
    main( )
    {
        static int n[3][3] = {

                                    2, 4, 3,
                                    6, 8, 5,
                                    3, 5, 1
                                } ;
        int i, j ;
        for ( i = 2 ; i = 0 ; i-- )
        {
            for ( j = 2 ; j = 0 ; j-- )
            printf ( "%d %d\n", n[i][j], *( *( n + i ) + j ) ) ;
        }
    }
```

(32)
```
    main( )
    {
        static int a[3][3] = {

                                    1, 2, 3,
                                    4, 5, 6,
                                    7, 8, 9
                                } ;
        int *ptr[3] = { a[0], a[1], a[2] } ;
        int **ptr1 = ptr ;
        int i ;
        for ( i = 0 ; i <= 2 ; i++ )
```

```
            printf ( "%d ", *ptr[i] ) ;

        printf ( "\n" ) ;
        for ( i = 0 ; i <= 2 ; i++ )
            printf ( "%d ", *a[i] ) ;

        printf ( "\n" ) ;
        for ( i = 0 ; i <= 2 ; i++ )
        {
            printf ( "%d ", **ptr1 ) ;
            ptr1++ ;
        }
    }
```

```
(33)  main( )
      {
          static int t[3][2][4] = {
                                    {
                                        2, 4, 3, 6,
                                        1, 6, 7, 9
                                    },
                                    {
                                        8, 2, 1, 1,
                                        2, 3, 7, 3
                                    },
                                    {
                                        1, 6, 2, 4,
                                        0, 7, 9, 5
                                    }
                                  } ;
          printf ("%d", t[2][1][3], *( *( *( t + 2 ) + 1 ) + 3 ) ) ;
      }
```

[B]   Attempt the following:

(1)   The first difference D1 of a sequence A of N elements is
       obtained by subtracting each element, except the last, from the

next element in the array. The second difference D2 is defined as the first difference of D1, and so on. For example, if

A: 1, 2, 4, 7, 11, 16, 22, then
D1: 1, 2, 3, 4, 5, 6
D2: 1, 1, 1, 1, 1
D3: 0, 0, 0, 0

Write a program that reads a sequence of 25 elements in an array and finds its first, second, and third differences.

(2)   A common problem in statistics is that of generating frequency distribution of the given data. Assuming that the data consists of 50 positive integers in the range 1 to 25, write a program that prints the number of times each integer occurs in the data.

(3)   A square matrix, that is, one having the same number of rows and columns, is called a diagonal matrix if its only non-zero elements are on the diagonal from upper left to lower right. It is called upper triangular, if all elements below the diagonal are zeroes, and lower triangular, if all elements above the diagonal are zeroes. Write a program that reads a matrix and determines if it is one of these three special matrices.

(4)   The Miniaturization Unlimited sells 5 types of memory chips through its retail outlets in 10 cities. The weekly sales of the company are stored in a 5 x 10 x 7 array SALES such that SALES(L, K, M) denotes the sales of the Lth memory chip in the Kth city on the Mth day of the week. Write a program that computes:

(a)   The total weekly sale of each type of memory chip
(b)   The total weekly sale in each city and
(c)   The average daily sale of the company

(5)   You have been called upon to write a match-making program for a marriage beaureau. The beaureau's questionnaire has 8

statements, and the applicant indicates her or his degree of agreement on a scale of 1 to 5. The response of the applicant is entered through the keyboard. Each response contains the applicant's code number, sex (F or M), and responses to the questionnaire (8 integers). You may assume that there are no more than 50 applicants.

Your program should match each person with the three most compatible persons of the opposite sex, and should print the code number of the applicants along with the code numbers of their prospective mates. As a measure of compatibility of two persons, use the cosine of difference between the responses; the larger the cosine, the more compatible the couple.

(6) A magic square is an n x n matrix, where each of the integers 1, 2, 3, ..., n^2, appear exactly once and the sums of every row column, and diagonal are equal. It has been proved that for even values of n, no magic square exists. Here is a magic square for n = 3:

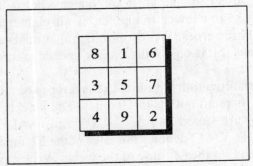

Figure 8.7 Magic square

The following is a procedure for constructing an n x n magic square for any odd integer n.

Place initial number in the middle of the top row. Then after integer k has been placed, move up one row and one column to the right to place the next integer $k + 1$, unless one of the following occurs:

(a)   If a move takes you above the top row in the jth column, move to the bottom of the jth column and place the integer there.

(b)   If a move takes you outside to the right of the square in the ith row, place the integer in the ith row at the left side.

(c)   If a move takes you to an already filled square or if you move out of the square at the upper-right-hand corner, place $k + 1$ immediately below k.

Write a program to construct a magic square for any odd integer n.

Answers

Answers to **[A]**

(1) *Output*

```
0 100 0
1 -75 0
2 123 0
3 1245 0
4 347 0
```

Explanation

Since the storage class of the array **a[ ]** has not been mentioned, the default storage class **auto** is assumed for it. As against this, the storage class of **b[ ]** has been explicitly mentioned as **static**. The default value of **auto** storage class variables is any garbage value and the default value of **static** storage class variables is 0. Therefore all zeroes are printed out for **b[ ]**, whereas garbage values are printed out for **a[ ]**.

(2) *Output*

No output

Explanation

Surprised? You expected numbers like 100, 400, 900, etc. to be printed. Then what went wrong? Look at the **for** loop carefully. There is a semicolon at the end of it. Thus the loop is reduced to the following form:

```
for ( i = 0 ; i <= 4 ; i++ )
```

This loop repeats the null statement (;) 5 times and then the control comes out of the loop. At this time the value of i has become 5 and hence the **if** condition fails and the control reaches the closing brace of **main( )**. The execution is therefore terminated without any output to the screen. Take care not to place a semicolon after **for**. If you do so, now you know whom to blame.

(3)   *Output*

```
0 0
0 0
0 0
0 0
0 0
```

Explanation

Default initial value of a **static** or **extern** storage class variable is 0. Thus, though the arrays **b[ ]** and **a[ ]** have not been initialised, the fact that their storage class is **extern** and **static** respectively causes their default initial values to be 0. Hence the output.

(4)   *Output*

1.200000 12.000000 2.400000 24.000000 3.500000 35.000000

Explanation

Were you expecting an error message because in the array initialisation some values are integers whereas others are **floats**? Well, the initialisation is perfectly alright. When we initialise **arr[1]** to a value 12, what really gets stored in **arr[1]** is 12.0. Same thing happens when we try to store 24 or 35 in the array. They are promoted to **floats** before storing the values. Thus the array contains all **floats**, thereby meeting the basic requirement of the array that all its elements must be similar. Since **printf( )** always prints a **float** with a precision of 6 digits after the decimal point, each array element has been printed with six places after the decimal point.

(5)   *Output*

Error message: Constant expression required in function main

Explanation

While declaring the array, its size should always be mentioned with a positive integer constant. Thus **arr[10]** is acceptable, whereas **arr[size]** is unacceptable, irrespective of whether **size** has been declared earlier to array declaration or not. Hence the error message.

(6)   *Output*

Error message: Constant expression required in function main

Explanation

Depending upon the value of **j**, we are attempting to determine the value of **arrsize**, and then expecting this value to be used in the array declaration. This is too ambitious, because when the array declaration statement is executed, C has to know how much space is to be reserved for the array. So, if we expect that the size of the array can be determined in **if**, and then this size should be used to declare the array, then by the time control reaches the **if** it has already lost the opportunity to declare the array. Moral is, nothing else except a positive integer is acceptable in the array size declaration.

Suppose we declare an array saying **int arr[25]** and then later in the program feel that this much space is not sufficient and we wish to store a few more elements in the array, then can we change the size of the array during execution of the program? By no means. Once you have declared the size of the array its size can never be changed during program execution. In that sense we can say that the memory allocation of an array is static, i.e. it cannot be changed on the run during execution. To overcome this limitation C provides functions like **malloc( )** and **calloc( )**, which dynamically allocate memory during execution. This memory can be increased or decreased as per the program's need during program execution.

(7)   *Output*

32 32 32 32 32 32 32 32 32 32

Explanation

arr1[ ] and **arr2[ ]** are declared as arrays capable of storing 10 integers. Through the **for** loop we are storing numbers from 65 to 74 in **arr1[ ]** and numbers from 97 to 106 in **arr2[ ]**. How come? Because whenever we mention 'A' it is replaced by its ascii value 65, whereas 'a' is replaced by its ascii value 97. Therefore, the operation 'A' + **i** is perfectly acceptable, as it just adds value of **i** to 65. Once the values are stored in the two arrays, the difference of the values, i.e. 32, is printed through the **printf( )**.

(8)   *Output*

10 20 30 40 50

Explanation

Using **i[b]** in any other language would have definitely resulted into an error. But not in C. Why? Because all other languages use pointers to access array elements, but somehow hide this fact from the user. Whereas C says that if I am going to use pointers internally to access array elements, then let the user as well know it.

When we mention the name of the array, we get its base address. When we say **b[i]**, internally C converts this to ***(b + i)**, which means value at the address which is **i** locations after the base address. Now you would agree that ***(b + i)** is same as ***(i + b)**, which is same as **i[b]**. Therefore, the above **for** loop prints the array elements stored in the array **b[ ]**.

(9) *Output*

1 2 3 4 5 6 0 0 0 0

Explanation

The array has been declared to be capable of holding 10 integers, but while initialising the array only 6 elements are stored in it. This is perfectly acceptable. What would be the values of the elements that have not been initialised? Garbage or zero? Since the storage class of the array has been declared as **static**, the rest of the elements have a value 0. This is because by default, any **static** storage class variable has a value 0. This fact is justified by the output of the program which shows the last four elements as 0, whereas the first six elements are having the values to which they have been initialised in the array declaration.

(10) *Output*

6 5 4 3 2

Explanation

'Dimension of the array not mentioned'. Possibly you expected this error message. But no such error message is displayed. Does that mean that we can drop the dimension while declaring the array? Yes, provided we are initialising the array at the same place where we are declaring it. And in this program this is what we are doing. So, the compiler gets past the declaration without faltering for a second.

In the **for** loop, **printf( )** uses the expression **a[--i]**. Can -- operator be used with an array subscript? By all means. Here, since -- precedes **i**, firstly **i** is decremented and then its value is used in accessing the array element. Thus, first time through the **for** loop, when the control reaches **a[--i]** with **i** equal to 5, firstly **i** is reduced to 4 and then this 4 is used to access the array element **a[4]**. This is done repeatedly through the **for** loop till all the array elements have been printed.

(11) *Output*

i = 11 j = 11 a[1] = 12
i = 2 m = 12
i = 3 n = 20

Explanation

In **i = ++a[1]**, since **++** precedes **a[1]**, firstly the value of **a[1]**, i.e. 10 would be incremented to 11, and then assigned to the variable **i**. As against this, in the next statement, firstly the element **a[1]** (i.e. 11) would be assigned to **j** and then the value of **a[1]** would be incremented to 12. The values of **i, j** and **a[1]** are then printed out.

Next, **i** is reset to 1. In **m = a[i++]**, since **++** succeeds **i**, firstly **a[i]**, i.e. 12 is assigned to variable **m**, and then the value of **i**, i.e. 1, is incremented to 2. The values of **i** and **m** are then printed out.

After that **i** is once again reset to 2. In **n = a[++i]** since **++** precedes **i**, firstly it is incremented to 3 and then the value of **a[3]**, i.e. 20 is assigned to the variable **n**. Finally, the values of **i** and **n** are printed out.

(12) *Output*

Error message: Function definition out of place in function main

Explanation

People who migrate to C from Basic or Fortran are likely to commit this error. For arrays, C uses square brackets, whereas Basic or Fortran use parentheses. The moment the compiler finds ( ), it expects a reference to a function, and **arr** has not been defined as a function. Hence the error message.

Would the program work if we change **arr(25)** and **arr(i)** to **arr[25]** and **arr[i]**? Well, we can't say. This is because in the **for** loop we are storing elements beyond **arr[24]**, which is the last legal array element. It means we are exceeding the bounds of the array. Would we get an error message? Certainly not. This is because C never performs bounds checking on an array. It is always the programmer's responsibility. When the array is declared, it would reserve 25 contiguous locations in memory. Through the **for** loop when we write beyond **arr[24]**, it might overwrite something important which might be present beyond this element. In worst possible case the computer would hang.

(13) *Output*

Error message: Lvalue required in function main

Explanation

Whenever we mention the name of the array, we get its base address. Therefore, first time through the loop, the **printf( )** should print the value at this base address. There is no problem upto this. The problem lies in the next statement, **a++**. Since C doesn't perform bounds checking on an array, the only thing that it remembers about an array once declared is its base address. And **a++** attempts to change this base address, which C won't allow because if it does so, it would be unable to remember the beginning of the array. Anything which can change - in compiler's langauage - is called lvalue. Since value of **a** cannot be changed through **++**, it flashes the error saying 'Lvalue required' so that **++** operator can change it.

(14) *Output*

Error message: Illegal use of pointer in function main

Explanation

j and **k** have been declared as pointer variables, which would contain the addresses of **floats**. In other words, **j** and **k** are **float** pointers. To begin with, the base address of the array **a[ ]** is stored in **j**. The next statement is perfectly acceptable; the address of the 4th **float** from the base address is stored in **k**. The next two statements are erroneous. This is because the only operations that can be performed on pointers are addition and subtraction. Multiplication or division of a pointer is not allowed. Hence the error message.

(15) *Output*

100 300

Explanation

n[ ] has been declared as an array capable of holding 25 elements numbered from 0 to 24. Then 100 and 200 are assigned to **n[0]** and **n[24]** respectively. Then comes the most important part - the **printf( )** statement. Whenever we mention the name of the array, we get its base address (i.e. address of the zeroth element of the array). Thus, ***n** would give the value at this base address, which in this case is 100. This is then printed out. Look at the next expression,

*(n + 24) + *(n + 0)

n gives the address of the zeroth element, **n + 1** gives the address of the next element of the array, and so on. Thus, **n + 24** would give the address of the last element of the array, and therefore ***(n + 24)** would give the value at this address, which is 200 in our case. Similarly, ***(n + 0)** would give 100 and the addition of the two would result into 300, which is outputted next.

(16) *Output*

10 20 30 40 50

Explanation

First look at Figure 8.8. The array elements are stored in contiguous memory locations and each element is an integer, hence is occupying 2 locations.

b[0]	b[1]	b[2]	b[3]	b[4]
10	20	30	40	50
4002	4004	4006	4008	4010

Figure 8.8

The expression **&b[4]** gives the address of **b[4]** (4010 in this case). From this address if we subtract 4, we get 4002. Or did you expect to get 4006? Remember that by subtracting 4 from 4010 what we mean is: get the address of an integer which is 4 integers to the left of the integer whose address is 4010. Now, address of the integer which is 4 integers to the left of the integer whose address is 4010, is the address 4002. This address, 4002, is stored in **k**, which has been declared as a variable capable of holding an integer's address. First time through the **for** loop ***k** would result into 10, i.e. value at the address contained in **k**. **k++** then increments **k** such that it contains the address of the next integer, i.e. 4004. Next time through the **for** loop ***k** would yield the value at address contained in **k**, i.e. value at the address 4004, which is 20. Similarly, the loop prints out the rest of the elements of the array.

(17) *Output*

4 8 12 16 20

Explanation

Imbibe the following two facts and the program becomes very simple to understand:

-    Mentioning the name of the array gives the base address of the array.
-    Array elements are stored in contiguous memory locations.On adding 1 to the address of an integer, we get the address of the next integer.

With those facts clearly laid out, let us now try to understand the program. Remember that internally C always accesses array elements using pointers. Thus, when we say **a[i]**, internally C converts it to *(**a + i**), which means value of ith integer from the base address. Now, if the expression **a[i]** is same as *(**a + i**) then *(**i + a**) must be same as **i[a]**. But *(**a + i**) is same as *(**i + a**). Therefore **a[i]** must be same as **i[a]**.

Thus **a[i]**, *(**a + i**), *(**i + a**) and **i[a]** refer to the same element - the ith element from the base address.

Therefore the expression used in the **for** loop, *(**a + i**) = **a[i]** + **i[a]** is nothing but **a[i] = a[i] + a[i]**. Thus all that is done in the **for** loop is each array element is doubled and then printed out through **printf( )**.

(18) *Output*

    2 7
    4 9
    6 11
    8 13
    10 15

Explanation

After initialising the array when the control enters the **for** loop, the function **f( )** gets called with value of **a[i]** and address of **b**. In **f( )** these are collected in variables **x** and **y**. Then comes the expression **x = *(y) += 2**. Here *(**y**) **+= 2** is evaluated first and then the result of this expression is assigned to **x**. The first time through the **for** loop ***(y)** gives 5, to which 2 is added and the result is stored at ***(y)**. It means 7 is assigned to **b**. Finally, the **=** operator assigns 7 to **x**. However, on assigning a new value to **x**, the array element **a[0]** in **main( )** remains unchanged. Thus, during every call to **f( )**, **b**'s value keeps getting updated whereas there is no change in the values of the array elements.

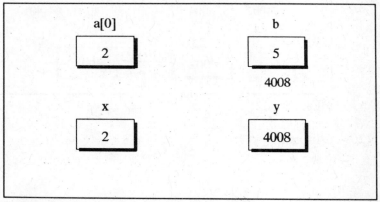

Figure 8.9

(19) *Output*

7 6 5 4 3

Explanation

While calling **change( )** we are passing the base address of the array, which as per Figure 8.10 is 4002. This address is collected in **b** in the function **change( )**. Then the control enters the **for** loop, where we meet the expression ***b = *b + 1**. This means replace the value at the address contained in **b**, with value at the address contained in **b** plus 1. Every time **b++** is executed, the address of the next integer gets stored in **b**. Thus, using the address stored in **b,** we get an access to array elements which are now changed to 3, 4, 5, 6 and 7. Once the control comes back from **change( ),** the current array contents are then printed out from end to beginning through the **for** loop.

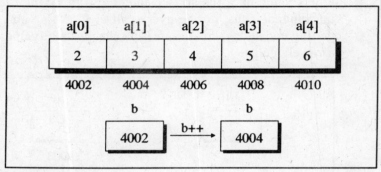

Figure 8.10

(20) *Output*

01234

Explanation

Refer to Figure 8.11 for a better understanding of the program.

Here **ptr** has been declared as an integer pointer, i.e. a variable capable of holding the address of an integer. In the **for** loop, in the initialisation part, this **ptr** is assigned the address of the zeroth element of the integer array. Suppose this address turns out to be 6004. Then address of the first element of the array would be 6006, address of the second element would be 6008, and so on. In the condition part of the **for** loop, the address stored in **ptr** is compared with the address of the fourth array element, i.e. 6012. Since for the first time the condition is satisfied (since 6004 is less than 6012), the control reaches **printf( )** where the value at address 6004, i.e. 0 gets printed.

After executing **printf( )** the control reaches **ptr++**, where **ptr** is incremented such that it contains the address of the next integer. Since the next integer is stored at 6006, **ptr** now contains 6006. Once again the condition is tested. Since 6006 is also smaller than 6012, the condition is satisfied hence the **printf( )** prints out the value at 6006, i.e. 1. And then **ptr++** is executed again so that it contains the address of the next integer, i.e. 6008. This process continues till all the array elements have been printed.

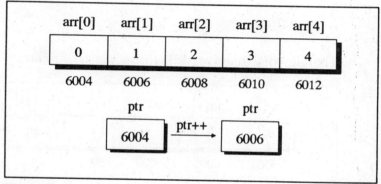

Figure 8.11

(21) *Output*

0 1 2 3 4

Explanation

In the initialisation part of the **for** loop, multiple initialisations are being done. Firstly, **ptr** is set up with the base address of the array and then **i** is set to 0. Since 0 is less than 4, the condition is satisfied for the first time and the control reaches **printf( )**. Here the value of the expression **ptr[i]** gets printed. Now **ptr[i]** is nothing but ***(ptr + i)**. Since **ptr** contains the base address of the array, (**ptr + i**) would give the address of the ith integer from the base address. Since **i** is going to vary from 0 to 4, this would give addresses of 0th, 1st, 2nd, 3rd and 4th integers from the base address of the array. Naturally, the expression ***(ptr + i)** would give values at these addresses. Thus, the **for** loop would print out all the array elements.

(22) *Output*

0 2 4

Explanation

The following figure would help in understanding the program.

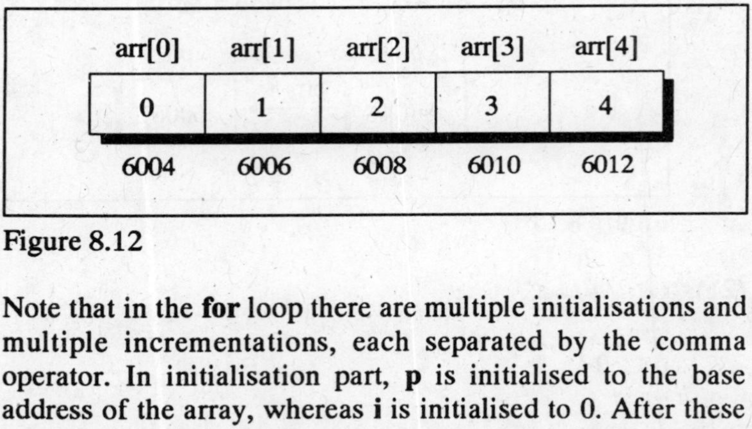

Figure 8.12

Note that in the **for** loop there are multiple initialisations and multiple incrementations, each separated by the comma operator. In initialisation part, **p** is initialised to the base address of the array, whereas **i** is initialised to 0. After these initialisations the control reaches the condition. The condition is a little complicated so let us isolate it for a clearer understanding.

p + i <= arr + 4

Here **+** enjoys a higher priority than **<=**. Therefore, first **p + i** and **arr + 4** are performed and then the **<=** goes to work. **p + i** yields 6004, whereas **arr + 4** evaluates to 6012. Since 6004 is

less than 6012, the condition is satisfied and the control reaches
printf( ), where value at (**p + i**), i.e. 0 gets printed. Then the
control reaches the incrementation part of the for loop, where
p++ increments **p** to 6006, and **i++** increments **i** to 1. Next,
once again the condition is tested. This time **p + i** gives 6008
(since **p** is 6006 and **i** is 1) and **arr + 4** gives 6012. Since the
condition once again gets satisfied, the **printf( )** prints out the
value at (**p + i**), i.e. 2. Similarly, next time around 4 gets
printed and then the condition fails therefore the execution is
terminated.

(23) *Output*

4 3 2 1 0

Explanation

The following figure would lead to a better understanding of
the program.

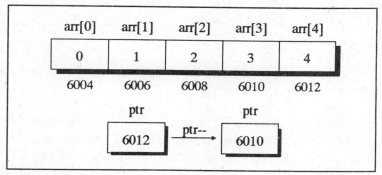

Figure 8.13

In the initialisation part, **ptr** is assigned the address of the last
element in the array. This is because **arr + 4** gives the address
of the fourth integer from the base address. First time through
the loop the condition evaluates to true, since the address of

the fourth element (6012) would certainly be bigger than the base address (6004) of the array. Next, the control reaches **printf( )**, which prints out the value at address contained in **ptr**, i.e. value at address 6012. Next, the statement **ptr--** gets executed which reduces **ptr** to 6010. Since 6010 is also bigger than 6004, the condition is satisfied once again, and the value at 6010 gets printed through the **printf( )**. This process is repeated for all the array elements.

(24)   *Output*

4 3 2 1 0

Explanation

arr[0]	arr[1]	arr[2]	arr[3]	arr[4]
0	1	2	3	4
6004	6006	6008	6010	6012

Figure 8.14

The above figure shows the arrangement of the array elements in memory.

In the initialisation part of the **for** loop, **ptr** is assigned a value 6012, since **arr + 4** gives the address of the fourth integer from the base address of the array. Here, the variable **i** is also initialised to 0. Since the condition is satisified for the first time (**i** being 0), the **printf( )** prints out the value of **ptr[-i]**. But what is **ptr[-i]**? Nothing but *(**ptr - i**). And since **i** is 0, *(**ptr - i**) evaluates to *(6012 - 0), i.e. 4. Then the control reaches **i++** where **i** is incremented to 1. Next, the condition is checked and since it evaluates to true, the **printf( )** prints out the value of **ptr[-i]**. Since this time **i** is 1, **ptr[-i]** becomes ***(ptr - 1)**, i.e. ***(6012 - 1)**, i.e ***(6010)**. Thus the value 3 gets printed. Likewise, 2, 1 and 0 also get printed subsequent times through the **for** loop.

(25) *Output*

4 3 2 1 0

Explanation

A picture is worth a thousand words. Going by this dictum, the following figure should add clarity to your understanding of the program.

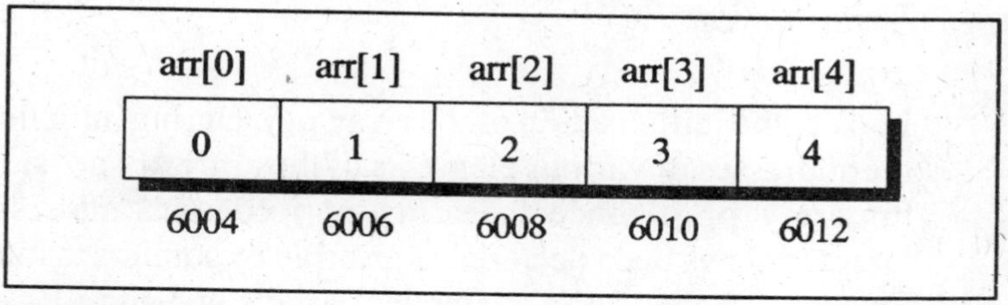

Figure 8.15

Now things are getting really complicated, as the **printf( )** would justify. Let us begin with the **for** loop. Firstly **ptr** is assigned the address 6012, the address of the fourth integer from the base address. Since this address is greater than the base address, the condition is satisfied and the control reaches **printf( )**. What does **arr [ptr - arr]** evaluate to? **ptr - arr** means **6012 - 6004**, which yields 4, and hence **arr[4]** prints out the fourth element of the array. Then **ptr--** reduces **ptr** to 6010. Since 6010 is greater than the base address 6004, the condition is satisfied and once again the control reaches the **printf( )**. This time **ptr - arr** becomes **6010 - 6004**, i.e. 3. Thus **arr[3]** prints out 3. This process is repeated till all the integers in the array have been printed out.

Possibly an easier way of understanding the expression **ptr - arr** would be as follows. Suppose **ptr** contains 6012 and **arr** contains 6004. We can then view the subtraction as (**arr + 4 - arr**), since **ptr** is nothing but **arr + 4**. Now I suppose its quite logical to expect the result of the subtraction as 4.

(26)   *Output*

```
6004 0
9016 6004 0
9016 6004 0
```

Explanation

Look at the initialisation of the array **p[ ]**. During initialisation, the addresses of various elements of the array **a[ ]** are stored in the array **p[ ]**. Since the array **p[ ]** contains addresses of integers, it has been declared as an array of pointers to integers. Figure 8.16 shows the contents of arrays **a[ ]** and **p[ ]**. In the variable **ptr**, the base address of the array **p[ ]**, i.e. 9016 is stored. Since this address is the address of **p[0]**, which itself is a pointer, **ptr** has been declared as pointer to an integer pointer.

Let us understand the **printf( )**s now. The first **printf( )** is quite simple.

```
printf ( "%d %d\n", a, *a ) ;
```

It prints out the base address of the array **a[ ]** and the value at this base address.

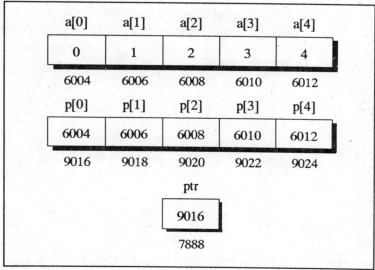

Figure 8.16

Looking at the figure, this would turn out to be 6004 and 0. When you execute the program, the address may turn out to be something other than 6004, but the value at the address would be surely 0.

Now look at the second **printf( )**.

printf ("%d %d %d\n", p, *p, **p) ;

Here **p** would give the base address of the array **p[ ]**, i.e. 9016; ***p** would give the value at this address, i.e. 6004; ****p** would give the value at the address given by ***p**, i.e. value at address 6004, which is 0.

Now on to the last **printf( )**.

printf ("%d %d %d\n", ptr, *ptr, **ptr) ;

Here **ptr** contains the base address of the array **p[ ]**, i.e. 9016; ***ptr** would give the value at this address, i.e. 6004; ****ptr** would give the value at the address given by ***ptr**, i.e. value at address 6004, which is 0.

(27)   *Output*

```
111
222
333
344
```

Explanation

Figure 8.17 would go a long way in helping to understand this program.

Here **ptr** has been declared as a pointer to an integer pointer and assigned the base address of the array **p[ ]**, which has been declared as an array of pointers. What happens when **ptr++** gets executed? **ptr** points to the next integer pointer in the array **p[ ]**. In other words, now **ptr** contains the address 9018. Now let us analyse the meaning of **ptr - p**, ***ptr - a** and ****ptr**.

ptr - p

Since **ptr** is containing the address 9018, we can as well say that **ptr** is containing the address given by **p + 1**. Then **ptr - p** is reduced to (**p + 1 - p**), which yields 1.

*ptr - a

*ptr means value at the address contained in **ptr**. Since **ptr** contains 9018, the value at this address would be 6006. Now 6006 can be imagined as (**a + 1**). Thus the expression becomes (**a + 1 - a**), which is nothing but 1.

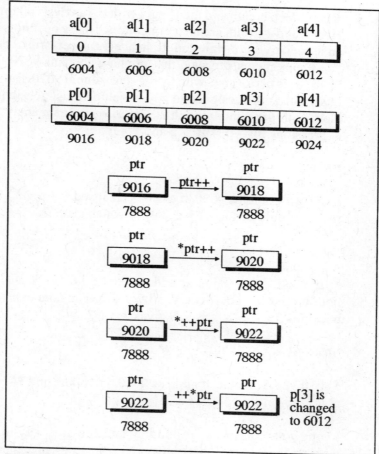

Figure 8.17

**ptr

ptr contains 9018, so ***ptr** yields 6006, and hence ****ptr** becomes ***(6006)**, which yields 1.

Thus the output of the first **printf( )** becomes 1 1 1.

Take a deep breath and then begin with the analysis of ***ptr++**. Here ***** and **++** both are unary operators. Unary operators have an associativity of right to left, hence **++** is performed before *****. **++** increments **ptr** such that **ptr** now contains 9020. Then ***(9020)** is performed, which gives the value at 9020. But since this value is not assigned to any variable, it just gets ignored. Now with **ptr** containing 9020, let us once again analyse the expressions **ptr - p**, ***ptr - a** and ****ptr**.

ptr - p

Since **ptr** contains 9020, it can be visualised as (**p + 2**). Thus **ptr - p** would become (**p + 2 - p**), which gives 2.

*ptr - a

*ptr would give value at address 9020, i.e. 6008, which is nothing but the address given by **a + 2**. Thus the expression becomes (**a + 2 - a**), which gives 2.

**ptr

*ptr gives the value at address 9020, i.e. 6008, and ***(6008)** gives the value at 6008, i.e. 2.

I hope your confidence is building and you are ready to meet head on the expression ***++ptr**. Here, since **++** precedes **ptr**, firstly **ptr** is incremented such that it contains the address 9022, and then the value at this address is obtained. Since the value is not collected in any variable, it gets ignored. Now having cooked enough pointer stew you can easily imagine that the output of the third **printf( )** would be 3 3 3.

Finally, let us understand the expression **++*ptr**. Here obviously, the priority goes to the *****. Thus, this expression increments the value given by ***ptr**. Since **ptr** contains 9022, ***ptr** gives value at 9022, i.e. 6010. This value is incremented to 6012. So **p[3]** now contains 6012, whereas value of **ptr** remains stationary at 9022. Let us now analyse the expressions **ptr - p**, ***ptr - a** and ****ptr**.

ptr - p

ptr contains 9022, therefore **ptr** can be imagined as (**p + 3**). Thus (**ptr - p**) becomes (**p + 3 - p**), which yields 3.

*ptr - a

***ptr** yields 6012 which can be thought of as (**a + 4**). Thus the expression is reduced to (**a + 4 - a**), which yields 4.

**ptr

***ptr** yields 6012, therefore ****ptr** would yield the value at ***ptr**, or the value at 6012, which is 4.

(28) *Output*

```
1 1 1
1 2 2
1 2 3
```

Explanation

To begin with, the array **a[ ]** is initialised and the array **p[ ]** is set up such that it contains the addressses of elements of array **a[ ]**. Thus array **p[ ]** becomes an array of pointers. The base address of this array of pointers is then assigned to **ptr**, which is rightly called a pointer to a pointer. The possible arrangement of the array elements in memory is shown in the following figure.

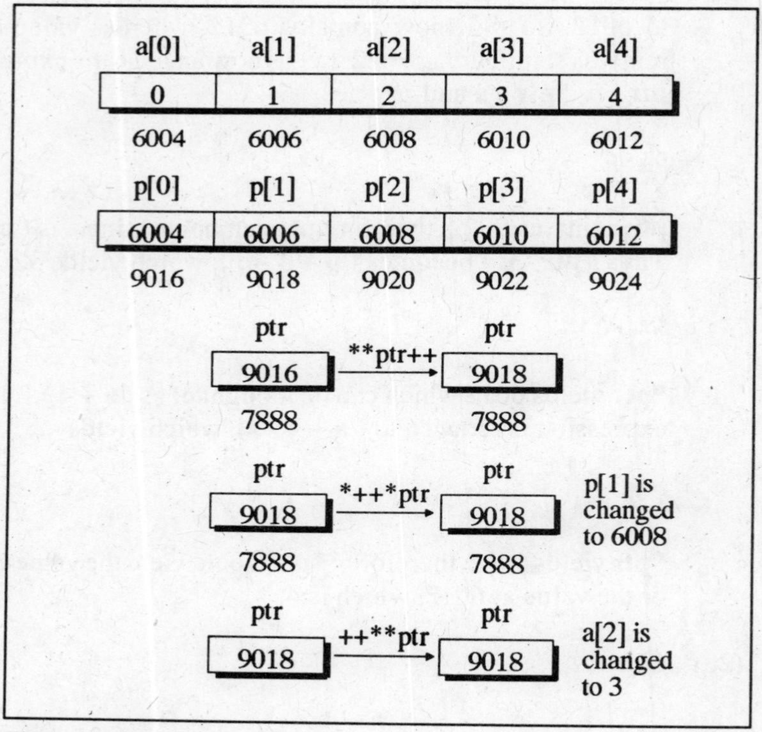

a[0]	a[1]	a[2]	a[3]	a[4]
0	1	2	3	4
6004	6006	6008	6010	6012

p[0]	p[1]	p[2]	p[3]	p[4]
6004	6006	6008	6010	6012
9016	9018	9020	9022	9024

ptr   ptr
┌──────┐   **ptr++   ┌──────┐
│ 9016 │ ──────────→ │ 9018 │
└──────┘   └──────┘
  7888   7888

ptr   ptr
┌──────┐   *++*ptr   ┌──────┐   p[1] is
│ 9018 │ ──────────→ │ 9018 │   changed
└──────┘   └──────┘   to 6008
  7888   7888

ptr   ptr
┌──────┐   ++**ptr   ┌──────┐   a[2] is
│ 9018 │ ──────────→ │ 9018 │   changed
└──────┘   └──────┘   to 3

Figure 8.18

Let us now analyse the expression **ptr++. Since the unary operators are associated from right to left, the above expression would evaluate in the order: *(*(ptr++)). ptr contains the address 9016, therefore incrementing ptr would store the address 9018 in ptr. *ptr would give the value at this address. This value turns out to be 6006, and *(6006) would give the value at 6006, i.e. 1. However, this value is not assigned to any variable while evaluating **ptr++. Once you are sure that ptr contains 9018, let us now proceed to find out what the output of printf( ) is. Let us take one expression at a time and analyse it step by careful step.

ptr - p

Since **ptr** is containing the address 9018, we can as well say that **ptr** is containing the address given by **p + 1**. Thus **ptr - p** is reduced to (**p + 1 - p**), which yields 1.

*ptr - a

*ptr means value at the address contained in **ptr**. Since **ptr** contains 9018, the value at this address would be 6006. Now 6006 can be imagined as (**a + 1**). Thus the expression becomes (**a + 1 - a**), which is nothing but 1.

**ptr

ptr contains 9018, so ***ptr** would yield 6006, and hence ****ptr** becomes *(**6006**), which would yield 1.

Thus the output of the first **printf( )** turns out to be 1 1 1.

The next statement needs a closer look. In ***++*ptr**, the order of evaluation would be *(++(*ptr)). Since **ptr** contains 9018, *(**ptr**) would yield the value at 9018, i.e. 6006. Then **++** goes to work on **6006** and increments it such that it is now 6008. Thus **p[1]** would now contain 6008. And finally *(**6008**) would give 2, which is ignored since it is not assigned to any variable.

Now, with **ptr** containing 9018, let us once again analyse the expressions **ptr - p**, **ptr - a** and ****ptr**.

ptr - p

Since **ptr** contains 9018, it can be visualised as (**p + 1**), thus **ptr - p** would become (**p + 1 - p**), which would be 1.

*ptr -a

*ptr would give value at address 9018, i.e. 6008, which is nothing but the address given by **a + 2**. Thus the expression becomes (**a + 2 - a**), which gives 2.

**ptr

*ptr gives the value at address 9018, i.e. 6008, and ***(6008)** gives the value at 6008, i.e. 2.

Thus the output of the second **printf( )** would be 1 2 2.

Finally, we reach the third expression **++**ptr**. As the unary operators are evaluated from right to left, the order of evaluation of the above expression becomes: (**++ (*(*ptr)))**. Since **ptr** contains 9018, ***ptr** yields 6008. ***(6008)** results into 2. This value at the address 6008 is then incremented from 2 to 3.

ptr - p

Since **ptr** contains 9018, it can be visualised as (**p + 1**), thus **ptr - p** would become (**p + 1 - p**), which would be 1.

*ptr -a

*ptr would give value at address 9018, i.e. 6008, which is nothing but the address given by **a + 2**. Thus the expression becomes (**a + 2 - a**), which gives 2.

**ptr

*ptr gives the value at address 9018, i.e. 6008, and ***(6008)** gives the value at 6008, i.e. 3.

Thus the output of the third **printf( )** is 1 2 3.

(29) *Output*

404 416 1

Explanation

n[ ][ ], to begin with, is declared as a two-dimensional array. Whenever we mention the name of the array, we get its base address. Therefore in **printf( )**, the first output would be the base adddress of the array. In our case it turned out to be 404. The array elements are arranged in the following manner in memory. Remember that there are no rows and columns in memory.

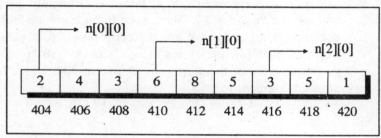

Figure 8.19

A two-dimensional array is nothing but an array of several one-dimensional arrays. The 2-D array contains addresses of these 1-D arrays. Thus **n[0]**, **n[1]** and **n[2]** contain the addresses 404, 410 and 416 respectively. Hence the second output of **printf( )**. The third output is quite straight forward. **n[2][2]** prints out the element in the second row and second column of the array.

(30) *Output*

416 3 3

Explanation

ptr has been declared as an integer pointer, and to begin with, assigned the base address of the array, which is 404.

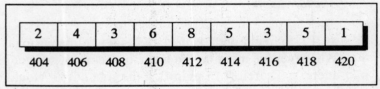

Figure 8.20

n[2] gives the base address of the second one-dimensional array, that is 416. Next comes the expression **ptr[2]**. Can we use such an expression? Yes, because ultimately **ptr[2]** is nothing but ***(ptr + 2)**. Thus, even though **ptr** has not been declared as an array, we are perfectly justified in using the expression **ptr[2]**. **ptr** stores the address 404, so *(ptr + 2) gives the value of the second integer from 404, which in this program happens to be 3.

(31) *Output*

    1 1
    5 5
    3 3
    5 5
    8 8
    6 6
    3 3
    4 4
    2 2

Explanation

The output of **n[i][j]** is as per the expectations, I believe. All that is done is, using the **for** loop, rows and columns are varied, **i** controlling the row and **j** controlling the column. What is definitely difficult to comprehend is the second expression in **printf( )**, ***(*(n + i) + j)**. Let us try to understand it. The following figure should prove helpful in doing so.

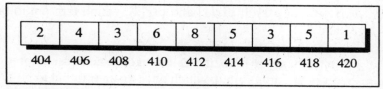

Figure 8.21

Imagine a 2-D array as a collection of several 1-D arrays. The only thing that the compiler needs to remember about a 1-D array is its base address. The compiler doesn't even have to remember the number of elements present in the array, since bounds checking is not the compiler's responsibility. Thus, if three 1-D arrays are to be remembered, the compiler should store somewhere the base addresses of these arrays. These base addresses are stored in **n[0]**, **n[1]** and **n[2]**. Now if **n[1]** gives the base address of the first array, then **n[1] + 2** would give the address of the second integer from this base address. In this case it turns out to be 414. The value at this address, that is 5, can be obtained through the expression ***(n[1] + 2)**. We know all too well that **n[1]** can also be expressed as ***(n + 1)**. Thus, the expression ***(n[1] + 2)** is same as ***(*(n + 1) + 2)**, which is same as **n[1][2]**. Therefore in general, we can say that **n[i][j]** is same as ***(*(n + i) + j)**. With that I suppose the output of the above program is quite simple.

(32) *Output*

```
147
147
147
```

Explanation

ptr[ ] has been declared as an array of pointers containing the base addresses of the three 1-D arrays as shown in Figure 8.22. Once past the declarations, the control reaches the first **for** loop. In this loop the **printf( )** prints the values at addresses stored in **ptr[0]**, **ptr[1]** and **ptr[2]**, which turn out to be 1, 4 and 7.

In the next **for** loop, the values at base addresses stored in the array **a[ ]** are printed, which once again turn out to be 1, 4 and 7. The third **for** loop is also simple. Since **ptr1** has been initialised to the base address of the array **ptr[ ]**, it contains the address 822.

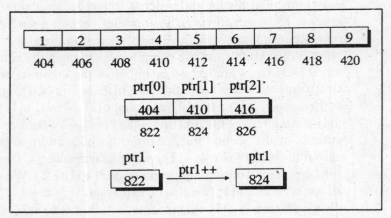

Figure 8.22

Therefore ***ptr1** would give the value at address 822, i.e 404, and ****ptr1** would give the value at address given by ***ptr1**, i,e. value at 404, which is 1. On incerementing **ptr1** it points to the next location after 822, i.e 824. Therefore next time through the **for** loop, ****ptr1** gives value at 410 (which is obtained through ***ptr1**), i.e. 4. Similarly, last time through the loop, the value 7 gets printed.

(33) *Output*

5 5

Explanation

In memory the 3-D array elements are arranged as shown in the following figure.

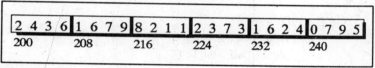

2 4 3 6	1 6 7 9	8 2 1 1	2 3 7 3	1 6 2 4	0 7 9 5
200	208	216	224	232	240

Figure 8.23

Here **t[ ][ ][ ]** has been declared as a three-dimensional array. A 3-D array can be considered as a collection of a number of 2-D arrays. Thus, the first expression in the **printf( )**, **t[2][1][3]** refers to the element in 1st row, 3rd column of the 2nd 2-D array. This turns out to be 5, which is printed through **printf( )**.

The next expression in **printf( )** is a little complicated. Since the only thing that the compiler needs to remember about the three 2-D arrays is their base addresses, these addresses are stored in **t[0]**, **t[1]** and **t[2]**. Therefore, the expression **t[2][1]** would give the address of the first row of the second 2-D array. Referring to the figure, this address turns out to be 240. To this address if we add 3, we would get the address of the third integer from this address. This address would be 246. Naturally, the value at this address (i.e. 5) can be obtained through the expression ***(t[2][1] + 3)**. But **t[2][1]** itself can be expressed as ***(t[2] + 1)**. And in this expression **t[2]** can be expressed as ***(t + 2)**. Thus the expression ***(t[2][1] + 3)** can be expressed as ***(*(*(t + 2) + 1) + 3)**.

Solutions to **[B]**

(1)   *Program*

```
main( )
{
    int a[25], d1[24], d2[23], d3[22], i ;

    printf ( "Enter 25 elements\n" ) ;
    for ( i = 0 ; i <= 24 ; i++ )
        scanf ( "%d", &a[i] ) ;

    printf ( "\nA: " ) ;
    for ( i = 0 ; i <= 24 ; i++ )
        printf ( "%d ", a[i] ) ;

    printf ( "\n\n1st, 2nd and 3rd differences are:\n" ) ;
    printf ( "\nD1: " ) ;
    for ( i = 0 ; i <= 23 ; i++ )
    {
        d1[i] = a[i+1] - a[i] ;
        printf ( "%d ", d1[i] ) ;
    }

    printf ( "\nD2: " ) ;
    for ( i = 0 ; i <= 22 ; i++ )
    {
        d2[i] = d1[i+1] - d1[i] ;
        printf ( "%d ", d2[i] ) ;
    }

    printf ( "\nD3: " ) ;
    for ( i = 0 ; i <= 21 ; i++ )
    {
        d3[i] = d2[i+1] - d2[i] ;
        printf ( "%d ", d3[i] ) ;
    }
}
```

Sample run

Enter 25 elements
1 2 4 7 11 16 22 2 4 5 6 7 8 9 10 1 2 3 4 5 6 2 6 7 8 9

A: 1 2 4 7 11 16 22 2 4 5 6 7 8 9 10 1 2 3 4 5 6 2 6 7 8 9

1st, 2nd and 3rd differences are:

D1: 1 2 3 4 5 6 -20 2 1 1 1 1 1 1 2 -9 1 1 1 -4 4 1 1 1
D2: 1 1 1 1 1 -26 22 -1 0 0 0 0 0 1 -11 10 0 0 -5 8 -3 0 0
D3: 0 0 0 0 -27 48 -23 1 0 0 0 0 1 -12 21 -10 0 -5 13 -11 3 0

Explanation

Firstly, the 25 array elements are read through the keyboard into an array **a[ ]**. Then through the **for** loops their first, second and third differences are calculated and then printed out.

(2) *Program*

```
main( )
{
    int data[50], i ;
    static int freq[26] ;

    printf ( "Enter data\n" ) ;
    for ( i = 0 ; i < 50 ; i++ )
    {
        scanf ( "%d", &data[i] ) ;
        if ( data[i] = 1 && data[i] <= 25 )
            freq[data[i]] = freq[data[i]] + 1 ;
    }

    printf ( "\nFrequency of occurrence:\n" ) ;
```

```
for ( i = 1 ; i < 26 ; i++ )
{
    if ( freq[i] != 0 )
        printf ( "%d - %d\n", i, freq[i] ) ;
}
```

Sample run

Enter data
1 1 1 2 2 2 3 3 3 4 4 4 4 4 4 4 4 45 45 45 45 22 22 22 22
6 6 6 6 6 6 6 6 6 6 2 2 2 2 2 2 2 17 17 17 17 17 43 43 43

Frequency of occurrence:
1 - 3
2 - 10
3 - 3
4 - 8
6 - 10
17 - 5
22 - 4
43 - 3
45 - 4

Explanation

To begin with, the data is read into the array **data[ ]** through
the first **for** loop. As each data item is read, it is tested for
validity and then the appropriate element in the array **freq[ ]**
is incremented by 1. To ensure that to begin with each element
of the array **freq[ ]** is 0, it has been declared as **static**. By the
time the entire data has been read, the **freq[ ]** array has also
been set up. Through the second **for** loop, the frequency of the
data items has been printed out. For want of space, frequencies
of only those data items have been printed out which occur at
least once.

(3)   *Program*

```
main( )
{
    int mat[10][10], n, r, c, lowertri = 0, uppertri = 0 ;

    printf ( "\nEnter no. of rows of matrix ( 1 to 10 ) " ) ;
    scanf ( "%d", &n ) ;
    printf ( "Enter elements of matrix\n" ) ;
    for ( r = 0 ; r < n ; r++ )
    {
        for ( c = 0 ; c < n ; c++ )
        scanf ( "%d", &mat[r][c] ) ;
    }

    /* check for lower triangular matrix */

    for ( r = 0 ; r < n - 1 ; r++ )
    {
        for ( c = r + 1 ; c < n ; c++ )
        {
            if ( mat[r][c] )
                break ;
        }
        if ( mat[r][c] )
            break ;
    }
    if ( r == n - 1 )
        lowertri = 1 ;

    /* check for upper triangular matrix */

    for ( r = 1 ; r < n ; r++ )
    {
        for ( c = 0 ; c < r ; c++ )
        {
```

```
                    if ( mat[r][c] )
                        break ;
            }
            if ( mat[r][c] )
                break ;
    }
    if ( r == n )
        uppertri = 1 ;

    if ( lowertri && uppertri )
        printf ( "\nDiagonal Matrix" ) ;
    else
    {
        if ( lowertri )
            printf ( "\nLower Triangular Matrix" ) ,
        else
        {
            if ( uppertri )
                printf ( "\nUpper Triangular Matrix" ) ;
            else
                printf ( "\nNot a special type of matrix" ) ;
        }
    }
}
```

Sample run

```
Enter no. of rows of matrix ( 1 to 10 ) 5
Enter elements of matrix
1 0 0 0 0
0 1 0 0 0
0 0 1 0 0
0 0 0 1 0
0 0 0 0 1

Diagonal matrix
```

Explanation

The program works for any square matrix whose number of rows and columns are less than or equal to 10. The program first asks for the size of the matrix, followed by matrix elements. Once these have been entered, through a pair of **for** loops it checks for any non-zero elements in the upper triangle of the matrix. If it finds a non-zero element, it breaks out of the **for** loops. Once outside the loops, it checks whether the control came out of the loops due to execution of **break** or a normal exit from the loops. If there is a normal exit it means that the upper triangle of the matrix contains all zeros, Hence the variable **lowertri** is set up with 1.

Similarly, through the next set of **for** loops, the lower triangle of the matrix is checked for non-zero elements. If there is a normal exit from these **for** loops, then **uppertri** is set up with 1.

Finally, through a series of **ifs** depending upon the value set up in **lowertri** and **uppertri**, it is decided whether the matrix is lower triangular, upper triangular or a diagonal matrix.

(4)   *Program*

```
main( )
{
    int sales[5][10][7] ;
    float wk_chip, wk_city, avg_dsales = 0 ;
    int i, j, k ;

    for ( i = 0 ; i < 5 ; i++ )
    {
        printf ( "\nChip no: %d", i ) ;
        wk_chip = 0 ;
        for ( j = 0 ; j < 10 ; j++ )
```

```
        {
                printf ( "\nCity no: %d", j ) ;
                printf ( "\nEnter weekly sale day by day\n") ;
                for ( k = 0 ; k < 7 ; k++ )
                {
                        scanf ( "%d", &sales[i][j][k] ) ;
                        wk_chip += sales[i][j][k] ;
                }
        }
        printf ( "\nChip no. %d sales = %f", i, wk_chip ) ;
        avg_dsales += wk_chip ;
    }
    avg_dsales /= 7 ;
    printf ( "\nAverage daily sales = %f", avg_dsales ) ;

    for ( j = 0 ; j < 10 ; j++ )
    {
        wk_city = 0 ;
        for ( i = 0 ; i < 5 ; i++ )
        {
            for ( k = 0 ; k < 7 ; k++ )
                wk_city += sales[i][j][k] ;
        }
        printf ( "\nCity no. %d sales = %f", j, wk_city ) ;
    }
}
```

Explanation

For want of space it is not possible to give a sample run of this program. However, the program is quite straightforward. Note that the variable **wk_chip** represents the total weekly sale chipwise, whereas **wk_city** represents total weekly sale citywise. You can imagine the 3-D array as a collection of five 2-D arrays. Each 2-D array contains day by day sale in each city for a particular chip. Behind this there is data of another chip, behind that data of another chip and so on. Once this is understood well, the rest of the program is simple.

In the first set of **for** loops the outermost loop controls the chip, the middle loop controls the city, and the innermost loop controls the daily sale. Through these loops the daily sale in each city for each chip is entered. As each daily sale figure is entered, a running sum is made using **wk_chip**. When the control comes out of the middle loop, **wk_chip** contains the total week's sale for a particular chip, which is printed out before receiving the sales figures for the next chip. Since **wk_chip** at this stage contains the total sale of a chip in all cities, this value is stored in **avg_dsales**. This variable is incremented everytime by an amount equal to the sale of a chip in a week as given by **wk_chip**. Once the control comes out of all the three loops, **avg_dsales** contains the total sale of all chips in all cities during the week. This is therefore divided by 7 to get the average daily sale of the company in that week.

The next set of **for** loops calculate the total sale of all chips in each city. I suppose you can now figure out how these loops work. Good luck!

(5) *Program*

```
#include "math.h"
#include "stdio.h"

int sex[50], sum[50], mcode[50][3], fcode[50][3] ;
float cosin[3] ;

main( )
{
    int i, j, ans, k, t_code, t ;
    float c, t_cosin, factor ;
```

```
for ( i = 0 ; i < 50 ; i++ )
{
    printf ( "\nEnter sex (M/F) " ) ;
    fflush ( stdin ) ;
    scanf ( "%c", &sex[i] ) ;

    printf ( "\nCode no. %d\n", i + 1 ) ;
    printf ( "Enter 8 responses (1-5) " ) ;
    for ( j = 0 ; j < 8 ; j++ )
    {
        scanf ( "%d", &ans ) ;
        sum[i] += ans ;
    }
}
for ( i = 0 ; i < 50 ; i++ )
{
    if ( sex[i] == 'M' )
    {
        for ( k = 0 ; k < 3 ; k++ )
            cosin[k] = 0 ;

        /* find three most compatible females */
        for ( j = 0 ; j < 50 ; j++ )
        {
            if ( sex[j] == 'F' )
            {
                factor = 3.14 / 180 ;
                c = cos ( ( sum[i] - sum[j] ) * factor ) ;
                t = j + 1 ;

                for ( k = 0 ; k < 3 ; k++ )
                {
                    if ( c > cosin[k] )
                    {
                        /* swap cosine values */
                        t_cosin = c ;
                        c = cosin[k] ;
```

```
                              cosin[k] = t_cosin ;

                              /* swap codes */
                              t_code = t ;
                              t = mcode[i][k] ;
                              mcode[i][k] = t_code ;
                         }
                    }
               }
          }
     }
     else
     {
          for ( k = 0 ; k < 3 ; k++ )
               cosin[k] = 0 ;

          /* find three most compatible males */
          for ( j = 0 ; j < 50 ; j++ )
          {
               if ( sex[j] == 'M' )
               {
                    factor = 3.14 / 180 ;
                    c = cos ( ( sum[i] - sum[j] ) * factor ) ;
                    t = j + 1 ;
                    for ( k = 0 ; k < 3 ; k++ )
                    {
                         if ( c > cosin[k] )
                         {
                              /* swap cosine values */
                              t_cosin = c ;
                              c = cosin[k] ;
                              cosin[k] = t_cosin ;

                              /* swap codes */
                              t_code = t ;
                              t = fcode[i][k] ;
                              fcode[i][k] = t_code ;
```

```
                            }
                        }
                    }
                }
            }
        }
        printf ( "\nMost compatible female mates for males:" ) ;
        printf ( "\n 0 means no mate" ) ;
        for ( i = 0 ; i < 50 ; i++ )
        {
            if ( sex[i] == 'M' )
            {
                printf ( "\nMale code no.: %d", i + 1 ) ;
                printf ( "\nFemale code nos.: " ) ;
                printf ( "%d %d %d", mcode[i][0], mcode[i][1], mcode[i][2] ) ;
            }
        }
        printf ( "\nMost compatible male mates for females:" ) ;
        printf ( "\n 0 means no mate" ) ;
        for ( i = 0 ; i < 50 ; i++ )
        {
            if ( sex[i] == 'F' )
            {
                printf ( "\nFemale code no.: %d", i + 1 ) ;
                printf ( "\nMale code nos.: " ) ;
                printf ( "%d %d %d", fcode[i][0], fcode[i][1], fcode[i][2] ) ;
            }
        }
    }
```

Explanation

In the first **for** loop the sex of each applicant and their responses
to the 8 questions are received through the keyboard and stored
in arrays **sex[ ]** and **sum[ ]**. The next **for** loop is the most
important part of this program. It finds out three most com-

patible females for each male and stores their code numbers in the array **mcode[ ][ ]**. Similarly, it finds the three most compatible males for each female and stores their code numbers in the array **fcode[ ][ ]**. While calculating the most compatible males for a female (or vice versa) the difference of the responses are used, with a basis that larger the cosine value more compatible is the couple. Finally, through a set of **for** loops the three most compatible females for each male (and vice versa) are printed out.

(6)   *Program*

```
#include "conio.h"
int a[81] ;
main( )
{
    int sr = 5, sc = 30, er, ec ;
    int n, num, row, col, i, j, l, k, sum = 0 ;

    printf ( "Enter the size of odd square matrix " ) ;
    scanf ( "%d", &n ) ;
    printf ( "Enter initial number of the series " ) ;
    scanf ( "%d", &num ) ;

    clrscr( ) ;
    gotoxy ( 35, 1 ) ;

    er = sr + n * 2 ; /* ending row */
    ec = sc + n * 3 ; /* ending column */

    drawbox ( sr, sc, er, ec ) ;

    i = 1 ; /* top row */
    j = 1 + n / 2 ; /* middle of top row */

    for ( k = 0 ; k < n * n ; k++ )
```

```
{
      /* find row & col where number is to be placed on screen */
      row = ( sr + 1 ) + ( i - 1 ) * 2 ;
      col = ( sc + 1 ) + ( j - 1 ) * 3 ;

      gotoxy ( col, row ) ;
      printf ( "%d", num ) ;

      /* calculate position where number is to be placed in array */
      l = ( i - 1 ) * n + ( j - 1 ) ;
      a[l] = num ;
      num++ ;

      /* go one row up */
      i-- ;

      /* go one column to right */
      j++ ;

      /* check if we reach outside the square */

      if ( i == 0 )
          i = n ;

      if ( i == n + 1 )
          i = 1 ;

      if ( j == 0 )
          j = n ;

      if ( j == n + 1 )
          j = 1 ;

      l = ( i - 1 ) * n + ( j - 1 ) ;

      /* if square already filled */
      if ( a[l] != 0 )
```

```
            /* increment row by 2, decrement col by 1 */
            i += 2 ;
            j-- ;

            /* adjust row and col if outside the box */

            if ( i > n )
                i = i - n ;

            if ( j == 0 )
                j = n ;
        }
    }

    for ( i = 0 ; i <= ( n * ( n - 1 ) ) ; i += n )
        sum = sum + a[i] ;

    gotoxy ( sc, er + 2 ) ;
    printf ( "Horizontal, Vertical & Diagonal sum = %d", sum )
}

/* draw squares into which numbers are to be displayed */
drawbox ( sr, sc, er, ec )
int sr, sc, er, ec ;
{
    int i, j ;

    for ( j = sr ; j <= er ; j += 2 )
    {
        for ( i = sc + 1 ; i < ec ; i++ )
        {
            gotoxy ( i, j ) ;
            printf ( "%c", 196 ) ;
        }
    }
    for ( i = sc ; i <= ec ; i += 3 )
```

```
        {
            for ( j = sr + 1 ; j < er ; j++ )
            {
                gotoxy ( i, j ) ;
                printf ( "%c", 179 ) ;
            }
        }

        for ( i = sc + 3 ; i < ec ; i += 3 )
        {
            gotoxy ( i, sr ) ;
            printf ( "%c", 194 ) ;
            gotoxy ( i, er ) ;
            printf ( "%c", 193 ) ;
        }

        for ( j = sr + 2 ; j < er ; j += 2 )
        {
            gotoxy ( sc, j ) ;
            printf ( "%c", 195 ) ;
            gotoxy ( ec, j ) ;
            printf ( "%c", 180 ) ;
        }

        for ( j = sr + 2 ; j < er ; j += 2 )
        {
            for ( i = sc + 3 ; i < ec ; i += 3 )
            {
                gotoxy ( i, j ) ;
                printf ( "%c", 197 ) ;
            }
        }

    gotoxy ( sc, sr ) ;
    printf ( "%c", 218 ) ;
    gotoxy ( ec, er ) ;
    printf ( "%c", 217 ) ;
```

```
        gotoxy ( ec, sr ) ;
        printf ("%c", 191 ) ;
        gotoxy ( sc, er ) ;
        printf ( "%c", 192 ) ;
}
```

Explanation

Even though this appears to a be problem of 2-D array, a 1-D array has been used. This is just to accomodate all problems beginning from a 3 x 3 square to a 9 x 9 square. The 1-D array **a[ ]** has been declared as external array so that to begin with its elements are initialised to 0.

Once into the **main( )**, the size of the matrix and the starting number of the series is received through the pair of **scanf( )**s. Depending upon the size of the square the ending row and ending column are calculated, and using these and the starting row and starting column, the box is constructed by calling the **drawbox( )** function.

Since there are **n * n** squares to be filled we use a **for** loop to do so. Within the **for** loop, first we calculate the row and column where the number is to be placed, reach there using **gotoxy( )**, and then print out the number. Next we calculate the position where the number should be placed in the array and then we place the number in the array. With this over, we go one row up and one column to the right by decrementing and incrementing **i** and **j** respectively. On doing this it is checked whether we reach outside the box. If so, the values of **i** and **j** are appropriately adjusted. If there is already a number present at this location, then once again **i** and **j** are readjusted so that the number is placed immediately below the number last placed in the square. This whole operation is carried through the loop till all the squares have been filled up.

9

Pulling the Strings

The way a group of integers can be stored in an integer array, likewise a group of characters can be stored in a character array. Character arrays are often called 'strings'. Character arrays are used by programming languages to manipulate text such as words and sentences. A string in C is always terminated by a null character ('\0'). The ascii value of '\0' is 0. The following figure illustrates how a string is stored and accessed.

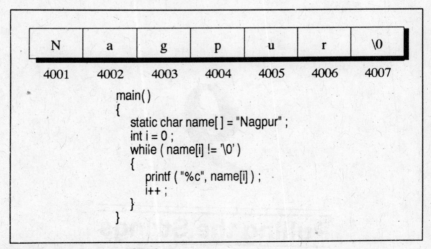

```
main( )
{
    static char name[ ] = "Nagpur" ;
    int i = 0 ;
    while ( name[i] != '\0' )
    {
        printf ( "%c", name[i] ) ;
        i++ ;
    }
}
```

Figure 9.1 Usage of string

Now a few tips about the usage of strings in C programs:

(a)   A string can also be initialised as,

static char[ ] = "Nagpur" ;

Here '\0' is not necessary. C inserts it automatically.

(b)   String elements can also be accessed using pointers as shown.

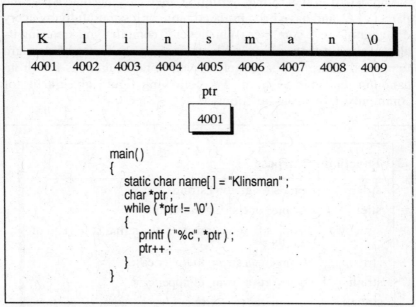

K	l	i	n	s	m	a	n	\0
4001	4002	4003	4004	4005	4006	4007	4008	4009

ptr

4001

```
main( )
{
    static char name[ ] = "Klinsman" ;
    char *ptr ;
    while ( *ptr != '\0' )
    {
        printf ( "%c", *ptr ) ;
        ptr++ ;
    }
}
```

Figure 9.2 Pointers and Strings

(c)   **scanf( )** and **printf( )** offer a simple way of doing string I/ O.

```
main( )
{
    char name[25] ;
    scanf ( "%s", name ) ;
    printf ( "%s", name ) ;
}
```

The **%s** is a format specification for handling a string.

Standard Library String Functions

Inspite of the awesome power that C puts in your hands, its vocabulary is limited to a mere 32 odd words. These words are supplemented by a set of library functions. Though these functions are not a part of C's formal definition, they have become a part and parcel of C, and have been imitated more or less faithfully by every designer of the C compiler. Whichever C compiler you are using its almost certain that you would have access to a library of standard functions. There is a large set of such library functions for string handling and manipulation. The following figure gives a list of commonly used string functions.

Function	Purpose
strlen	Finds length of a string
strcpy	Copies one string into another
strncpy	Copies first n characters of a string at the end of another
strlwr	Converts a string to lower case
strupr	Converts a string to upper case
strcmp	Compares two strings
strncmp	Compares first n characters of two strings
strcat	Appends one string at the end of another
strncat	Appends first n characters of a string at the end of another
strstr	Finds first occurrence of a given string in another string
strrev	Reverses a string
strset	Sets all characters of string to a given character

Figure 9.3 Standard library string functions

Array of Pointers to Strings

A pointer can point to a string. If we collect a number of such pointers pointing to different strings in an array we get an array of pointers to strings. The following figure shows array of pointers to strings at work.

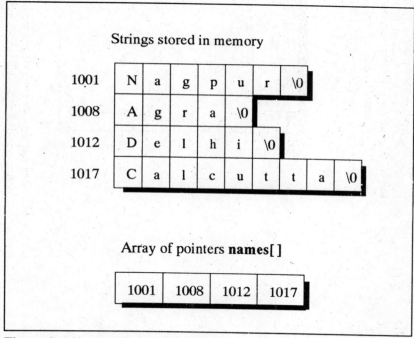

Figure 9.4 Array of pointers to strings

As can be observed from the figure the strings themselves are stored at different locations but their base addresses are stored in adjacent locations in the array of pointers **names[ ]**. These strings can be accessed through the array of pointers as shown in the following program.

```
main( )
```

```
{
    static char *names[ ] = {
                            "Nagpur",
                            "Agra",
                            "Delhi",
                            "Calcutta"
                        } ;
    int i ;

    for ( i = 0 ; i <= 3 ; i++ )
        printf ( "%s\n", names[i] ) ;
}
```

Exercise

[A]   What will be the output of the following programs:

(1)
```
main( )
{
    static char s[ ] = "Rendezvous !" ;
    printf ( "%d", *( s + strlen ( s ) ) ) ;
}
```

(2)
```
main( )
{
    char ch[20] ;
    int i ;
    for ( i = 0 ; i < 19 ; i++ )
        *( ch + i ) = 67 ;
    *( ch + i ) = '\0' ;
    printf ( "%s", ch ) ;
}
```

(3)
```
main( )
{
    char str[20] ;
    int i ;
    for ( i = 0 ; i <= 18 ; i++ )
        i[str] = 'C' ;
    i[str] = '\0' ;
    printf ( "%s", str ) ;
}
```

(4)
```
main( )
{
    char str[20] ;
    static int i ;
    for ( ; ; )
```

```
        {
                i++[str] = 'A' + 2 ,
                if ( i == 19 )
                        break ;
        }
        i[str] = '\0' ;
        printf ( "%s", str ) ;
}
```

(5)   main( )
```
        {
                static char str[ ] = { 48, 48, 48, 48, 48, 48, 48, 48, 48, 48 } ;
                char *s ;
                int i ;
                s = str ;
                for ( i = 0 ; i <= 9 ; i++ )
                {
                        if ( *s )
                                printf ( "%c ", *s ) ;
                        s++ ;
                }
        }
```

(6)   main( )
```
        {
                static char str[10] = { 0, 0, 0, 0, 0, 0, 0, 0, 0, 0 } ;
                char *s ;
                int i ;
                s = str ;
                for ( i = 0 ; i <= 9 ; i++ )
                {
                        if ( *s )
                                printf ( "%c", *s ) ;
                        s++ ;
                }
        }
```

```
(7)    main( )
       {
            static char s[ ] = "C smart !!" ;
            int i ;
            for ( i = 0 ; s[i] ; i++ )
                 printf ( "%c %c %c %c\n", s[i], *( s + i ) , i[s], *( i + s ) ;
       }

(8)    main( )
       {
            static char s[ ] = "Oinks Grunts and Guffaws" ;
            printf ( "%c\n", *( &s[2] ) ) ;
            printf ( "%s\n", s + 5 ) ;
            printf ( "%s\n", s ) :
            printf ( "%c\n", *( s + 2 ) ) ;
            printf ( "%d\n", s ) ;
       }

(9)    main( )
       {
            static char s[25] = "The cocaine man" ;
            int i = 0 ;
            char ch ;
            ch = s[++i] ;
            printf ( "%c %d\n", ch, i ) ;
            ch = s[i++] ;
            printf ( "%c %d\n", ch, i ) ;
            ch = i++[s] ;
            printf ( "%c %d\n", ch, i ) ;
            ch = ++i[s] ;
            printf ( "%c %d\n", ch, i ) ;
       }

(10)   main( )
       {
            static char arr[ ] = "Pickpocketing my peace of mind.."
```

```
            int i ;
            printf ( "%c\n", *arr ) ;
            arr++ ;
            printf ( "%c\n", *arr ) ;
    }
```

(11) ```
      main( )
      {
            static char str[ ] = "Limericks" ;
            char *s ;
            s = &str[6] - 6 ;
            while (*s)
                  printf ("%c", *s++) ;
      }
      ```

(12)  ```
      main( )
      {
            static char *s[ ] = {
                                    "ice",
                                    "green",
                                    "cone",
                                    "please"
                                } ;
            staic char **ptr[ ] = { s + 3 , s + 2 , s + 1 , s } ;
            char ***p = ptr ;
            printf ( "%s\n" , **++p ) ;
            printf ( "%s\n" , *--*++p + 3 ) ;
            printf ( "%s\n" , *p[-2] + 3 ) ;
            printf ( "%s\n" , p[-1][-1] + 1 ) ;
      }
      ```

(13) ```
      main( )
      {
            static char s[ ] = "C it for yourself" ;
            int i = 0 ;
            while (s[i])
      ```
      ```

```
        {
            if ( s[i] != ' ' )
                s[i] = s[i] + 1 ;
            i++ ;
        }
        printf ( "%s", s ) ;
    }
```

(14)
```
    main( )
    {
        static char str[ ] = "For your eyes only" ,
        int i ;
        char *p ;
        for ( p = str, i = 0 ; p + i <= str + strlen ( str ) ; p++, i++ )
            printf ( "%c", *( p + i ) ) ;
    }
```

(15)
```
    main( )
    {
        static char str[ ] = "MalayalaM" ;
        char *s ;
        s = str + 8 ;
        while ( s >= str )
        {
            printf ( "%c", *s ) ;
            s-- ;
        }
    }
```

(16)
```
    main( )
    {
        static char a[ ] = "Able was I ere I saw elbA" ;
        char *t, *s, *b ;
        s = a ;
        b = a + strlen ( a ) - 1 ;
        t = b ;
```

```
        while ( s != t )
        {
            printf ( "%c", *s ) ;
            s++ ;
            printf ( "%c", *t ) ;
            t-- ;
        }
    }

(17)  main( )
    {
        static char str[ ] = "Shall we tell the Deputy Director?" ;
        printf ( "%s\n%s\n%s", str, str + 6, str + 9 ) ;
    }


(18)  main( )
    {
        static char s[ ] = "C is a philosophy of life" ;
        char t[40] ;
        char *ss, *tt ;
        ss = s ;
        tt = t ;
        while ( *ss )
            *tt++ = *ss++ ;
        *tt = '\0' ;
        printf ( "%s", t ) ;
    }


(19)  main( )
    {
        static char s[ ]= "Lumps, bumps, swollen veins, new pains" ;
        char t[40] ;
        char *ss, *tt ;
        tt = t ;
        ss = s ;
        while ( *tt++ = *ss++ ) ;
```

```
            printf ( "%s", t ) ;
        }

(20)    main( )
        {
            static char str1[ ] = "dills" ;
            static char str2[20] ;
            static char str3[20] = "Daffo" ;
            int I ;
            I = strcmp ( strcat ( str3, strcpy ( str2, str1 ) ), "Daffodills" )
            printf ( "I = %d", I ) ;
        }

(21)    main( )
        {
            static int arr[12] ;
            printf ( "%d", sizeof ( arr ) ) ;
        }

(22)    main( )
        {
            static char *mess[ ] = {
                                    "Some love one",
                                    "Some love two",
                                    "I love one",
                                    "That is you"
                                } ;
            printf ( "%d %d", sizeof ( mess ), sizeof ( mess [1] ) ) ;
        }

(23)    main( )
        {
            char names[3][20] ;
            int i ;
            for ( i = 0 ; i <= 2 ; i++ )
            {
```

```
            printf ( "\nENTER NAME: " ) ;
            scanf ( "%s", names[i] ) ;
            printf ( "\nYou entered %s", names[i] ) ;
        }
    }

(24)  main( )
    {
        static char names[5][20] = {
                                    "Roshni",
                                    "Manish",
                                    "Mona",
                                    "Baiju",
                                    "Ritu"
                                } ;
        int i ;
        char *t ;
        t = names[3] ;
        names[3] = names[4] ;
        names[4] = t ;
        for ( i = 0 ; i <= 4 ; i++ )
            printf ( "%s\n", names[i] ) ;
    }

(25)  main( )
    {
        static char mess[6][30] = {
                                    "Don't walk in front of me ...",
                                    "I may not follow ;",
                                    "Don't walk behind me ...",
                                    "I may not lead ;",
                                    "Just walk beside me ...",
                                    "And be my friend."
                                } ;
        printf ( "%c %c", *( mess[2] + 9 ), *( *( mess + 2 ) + 9 ) ) ;
    }
```

```
(26)   main( )
       {
           static char mess[2][2][20] = {
                                          {
                                            "A chink in your armour",
                                            "A voice in your mailbox"
                                          },
                                          {
                                            "A foot in your tooth",
                                            "A hole in your pocket"
                                          }
                                        } ;
           printf ( "%s\n%s", mess[1][0], mess[0][1] ) ;
       }
```

[B]   Attempt the following:

(1)   Write a function **xstrstr( )** that will return the position where one string is present within another string. If the second string doesn't occur in the first string **xstrstr( )** should return a 0.

For example, in the string "somewhere over the rainbow", "over" is present at position 11.

(2)   Write a program to encode the following string such that it gets converted into an unrecognizable form. Also write a decode function to get back the original string.

"Man's reach must always exceed his grasp.... or what is the heaven for?"

(3)   Write a program to count the number of capital letters in the following array of pointers to strings:

```
static char *str[ ] = {
                        "A FRiend Is...",
                        "SomEOne Loving & trUE...",
```

```
                        "fOr insTance somEONE....",
                        "exactlY likE yoU !!"
            };
```

(4)   Write a program to print those strings which are palindromes from a set of strings stored in the following array of pointers to strings.

```
static char *s[ ] = {
                    "MalayalaM",
                    "To really mess things up...",
                    "One needs to know C !!"
                    "able was I ere I saw elba"
            };
```

(5)   Write a program to compress the following string such that the the multiple blanks are eliminated. Store the compressed message in another string. Also write a decompressant program to get back the original string with all its spaces restored.

"Imperial   Palace.   Rome. Attention Julius   Caesar. Dear Caesar,   we   have   the   clarification you requested. Details to follow by courier. Meanwhile   stay   clear of Brutus."

Answers

Answers to [A]

(1)   *Output*

0

Explanation

No 'Rendezvous !', but a zero is printed out. Mentioning the name of the string gives the base address of the string. The function **strlen(s)** returns the length of the string s[ ], which in this case is 12. In **printf( )**, using the 'contents of' operator (often called 'value at address' operator), we are trying to print out the contents of the 12th address from the base address of the string. At this address there is a '\0', which is automatically stored to mark the end of the string. The ascii value of '\0' is 0, which is what is being printed by the **printf( )**.

(2)   *Output*

CCCCCCCCCCCCCCCCCCC

Explanation

Mentioning the name of the array always gives its base address. Therefore (**ch + i**) would give the address of the ith element from the base address, and *(**ch + i**) would give the value at this address, i.e. the value of the ith element. Through the **for** loop we store 67, which is the ascii value of upper case 'C', in all the locations of the string. Once the control reaches outside the **for** loop the value of **i** would be 19, and in the 19th location from the base address we store a '\0' to mark the end of the string. This is essential, as the compiler has no other way of knowing where the string is terminated. In the **printf( )** that follows, **%s** is the format specification for printing a string, and **ch** gives the base address of the string. Hence starting from the first element, the complete string is printed out.

(3)   *Output*

CCCCCCCCCCCCCCCCCCCC

Explanation

If your concept of arrays is fool-proof, you should find the above output only natural. If not, here's your chance to make it so. C makes no secret of the fact that it uses pointers internally to access array elements. With the knowledge of how array elements are accessed using pointers, we can think of **str[i]** as ***(str + i)**. Basic maths tells us that ***(str + i)** would be same as ***(i + str)**. And if **str[i]** is same as ***(str + i)**, then naturally ***(i + str)** would be same as **i[str]**.

Thus, we can conclude that all the following expresssions are different ways of referring the ith element of the string:

```
str[i]
*( str + i )
*( i + str )
i[str]
```

Hence, through the **for** loop upper case C is stored in all the elements of the string. A '\0' is stored to mark the end of the string, and then the string is printed out using **printf( )**.

(4)   *Output*

CCCCCCCCCCCCCCCCCCCC

Explanation

Here, the structure of the **for** loop has been reduced to only 2 semi-colons. We can afford to do so because all the three tasks (initialisation, testing and incrementation) of the **for** are being accomplished by three different statements in the program: declaring **i** as a **static int** ensures that **i** is initialised to 0, the **if** condition tests when to get out of the loop, and **i++** takes care of the incrementation part.

As the **++** operator succeeds **i**, first the value of **i** gets used in the expression **i++[str]** and only then it gets incremented. Since we know that **str[i]** is same as **i[str]**, **i[str]** denotes the **i**[th] element of the string. Starting from 0, **i** takes values upto 18, and each time **'A' + 2** is stored in the string elements. Can we add a character and an integer? Yes, as any character is stored as its corresponding ascii value. The ascii value of 'A' is 65, and on adding 2 to this we get 67, which happens to be the ascii value of 'C'. Thus, upper case 'C' is stored in elements 0 to 18 of the string. When **i** becomes 19, **break** takes the control out of the **for** loop, where a '\0' is inserted in the string to mark its end. The string is then printed out using **printf( )**.

(5) *Output*

0000000000

Explanation

In all 10 elements of **str[ ]**, an integer, 48 is stored. Wondering whether a **char** string can hold **int**s? The answer is yes, as 48 does not get stored literally in the elements. 48 is interpreted as the ascii value of the character to be stored in the string. The character corresponding to ascii 48 happens to be 0, which is assigned to all the locations of the string.

s, a character pointer, is assigned the base address of the string **str[ ]**. Next, in the **if** condition, the value at address contained in s is checked for truth/falsity. As 0 represents ascii 48, the condition evaluates to true everytime, until the end of the string is reached. At the end of the string a '\0', i.e. ascii 0 is encountered, and the **if** condition fails. Irrespective of whether the condition is satisfied or not, s is incremented so that each time it points to the subsequent array element. This entire logic is repeated in the **for** loop, printing out 10 zeroes in the process.

(6) *Output*

No output

Explanation

Though you may not have expected zeroes to be outputted this time, you surely did expect some output! We stored the character corresponding to ascii 0 in all 10 elements of the string. Next, we assign s, a **char** pointer, the base address of the string. Through the **for** loop, we are attempting to print out all elements one by one, but not before imposing the **if** condition.

The **if** is made to test the value at address contained in s before the execution of the **printf( )**. The first time, ***s** yields ascii 0. Therefore the **if** statement reduces to **if(0)**, and as 0 stands for falsity, the condition fails. Hence, s is incremented and control loops back to **for** without executing the **printf( )**. The same thing happens the next time around, and the next, and so on, till the **for** loop ends, resulting in no output at all.

(7) *Output*

C C C C

```
s s s s
m m m m
a a a a
r r r r
t t t t

! ! ! !
```

Explanation

The above program rubs in the point that **s[i]**, **i[s]**, ***(s + i)** and ***(i + s)** are various ways of referring to the same element, that is the ith element of the string **s**. Each element of the string is printed out four times, till the end of the string is encountered. Note that in the **for** loop there is an expression **s[i]** in the condition part. This means the loop would continue to get executed till **s[i]** is not equal to zero. We can afford to say this because a string always ends with a '\0', whose ascii value is 0. Thus the **for** loop will be terminated when the expression **s[i]** yields a '\0'.

(8) *Output*

```
n
 Grunts and Guffaws
Oinks Grunts and Guffaws
n
404
```

Explanation

In the first **printf( )** the 'address of' operator, **&**, gives the address of the second element of the string. Value at this address is 'n', which is printed out by the **printf( )** using **%c**.

Since **s** gives the base address of the array, (**s + 5**) would give the address of the fifth element from the base address. This address is passed to the second **printf( )**. Using the format specification **%s**, the contents of the string are printed out the 5th element onwards.

The third **printf( )** prints the entire string, as the base address of the string is being passed to it.

The fourth **printf( )** is made to print the second character of the string, as ***(s + 2)** is nothing but **s[2]**. Thus 'n' gets printed.

Does the output of the final **printf( )** surprise you by printing out a number, 404? Note that the format specification **%d** is used with **s**, which gives the base address of the string. It happened to be 404 when we executed the program, which got printed out. On executing the same yourself, you may get any other address, depending on what address is allotted to the string by the compiler.

(9)   *Output*

```
h 1
h 2
e 3
! 3
```

Explanation

At first, **ch** is set up with the value of the expression **s[++i]**. As **++** precedes **i**, first **i** is incremented to 1, and then **s[1]** is assigned to **ch**. **s[1]**, the first element of the string **s[ ]**, is 'h'. So the first **printf( )** prints out 'h' for **ch** and 1 for **i**.

Next, **ch** is assigned the value given by the expression s[i++]. This time, first the value of **i** is used and then **i** is incremented to 2. Therefore **ch** still remains s[1], i.e. 'h', while **i** is now 2.

The third time, i++[s] is assigned to **ch**. This is evaluated just as s[i++] was, as saying i[s] is same as saying s[i]. Firstly, value of **i**, i.e. 2, is used to give 2[s] i.e. 'e', the second element of the string. After this, **i** is incremented to 3.

Finally, **ch** is assigned the value of the expression ++i[s]. This time it is not **i** that is getting incremented, but the value i[s]. Firstly i[s] is evaluated, which gives the 3rd element of the string, since **i** is presently 3. This happens to be the blank following the word 'the' in the string. Ascii value of the blank character is 32, which is incremented by the ++ operator, and thus 33 is assigned to **ch**. 33 is the ascii value of the character '!', which the **printf**( ) displays. **i** remains stationary at 3.

(10) *Output*

Error message: Lvalue required in function main

Explanation

Though everything seems to be in order at first glance, there lies a fundamental error in our program. When we say **arr**, we are referring to the base address of the string. This is the only information that helps the C compiler keep track of the string **arr[ ]**. If this information is lost, there is no way the compiler can access the string. So, this particular address is given a favoured status, that of a constant. The statement **arr++** is essentially wrong because a constant can't be incremented and hence the compiler asks for an lvalue, which is a value that can be changed.

(11) *Output*

Limericks

Explanation

The following figure should help in analyzing this program.

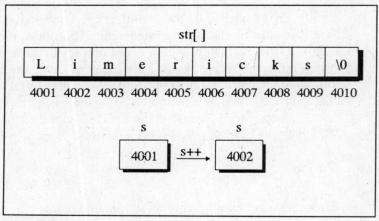

Figure 9.5

s has been declared as a pointer to a **char**, whereas **str[ ]** has been declared as a character string. Let us now evaluate the expression **&str[6] - 6**. Here **&str[6]** gives the address of the sixth element of the string. This address can also be obtained by the expression **str + 6**. On subtracting 6 from this, we end up with good old **str**, the address of the zeroth element, which is assigned to **s**.

In the **printf( )**, the value at address contained in **s** is printed, and then **s** gets incremented so that it points to the next character in the string. The **while** loop continues till s doesn't point to '\0', which marks the end of the string. When s points to '\0', the value of ***s** would be 0, a falsity. Hence the **while** loop will be terminated.

(12) *Output*

cone

ase
reen

Explanation

This time we seem to be faced with a galaxy of stars! We would do well to take the help of a figure in crossing them one by one. At the outset, **s[ ]** has been declared and initialised as an array of pointers. Simply saying **s** gives us the base address of this array, 4006 as can be seen from Figure 9.6. **ptr[ ]** stores the addresses of the locations where the base addresses of strings comprising **s[ ]** have been stored, starting with the last string. To put it more clearly, **ptr[0]** stores the address 4012, which is the address at which base address of the string "please" is stored. Similarly, **ptr[1]** stores the address 4010, which is where the base address of the string "cone" is stored, and so on. Since **ptr[ ]** essentially stores addresses of addresses, it is a pointer to a pointer, and has been declared as such using ******.

Finally, the base address of **ptr[ ]** is asssigned to a pointer to a pointer to a pointer, **p**. Reeling?! Going through the figure would decidedly aid you to get disentangled. Thus, **p** is assigned the address 6020.

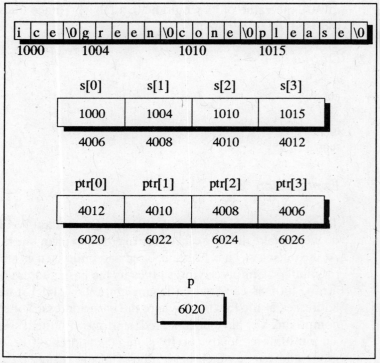

Figure 9.6

Having sorted out what is present where, we now proceed to the **printf( )**s. Let us tackle the expressions one by one.

**++p

The first one prints out the string starting from the address ****++p**. The **++** goes to work first and increments **p** not to 6021, but to 6022. The C compiler has been made to understand that on incrementing a pointer variable, it is to point to the next location of its type. The words 'of its type' hold significance here. A pointer to a **char** on incrementing goes one byte further, since a **char** is a 1-byte entity. A pointer to an **int** points 2 bytes further, as an **int** is a 2-byte entity. Also, a pointer by itself is always a 2-byte entity, so incrementing a pointer to a pointer would advance you by 2 bytes.

Having convinced ourselves that **p** now stores 6022, we go on to evaluate the expression further. ***p** signifies contents of 6022, i.e. 4010. ****p** means value at this address, i.e. value at 4010, which is the address 1010. The **printf( )** prints the string at this address, which is "cone".

--++p + 3

p, presently containing 6022, which on incrementing becomes 6024. Value at this address is the address 4008, or in terms of **s, s + 1**. On this the decrement operator -- works to give 4006, i.e. **s**. Value at 4006, or ***(s)** is 1000. Thus the expression is now reduced to (1000 + 3), and what finally gets passed to **printf( )** is the address 1003. Value at this address is a '\0', as at the end of every string a '\0' is inserted automatically. This '\0' is printed out as a blank by **printf( )**.

*p[-2] + 3

The current address in **p** is 6024. ***p[-2]** can be thought of as ***(*(p - 2))**, as **num[i]** is same as ***(num + i)**. This in turn evaluates as ***(*(6024 - 2))**, i.e. ***(*(6020))**, as **p** is a pointer to a pointer. This is equal to ***(4012)**, as at 6020 the address 4012 is present. Value at 4012 is 1015, i.e. the base address of the fourth string, "please". Having reached the address of letter 'p', 3 is added, which yields the address 1018. The string starting from 1018 is printed out, which comprises of the last three letters of "please", i.e. 'ase'.

p[-1][-1] + 1

The above expression can be thought of as ***(p[-1] - 1) + 1**, as **num[i]** and ***(num + i)** amounts to the same thing. Further, **p[-1]** can itself be simplified to ***(p - 1)**. Hence we can interpret the given expression as ***(*(p - 1) - 1) + 1**. Now let us evaluate this expression.

After the execution of the third **printf( )**, **p** still holds the address 6024. ***(6024 - 1)** gives ***(6022)**, i.e. address 4010. Therefore the expression now becomes ***(4010 - 1) + 1**. Looking at the figure you would agree that 4010 can be expressed as **s + 2**. So now the expression becomes ***(s + 2 - 1) + 1** or ***(s + 1) + 1**. Once again the figure would confirm that ***(s + 1)** evaluates to ***(4008)** and ***(4008)** yields 1004, which is the base address of the second string "green". To this, 1 is added to yield the address of the first element, 'r'. With this as the starting address, **printf( )** prints out what is remaining of the string "green".

(13)   *Output*

D ju gps zpvstfmg

Explanation

No, your computer hasn't caught a virus! It has done just what you instructed it to. The **while** loop tests the value of the ith element of the string. Since **i** has been initialised to 0, the first time **s[0]**, i.e. C is used. Since 'C' has a non-zero ascii value, the condition evaluates to true, and control passes to the **if** statement. The condition to be satisfied here is that the ith element is not a blank space. **s[0]** satisfies this condition hence the contents of the 0th element are incremented by 1. Thus **s[0]**, i.e. 'C' having ascii value 67, is incremented to 68, which is the ascii value of upper case 'D'. The new value of **s[0]** is therefore 'D'. Next **i** is incremented to 1, and the **while** repeats for **s[1]**. However, the **if** condition fails this time, as **s[1]** is a blank space, so this element remains unchanged. Similarly, all non-blank elements are incremented, and the **while** ends when the '\0' is reached. Lastly, the **printf( )** outputs the changed string.

(14) *Output*

Fryu ysol<space>

Explanation

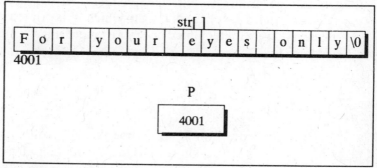

Figure 9.7

The **for** loop here hosts two initialisations and two incremen-tations, which is perfectly acceptable. However, there must always be a unique test condition.

In the initialisation part, **p** is assigned the base address of the string, and **i** is set to 0. Next the condition is tested. Let us isolate this condition for closer examination.

p + i <= str + strlen (str)

Since length of **str[ ]** is 18, **str + strlen (str)** would give the address of '\0' present at the end of the string. If we assume that the base address of the string is 4001, then the address of '\0' would be 4019. Since **p** has been assigned the base address of the string, in the first go, **p + 0** would yield 4001. Since this is less than 4019, the condition holds good, and the character present at the address (**p + 0**), i.e. 'F', is printed out. This can be understood better with the aid of the Figure 9.7.

After this, both **p** and **i** are incremented, so that **p** contains 4002 and **i** contains 1, and once again the condition in the **for** loop is tested. This time (**p + i**) yields 4003, whereas the expression **str + strlen (str)** continues to yield 4019. Therefore again the condition is satisfied and the character at address 4003, i.e. 'r' gets printed. Likewise, alternate elements of the string are outputted till **i** is 8, corresponding to which 'l' is printed. Now, when **p** and **i** are incremented one more time, the test condition evaluates to:

```
p + i <= str + strlen ( str )
4019 <= 4019
```

The 18th element of **str** is of course the '\0', which is also printed out as a blank. On further incrementation of **p** and **i**, control snaps out of the **for** and the program execution is terminated.

(15) *Output*

MalayalaM

Explanation

s, a pointer to a **char**, is assigned an address 8 locations ahead of the base address of the string. That means **s** is currently pointing to the last element 'M' of the string. If we assume the base address to be 4001, then **s** would contain the address 4009. Since this address is greater than the base address, first time through the loop the condition is satisfied. Next the value of the expression ***s** is printed. Since **s** contains the address 4009, the value at this address, i.e. 'M', gets printed. Then **s** is decremented to point to the preceding element, i.e. the element at address 4008.

This way one by one, the elements of the string are printed out in the reverse order, till **s** equals **str**, the address of the zeroth element. That the output is indeed the reverse of the original string can be verified if you read "MalayalaM" backwards. You have been presented with a string that reads the same from either end. Such strings, incidentally, go by the name 'Palindrome'.

(16) *Output*

AAbbllee waass ll ee

Explanation

The **char** pointer s is assigned the base address of string **a[ ]**. The **char** pointer **b** is assigned the address 24 elements ahead of the base address. Why 24? Because the function **strlen(a)** yields the length of the string **a[ ]**, which in this case turns out to be 25. Thus **b** points to 'A' present at the end of the string. Another character pointer, **t**, is also initialised to the same value as **b**. Assuming the base address of the string to be 5001, s would be assigned 5001 and **b** and **t** would be assigned the address 5025.

Naturally, first time through the **while** loop since s and **t** are not equal, the condition is satisfied. Hence the **printf( )** prints out the character at which s is pointing. Thus the character 'A' gets printed. Now s is incremented, so that it points to the character 'b'. The next **printf( )** prints the value at the address contained in **t**. Therefore another 'A' appears on the screen. After printing, **t** is decremented so that it starts pointing to 'b'. This goes on till s and **t** meet each other, whence the **while** ends. At this instance, **s** and **t** both are pointing to 'r', the middle character of the entire string.

(17) *Output*

Shall we tell the Deputy Director?
we tell the Deputy Director?
tell the Deputy Director?

Explanation

Using **%s**, the format specification for a string, the **printf( )** prints three strings. The addresses being passed to **printf( )** are **str, str + 6** and **str + 9**. Since **str** is the base address of the string, the complete message gets printed out, starting from the zeroth element. **str + 6** is the address 6 elements ahead of **str**, i.e. address of 'w'. With this as starting address, the second output 'we ... ' is obtained. Lastly, the part of the string 9th element onwards is printed out, as **str + 9** denotes the address of the 9th character from the base address of the string.

(18) *Output*

C is a philosophy of life

Explanation

To begin with, **ss** and **tt** are assigned the base addresses of the two strings **s[ ]** and **t[ ]**. In the **while**, the value at address contained in **ss** is tested for operating the loop. The first time through the loop **ss** contains the base address of the string. Hence ***ss** gives 'C', whose ascii value is 67. As any non-zero value is a truth value, the condition evaluates to true, and this value is stored at the address contained in **tt**, i.e. at the base address of the string **t[ ]**. Note that the **++** operator occurs after the variables, so after 'C' has been stored in the first location of the string **t[ ]**, both **ss** and **tt** are incremented, so that both now point to the first elements of **s[ ]** and **t[ ]** respectively. In the second go, value at the address contained in **ss** is tested in the **while**, and this time a blank is encountered, whose ascii value is 32. The condition again holds good, therefore the blank is stored in string **t[ ]**, and **ss** and **tt** are incremented. This goes on till the end of the string is encountered. At the end of any string, a '\0' is stored. Ascii value of '\0' is 0, which when tested in the **while**, evaluates to falsity, and the control comes out of the loop.

Note that the '\0' has not been stored into string **t[ ]**, hence the compiler does not know where the string ends. We do so by inserting a '\0' on leaving the **while**. Finally, the contents of the string **t[ ]** are printed out.

(19) *Output*

Lumps, bumps, swollen veins, new pains

Explanation

The program begins by assigning the base addresses of strings **s[ ]** and **t[ ]** to the character pointers **ss** and **tt**. The **while** loop that follows next may raise a few eyebrows. We have made it compact by combining the assignment, test condition and the incrementation in the **while** loop itself. In effect, the **while** has been reduced to:

```
while ( *tt++ = *ss++ )
```

Here the null statement is executed so long as the condition remains true. How the condition is evaluated is like this...

In the **while** the value at the address stored in **ss** replaces the value at the address stored in **tt**. After assignment the test is carried out to decide whether the **while** loop should continue or not. This is done by testing the expression ***tt** for truth/falsity. Since currently **tt** is pointing to 'l' of 'lumps', ***tt** gives 'l' which is a truth value. Following this **ss** and **tt** both are incremented, so that they have the addresses of the first elements of strings **s[ ]** and **t[ ]** respectively. Since the condition has been satisfied the null statement is executed. This goes on till the end of the string **s[ ]** is encountered, which is marked by the presence of a '\0', having ascii value 0. When this character is stored in **t[ ]**, ***tt** would give '\0'. This time when the condition is tested, it evaluates to false since ***tt** yields a 0 (ascii value of '\0'). Thus, all elements of the first string are faithfully copied into the second one, including the '\0'. On printing out string **t[ ]**, we get the entire string as it was in **s[ ]**.

(20) *Output*

I = 0

Explanation

This example uses 3 string functions. If **t[ ]** is the target string and **s[ ]** the source string, then the functions behave as mentioned below.

strcpy (t, s): Copies the contents of **s[ ]** into **t[ ]** and returns the base address of the target string **t[ ]**.

strcat (t, s): Concatenates or appends the source string at the end of target string. This also returns the base address of the target string.

strcmp (t, s): Compares the two strings and returns a 0 if they are equal and a non-zero value if they are unequal.

Evaluating the parentheses outwards from inside, let's see what **strcpy( )** succeeds in doing. The string **str1[ ]**, i.e. "dills" gets copied into **str2[ ]**, and the base address **str2** is returned. The expression now looks like:

```
l = strcmp ( strcat ( str3, str2 ), "Dafodills" ) ;
```

Next, **strcat( )** writes the contents of **str2[ ]**, i.e. "dills" at the end of **str3[ ]**, which has been initialised to "Daffo". After concatenation **strcat( )** returns the base address of the target string, **str3**. Once copying and concatenation is over, the string comparison is carried out using the function **strcmp( )**. This function has the arguments as shown below.

```
l = strcmp ( str3, "Daffodills" ) ;
```

Since **str3[ ]** does contain "Daffodills" now, the result of the comparison is a 0, which is assigned to l. On printing out, we get the output **l = 0**.

(21) *Output*

24

Explanation

The **sizeof( )** operator gives the size of its argument. As **arr[ ]** is an integer array of 12 elements, saying **sizeof (arr)** gives us the size of this array. Each integer is 2 bytes long, hence the array **arr[ ]** engages twice the number of elements, i.e. 24 bytes.

(22) *Output*

82

Explanation

mess[ ] has been declared as an array of pointers to strings. This signifies that the array **mess[]** stores the starting addresses of the four strings initialised in the program. **mess[0]** has the starting address of the string "Some love one", **mess[1]** the starting address of the second string "Some love two" and so on. As each address is 2 bytes long, four base addresses need 8 bytes, hence the array **mess[ ]** is 8 bytes long.

The **sizeof( )** operator gives the size of the datatype that is supplied as its argument. Therefore, **sizeof (mess)** is reported as 8.

mess[1], the first element of the array of pointers stores an address, which is invariably 2 bytes long. Therefore **printf( )** reports **sizeof (mess[1])** as 2.

(23) *Output*

```
ENTER NAME: Parag
You entered Parag
ENTER NAME: Veenu
You entered Veenu
ENTER NAME: Jaina
You entered Jaina
```

Explanation

names[5][20] has been declared as a two-dimensional array of characters. We can think of it as an array of 5 elements, each element itself being an array of 20 characters.

Let the base address of the 2-D array, i.e. **names** be 4001. In the **scanf( )** and **printf( )** statements, **names[i]** refers to the address of the ith string in the array. **names[0]** refers to the zeroth element of the 2-D array, or the base address of the string of characters starting from 4001. **names[1]** denotes the address of the first element of the 2-D array, which is 20 bytes ahead, i.e. 4021, and so on.

Assured that **names[i]** stands for the base address of the ith string, we proceed to see what actually is going on in this program.

The first time through the **for** loop, when you are prompted "ENTER NAME:", say you entered 'Parag'. The **scanf( )** accepts this name and stores it at the address given by **names[0]**. The **printf( )** immediately reads from the same address **name[0],** and prints the name starting at this address on to the screen. This is repeated by incrementing the value of **i** each time through the loop. When **i** is incremented for the third time, the process is terminated.

(24) *Output*

Error message: Lvalue required in function main

Explanation

Apparently, what the program attempts to do is interchange the addresses stored in **names[3]** and **names[4]** using an auxiliary variable **t**. Sounds straight forward, but is essentially against the very concept of how the C compiler deals with strings. The compiler keeps track of any string by remembering only the base address of the string. So it has its reservations when it comes to changing this information, as it anticipates that there would be no one to blame but itself once this information is waylaid and we demand an access to the string later. And this is what is being attempted in the statement **names[3] = names[4]**. Here we are trying to change the base address stored in **names[3]**. As said earlier, this will not be allowed. Thus the starting address of a string is an indelible entity, in no way an lvalue, which is a value that can change. Hence the error message.

(25) *Output*

k k

Explanation

The two-dimensional array comprises of one-dimensional arrays, each of which is 30 characters long. We know, **mess[2][9]** refers to the 9th element of the 2nd 1-D array.

Recall that **mess[2]** would give the base address of the second string. If this address turns out to be 4001, then the expression **mess[2] + 9** would become (4001 + 9), which would give the address of the ninth character from the address 4001. This address happens to be the address of the letter 'k' in the string "Don't walk behind me". Hence this letter 'k' can be accessed by the expression *(**mess[2] + 9**). But we already know that whenever we use the notation **mess[2]**, it is internally converted to *(**mess + 2**) by the compiler. Therefore *(**mess[2] + 9**) can also be expressed as *(*(**mess + 2**) + 9).

Thus, **mess[2][9]**, *(**mess[2] + 9**) and *(*(**mess + 2**) + 9) are one and the same, i.e. the 9th element of the 2nd string in the array. The same array element can thus be accessed in any of these three ways. The **printf( )** on execution outputs the letter 'k' twice.

(26) *Output*

A voice in your mailbox
A foot in your tooth

Explanation

The array **mess[ ][ ][ ]** is a three-dimensional array. Taken
apart, we can think of it as an array of two 2-D arrays. Each of
these two 2-D arrays is itself comprised of two 1-D arrays.
Lastly, these 1-D arrays are each 20 elements long.

mess[0][1] refers to the first element of zeroth 2-D array. This
element happens to be the base address of the string "A voice
...". Since **mess[0][1]** is an address, the **printf( )** prints out the
string starting here. Similarly, **mess[1][0]** refers to the zeroth
element of the first 2-D array. This element is the base address
of the string "A foot ...". Hence this string is outputted next.

Solutions to **[B]**

(1) *Program*

```
main( )
{
      static char str1[ ] = "somewhere over the rainbow" ;
      static char str2[ ] = "over" ;

      printf ( "String found at %d", xstrstr ( str1, str2 ) ) ;
}

xstrstr ( s1, s2 )
char *s1, *s2 ;
{
      int i, a, len1, len2 ;
```

```
len1 = strlen ( s1 ) ;
len2 = strlen ( s2 ) ;

for ( i = 0 ; i <= ( len1 - 1 ) ; i++ )
{
    a = strncmp ( ( s1 + i ), s2, len2 ) ;

    if ( a == 0 )
        return ( i + 1 ) ;
}
return ( 0 ) ;
}
```

Sample run

String found at 11

Explanation

The two strings have been declared as **str1[ ]** and **str2[ ]** in **main( )**, from where the base addresses are sent to the function **xstrstr( )** for searching the second string in the first one. In **xstrstr( )**, **len1** and **len2** store the lengths of the 2 strings with base addresses **s1** and **s2** respectively. In the **for** loop, **i** is incremented **len1** number of times. As many times, the standard library function **strncmp (t, s, n)** gets called. This function compares the first **n** elements of strings starting from **t** and **s** and returns 0 if they are equal.

The first time through the **for** loop, **i** is 0. Hence **strncmp( )** compares the first **len2** (here len2 is equal to 4) elements of strings starting from (**s1 + 0**) (i.e. **s1**) and **s2**. **a** collects a non-zero value, as the first four elements of the two strings are found to be different. The control therefore reverts back to the **for** where **i** is incremented to 1. So the second time through the loop **strncmp( )** compares first **len2** elements of strings start-ing from **s1 + 1** and **s2**. Literally, first 4 elements of "omewhere over the rainbow" and "over" are compared. Once again **a** collects a non-zero value and **i** is incremented a second time.

This goes on similarly till **i** is 10, when **s1 + 10** denotes the base address of the string "over the rainbow". This time **a** is assigned a 0, as both the strings have o, v, e, and r as the first four elements, and control returns to **main( )** with **i + 1**, i.e. 11. This is the position of the second string in the first one.

Suppose the second string is not present in the first string at all, then at no time **a** would contain 0. Thus the **return** statement within the **for** loop would never get executed. In such cases the **return** statement after the loop would return 0, signifying that the second string was not found in the first one.

(2)   *Program*

```
main( )
{
      static unsigned char s1[] = "Man's reach must always \
exceed his grasp.... or what is the heaven for?" ;

      unsigned char s2[80], s3[80] ;

      printf ( "%s", s1 ) ;

      codestr ( s1, s2 ) ;
      printf ( "\n%s", s2 ) ;

      decodestr ( s2, s3 ) ;
      printf ( "\n%s", s3 ) ;
}

codestr ( s, t )
```

```
unsigned char *s, *t ;
{
    while ( *s )
    {
        *t = *s + 127 ;
        t++ ;
        s++ ;
    }
    *t = 0 ;
}

decodestr ( s, t )
unsigned char *s, *t ;
{
    while ( *s )
    {
        *t = *s - 127 ;
        t++ ;
        s++ ;
    }
    *t = 0 ;
}
```

Sample run

Man's reach must always exceed his grasp.... or what is the heaven for?

[graphic characters]

Man's reach must always exceed his grasp.... or what is the heaven for?

Explanation

The program uses two functions; **codestr( )** for coding the string into an illegible form, and **decodestr( )** for retrieving the original string.

In both functions, the **while** loop tests for the end of the source string. In **codestr( )**, each character of the source string is given an offset of 127, and then stored in the target string. If you refer to the ascii chart in the appendix, you'll find that values 127 onwards correspond to graphic characters. By adding 127 to any character, we transform the same into some graphic symbol. In this manner, the whole string is transformed into a group of graphic characters, which you'll appreciate would certainly be unreadable!

In **decodestr( )**, just the reverse is done. From the contents of source string, 127 is subtracted and then the resultant character, which is invariably what the original one was, is stored in the target string.

On printing out **s1[ ]** and **s3[ ]**, we get our familiar message, while **s2[ ]** prints out nonsensical characters.

(3) *Program*

```
main( )
{
     static char *str[ ] = {
                              "A FRiend iS...",
                              "SomEOne Loving & trUE...",
                              "fOr insTance somEONE....",
                              "exactlY likE yoU !!"
                      } ;

     printf ( "No. of capitals = %d", capcount ( s, 4 ) ) ;
```

```
}

capcount ( s, c )
char **s ;
int c ;
{
    int i, cap = 0 ;
    char *t ;

    for ( i = 0 ; i < c ; i++ )
    {
        t = *( s + i ) ;

        while ( *t )
        {
            if ( *t >= 65 && *t <= 90 )
                cap ++ ;

            t++ ;
        }
    }
    return ( cap ) ;
}
```

Sample run

No. of capitals = 19

Explanation

The string **str[ ]** is an array of pointers. This means it stores the base addresses of the four strings initialised in the declaration. **str[0]** has the starting address of "A FRiend iS...", **str[1]** that of "SomEOne Loving & trUE...", and so on. The base address of this array of pointers and the number of strings are passed to the function **capcount( )**, which we have written for count-ing the number of capital letters in the four strings.

In **capcount( )**, these are collected in **s** and **c**. Essentially, s contains the address of the location where **str[0]** is stored. But **str[0]** contains the base address of the first string. Hence s is declared as a pointer to a pointer.

In the **for** loop **i** varies from 0 to 3, each time assigning the base address of the **i**[th] string to **t**. Once the base address of the string is stored in **t**, the **while** loop scans the entire string for a capital letter until **t** reaches the end of string. Each time the condition evaluates to true the variable **cap**, which counts the number of capital letters, is incremented. Subsequently, the **++** operator increments **t**, so that it points to the next character in the string.

When the **for** loop terminates the value of **cap**, which is nothing but the number of capital letters in the strings, is returned. The same is then printed out in **main( )**.

(4) *Program*

```
main( )
{
    static char *s[ ] = {
                        "MalayalaM",
                        "to really mess things up...",
                        "one needs to know C !!",
                        "able was I ere I saw elba"
                    } ;
    char rev[30] ;
    int i, a ;

    for ( i = 0 ; i <= 3 ; i++ )
    {
```

```
        strcpy ( rev, s[i] ) ;
        strrev ( rev ) ;
        a = strcmp ( s[i], rev ) ;

        if ( a == 0 )
            printf ( "%s\n", s[i] ) ;
    }
}
```

Sample run

MalayalaM
able was I ere I saw elba

Explanation

A string is said to be a 'palindrome' if on reversing it you again
end up with the original string. For instance, 'MalayalaM' on
reversing gives 'MalayalaM' itself.

Our program makes use of the following standard library string
functions:

If **s** and **t** are the base addresses of source and target strings
respectively, then the functions work as follows:

strcpy (t, s): Copies the source string into the target string.

strrev (s): Reverses the source string.

strcmp (t, s): Compares the two strings and returns 0 if they
are equal, and a non-zero value if unequal.

Since there are four strings to be dealt with in the array of
pointers **s[ ]**, we set up a **for** loop with **i** taking values from 0

to 3. The first time, **s[0]** provides the base address of the first string, "MalayalaM", and **rev**, that of the target string. After copying "MalayalaM" into **rev[ ]**, **rev[ ]** is reversed using **strrev( )**. Now **rev[ ]** contains the reversed string while the original string is intact at **s[i]**. We compare the two strings making use of **strcmp( )**, and receive the returned value in the variable **a**. **a** is assigned a value 0 if the string is indeed a Palindrome. If so, the corresponding string is printed out.

(5)   *Program*

```
main( )
{
    static unsigned char str1[ ] = "Imperial   Palace.      Rome.
Attention  Julius   Caesar. Dear Caesar, we   have  the  clarifica-
tion  you requested. Details to follow by courier. Meanwhile   stay
clear of Brutus." ;

    unsigned char str2[500], str3[500] ;

    printf ( "%s\n", str1 ) ;

    compress ( str1, str2 ) ;
    printf ( "%s\n", str2 ) ;

    decompress ( str2, str3 ) ;
    printf ( "%s", str3 ) ;
}

compress ( s, t )
unsigned char *s, *t ;
{
    int spcount ;

    while ( *s )
    {
```

```
if ( *s == '' )
{
    spcount = 1 ;
    s++ ;
    while ( *s == '' )
    {
        spcount++ ;
        s++ ;
        if ( spcount == 10 )
        {
            *t = 23 ;
            t++ ;
            spcount = 0 ;
        }
    }
    if ( spcount )
    {
        if ( spcount == 1 )
        {
            *t = *s + 127 ;
            s++ ;
        }
        else
            *t = 13 + spcount ;

        t++ ;
    }
}
else
{
    *t = *s ;
    t++ ;
    s++ ;
}
}
*t = 0 ;
}
```

```
decompress ( s, t )
unsigned char *s, *t ;
{
    int i ;
    while ( *s )
    {
        if ( *s >= 127 )
        {
            *t = '' ;
            t++ ;
            *t = *s - 127 ;
            t++ ;
        }
        else
        {
            if ( *s > 13 && *s < 24 )
            {
                for ( i = 0 ; i < ( *s - 13 ) ; i++ )
                {
                    *t = '' ;
                    t++ ;
                }
            }
            else
            {
                *t = *s ;
                t++ ;
            }
        }
        s++ ;
    }
    *t = 0 ;
}
```

Explanation

The logic used for the compression is like this:

Each character is copied into the string **str2[ ]** as it is, provided it is not a blank space. If a single blank occurs between two words, then a graphic character is stored in **str2[ ]**, which is derived by adding 127 to the ascii value of the character immediately after the blank. Following this, the characters are again copied as they come, till another blank comes across. Thus, when **str2[ ]** is sent for decompression, the presence of a graphic character indicates that the original string had a character having an an ascii value which is 127 less than that of the graphic character, and that one blank space preceded it.

In case of multiple blanks, a variable **spcount** is used to count their number. For instance, if there are 8 blank spaces before 'Rome', then **spcount** gets incremented 8 times through the **while** loop. Again, no spaces are copied into **str2[ ]**. Instead a character corresponding to ascii value **spcount + 13** is written into **str2[ ]**. In the ascii table, values from 14 to 23 are reserved for special control characters. Thus, for **spcount** equal to 8, ascii 21 is written into **str2[ ]**. Next, 'Rome' is copied as it is. In **decompress( )**, when a control character having an ascii value between 13 and 24 is encountered, it signifies that the original string had multiple spaces in its place. The number of spaces is calculated by subtracting 13 from the ascii value of the control character.

Further, multiple spaces are kept track of in units of 10. This is done by inserting ascii 10 + 13, i.e. 23 in **str2[ ]** whenever **spcount** becomes 10, and then resetting it to 0. What that means is, if there are 14 spaces, then two control characters are stored: one corresponding to the first 10 spaces, i.e. 23, and the second for the remaining 4 spaces, having ascii value 4 + 13, i.e. 17. Finally, in case of just one space after a unit of 10, it is treated with the same logic as for a single isolated space.

10

Structures and Unions

W hile handling real world data, we usually deal with a collection of integers, **char**s and **float**s rather than isolated entities. For example, an entity we call a 'book' is a collection of things like a title, an author, a call no., a publisher, number of pages, date of publication, price etc. As you can see, all this data is dissimilar; author is a string, price is a **float**, whereas number of pages is an **int**. For dealing with such collections, C provides a datatype called 'structure'. A structure gathers together different atoms of information that form a given entity.

Look at the following program that combines dissimilar datatypes into an entity called structure.

```
main( )
{
    struct account
    {
        int no ;
        char acc_name[15] ;
        float bal ;
    } ;
    struct account a1, a2, a3 ;

    printf ( "Enter acc nos., names, and balances \n" ) ;
    scanf ( "%d %s %f", &a1.no, a1.acc_name, &a1.bal ) ;
```

```
            scanf ( "%d %s %f", &a2.no, a2.acc_name, &a2.bal ) ;
            scanf ( "%d %s %f", &a3.no, a3.acc_name, &a3.bal ) ;

            printf ( "\n%d %s %f", a1.no, a1.acc_name, a1.bal ) ;
            printf ( "\n%d %s %f", a2.no, a2.acc_name, a2.bal ) ;
            printf ( "\n%d %s %f", a3.no, a3.acc_name, a3.bal ) ;
        }
```

Now a few tips about the program:

(a)   The declaration at the beginning of the program combines dissimilar datatypes into a single entity called **struct account**. Here **struct** is a keyword, **account** is the structure name, and the entities are structure elements.

(b)   **a1, a2** and **a3** are structure variables of the type **struct account**.

(c)   The structure elements are accessed using a '.' operator. So to refer **no** we use **a1.no** and to refer to **acc_name** we use **a1.acc_name**. Before the dot there must always be a structure variable and after the dot there must always be a structure element.

(d)   Since **a1.acc_name** is a string, its base address can be obtained just by mentioning **a1.acc_name**. Hence the 'address of' operator **&** has been dropped while receiving the account name in **scanf( )**.

(e)   The structure elements are always arranged in contiguous memory locations. This arrangement is shown in the following figure.

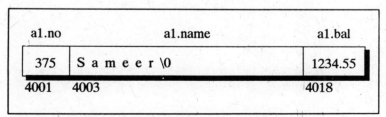

Figure 10.1 Structure elements in memory

An Array of Structures

In the above example if we were to store data of 100 accounts, we would be required to use 100 different structure variables from **a1** to **a100**, which is definitely not very convenient. A better approach would be to use an array of structures. The following program shows how to use an array of structures.

```
main( )
{
    struct employee
    {
        int no ;
        float bal ;
    } ;

    struct employee a[10] ;
    int i ;

    for ( i = 0 ; i <= 9 ; i++ )
    {
        printf ( "Enter account number  and balance " ) ;
        scanf ( "%d %f", &a[i].no,  &a[i].bal ) ;
    }

    for ( i = 0 ; i <= 9 ; i++ )
        printf ( "%d %f\n", a[i].no, a[i].bal ) ;
}
```

The arrangement of the array of structures in memory is shown in the following figure.

a[0].no	a[0].bal	a[1].no	a[1].bal		a[9].no	a[9].bal
007	2000.55	134	4892.30		122	6432.90
4000	4002	4006	4008		4054	4056

Figure 10.2 Array of structures in memory

More about Structures

Let us now explore the intricacies of structures with a view of programming convenience.

(a)   The declaration of structure type and the structure variable can be combined in one statement. For example,

```
struct player
{
    char name[20] ;
    int age ;
} ;
struct player p1 = { "Nick Yates", 30 } ;
```

is same as...

```
struct player
{
    char name[20] ;
    int age ;
} p1 = { "Nick Yates", 30 } ;
```

or even...

```
struct
{
```

```
        char name[20] ;
        int age ;
} p1 = { "Nick Yates", 30 } ;
```

(b)   The values of a structure variable can be assigned to another
      structure variable of the same type using the assignment
      operator. It is not necessary to copy the structure elements
      piece-meal. For example,

```
struct player
{
    char name[20] ;
    int age ;
} ;
struct player p2, p1 = { "Nick Yates", 30 } ;
p2 = p1 ;
```

(c)   One structure can be nested within another structure as shown
      below.

```
struct part
{
    char type ;
    int qty ;
} ;
struct vehicle
{
    char maruti[20] ;
    struct part bolt ;
} ;
struct vehicle v ;
v.bolt.qty = 300 ;
```

(d)   Like an ordinary variable, a structure variable can also be
      passed to a function. We may either pass individual structure
      elements or the entire structure at one go. If need be we can

also pass addresses of structure elements or address of a structure variable as shown below.

```
struct player
{
    char nam[20] ;
    int age ;
} ;
struct player p1 = { "Nick Yates", 30 } ;

display ( p1.nam, p1.age ) ;  /* passing individual elements */
show ( p1 ) ;  /* passing structure variable */
d ( p1.nam, &p1.age ) ;  /* passing addresses of structure elements */
print ( &p1 ) ;  /* passing address of structure variable */
```

(e)   To access structure elements through a structure variable we use the '.' operator. Whereas to access structure elements through a pointer to a structure we use the '->' operator. This is shown below.

```
struct book
{
    char name[25] ;
    int callno ;
} ;
struct book b1 = { "let us C", "C.Iyer", 101 } ;
struct book *b2 ;
printf ( "%s %d\n", b1.name, b1.callno ) ;
b2 = &b1 ;
printf ( "%s %d", b2->name, b2->callno ) ;
```

Unions

Unions, like structures, are derived datatypes which group together a number of variables. However, the way the two treat these variables is totally different. While the elements of a structure enable us to access different locations in memory, the elements of a **union** serve as different names by which the same portion of memory can be accessed. Consider the following program.

```
main( )
{
    union demo
    {
        int i ;
        char ch[2] ;
    } ;
    union demo a ;
    a.i = 512 ;
    printf ( "a.i = %d\n", a.i ) ;
    printf ( "a.ch[0] = %d\n", a.ch[0] ) ;
    printf ( "a.ch[1] = %d", a.ch[1] ) ;
}
```

The output of this program would be:

```
a.i = 512
a.ch[0] = 0
a.ch[1] = 2
```

Note that the declaration of the datatype **union** and the **union** variable **a** is just like the way it is done for structures. So is the accessing of the elements of the union using dot operators. But the analogy ends here, as the following figure illustrates.

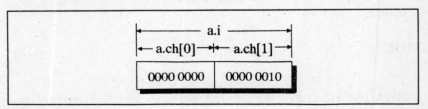

Figure 10.3

Where a structure would have employed a total of four bytes for **a.i** and **a.ch[ ]**, the union engages only two bytes. The same two bytes which comprise **a.i** also comprise the array **a.ch[ ]**. Hence, we can access the two bytes together by mentioning **a.i**, or individually by mentioning **a.ch[0]** and **a.ch[1]**.

On assigning 512 to **a.i**, the binary equivalent of 512, i.e. 0000 0010 0000 0000 is what is actually stored in the two bytes of the **int**. Of the 16 bit number, first the lower 8 bits are stored in **ch[0]**, and next the higher 8 bits are assigned to **ch[1]**. Taken bytewise, **a.ch[0]** contains decimal 0, and **a.ch[1]** contains decimal 2.

This datatype proves very useful while interacting with the hardware of the computer, which lies beyond the scope of this book.

Exercise

[A]   What will be the output of the following programs:

(1)
```
main( )
{
    struct employee
    {
        char name[25] ;
        int age ;
        float bs ;
    }
    struct employee e ;
    e.name = "Hacker" ;
    e.age = 25 ;
    printf ( "%s %d", e.name, e.age ) ;
}
```

(2)
```
main( )
{
    struct
    {
        char name[25] ;
        char language[10] ;
    } a ;
    static struct a = { "Hacker", "C" } ;
    printf ( "%s %s", a.name, a.language ) ;
}
```

(3)
```
struct virus
{
    char signature[25] ;
    int size ;
} v[2] ;
main( )
```

```
        {
                static struct v[0] = { "Yankee Doodle", 1813 } ;
                static struct v[1] = { "Dark Avenger", 1795 } ;
                int i ;

                for ( i = 0 ; i <= 1 ; i++ )
                        printf ( "%s %d\n", v[i].signature, v[i].size ) ;
        }
```

(4)   ```
        struct s
        {
                char ch ;
                int i ;
                float a ;
        } ;
        main( )
        {
                static struct s var = { 'C', 100, 12.55 }
                f (var) ;
                g (&var) ;
        }

        f (v)
        struct s v ;
        {
                printf ("%c %d %f", v->ch, v->i, v->a) ;
        }

        g (v)
        struct s *v ;
        {
                printf ("%c %d %f", v.ch, v.i, v.a) ;
        }
```

(5)    ```
        main( )
        {
                static char str1[ ] = "Ransacked" ;
```

```
            char str2[20] ;

            struct word
            {
                char str[20] ;
            } ;

            static struct word s1 = { "Ransacked" } ;
            struct word s2 ;

            strcpy ( str2, str1 ) ;
            s2 = s1 ;

            printf ( "%s %s\n", s1.str, s2.str ) ;
            printf ( "%s %s\n", str1, str2 ) ;
      }

(6)   main( )
      {
            struct
            {
                int num ;
                float f ;
                char mess[50] ;
            } m ;

            m.num = 1 ;
            m.f = 3 14 ;
            strcpy ( m.mess, "Everything looks rosy" ) ;

            printf ( "%d %d %d\n", &m.num, &m.f, m.mess ) ;
            printf ( "%d %f %s\n", m.num, m.f, m.mess ) ;
      }

(7)   main( )
      {
            static struct emp
```

```
             {
                 char name[20] ;
                 int age ;
                 struct address
                 {
                     char city[20] ;
                     long int pin ;
                 } a ;
             } e = { "abhijeet", 30, "nagpur", 440010 } ;

             printf ( "%s %s", e.name, e.a.city ) ;
         }
```

(8)   main( )
```
         {
             struct a
             {
                 char arr[10] ;
                 int i ;
                 float b ;
             } v[2] ;

             /* assume that first structure begins at address 1004 */
             printf ( "%d %d %d\n", v[0].arr, &v[0].i, &v[0].b ) ;
             printf ( "%d %d %d\n", v[1].arr, &v[1].i, &v[1].b ) ;
         }
```

(9)   main( )
```
         {
             struct a
             {
                 char ch[7] ;
                 char *str ;
             } ;

             static struct a s1 = { "Nagpur", "Bombay" } ;
```

```
            printf ( "%c %c\n", s1.ch[0], *s1.str ) ;
            printf ( "%s %s\n", s1.ch, s1.str ) ;
      }

(10)  main( )
      {
            struct a
            {
                 char ch[7] ;
                 char *str ;
            } ;

            struct b
            {
                 char *c ;
                 struct a ss1 ;
            } ;

            static struct b s2 = { "Raipur", "Kanpur", "Jaipur" } ;

            printf ( "%s %s\n", s2.c, s2.ss1.str ) ;
            printf ( "%s %s\n", ++s2.c, ++s2.ss1.str ) ;
      }

(11)  main( )
      {
            struct s1
            {
                 char *z ;
                 int i ;
                 struct s1 *p ;
            } ;
            static struct s1 a[ ] = {
                                     { "Nagpur", 1, a + 1 },
                                     { "Raipur", 2, a + 2 },
                                     { "Kanpur", 3, a }
                            } ;
```

```
            struct s1 *ptr = a ;
            printf ( "%s %s %s\n", a[0].z, ptr->z, a[2].p->z ) ;
      }

(12)  main( )
      {
            struct s1
            {
                char *str ;
                int i ;
                struct s1 *ptr ;
            } ;
            static struct s1 a[ ] = {
                                        { "Nagpur", 1, a + 1 },
                                        { "Raipur", 2, a + 2 },
                                        { "Kanpur", 3, a }
                                } ;
            struct s1 *p = a ;
            int j ;

            for ( j = 0 ; j <= 2 ; j++ )
            {
                printf ( "%d " , --a[j].i ) ;
                printf ( "%s\n" , ++a[j].str ) ;
            }
      }

(13)  main( )
      {
            struct s1
            {
                char *z ;
                int i ;
                struct s1 *p ;
            } ;
            static struct s1 a[ ] = {
                                        { "Nagpur", 1, a + 1 },
```

```
                                    { "Raipur", 2, a + 2 },
                                    { "Kanpur", 3, a }
                              } ;
        struct s1 *ptr = a ;

        printf ( "%s\n", ++( ptr->z ) ;
        printf ( "%s\n", a[( ++ptr )->i].z ) ;
        printf ( "%s\n", a [--( ptr->p->i )].z ) ;
    }


(14)  main( )
    {
        struct s1
        {
            char *str ;
            struct s1 *ptr ;
        } ;
        static struct s1 arr[ ] = {
                                    { "Nikhil", arr+1 } ,
                                    { "Aditya", arr+2 },
                                    { "Sudheer", arr }
                              } ;

        struct s1 *p[3] ;
        int i ;

        for ( i = 0 ; i <= 2 ; i++ )
            p[i] = arr[i].ptr ;

        printf ( "%s\n", p[0]->str ) ;
        printf ( "%s\n", (*p)->str ) ;
        printf ( "%s\n", (**p) ) ;
    }

(15)  struct s1
    {
        char *str ;
```

```
        struct s1 *next ;
} ;
main( )
{
    static struct s1 arr[ ] = {
                                    { "Akhil", arr+1 },
                                    { "Nikhil", arr+2 },
                                    { "Anant", arr }
                        } ;

    struct s1 *p[3] ;
    int i ;

    for ( i = 0 ; i <= 2 ; i++ )
        p[i] = arr[i].next ;

    printf ( "%s %s %s", p[0]->str, *p->str, **p.str ) ;

    swap ( *p, arr ) ;

    printf ( "\n%s", p[0]->str ) ;
    printf ( "\n%s", ( *p )->str ) ;
    printf ( "\n%s", ( *p )->next->str ) ;

    swap ( p[0], p[0]->next ) ;

    printf ( "\n%s", p[0]->str ) ;
    printf ( "\n%s", ( *++p[0] ).str ) ;
    printf ( "\n%s", ++( *++( *p )->next ).str ) ;
}

swap ( p1, p2 )
struct s1 *p1, *p2 ;
{
    char *temp ;

    temp = p1->str ;
```

```
            p1->str = p2->str ;
            p2->str = temp ;
      }

(16)  main( )
      {
            struct node
            {
                int data ;
                struct node *link ;
            } ;
            struct node *p, *q ;

            p = malloc ( sizeof ( struct node ) ) ;
            q = malloc ( sizeof ( struct node ) ) ;

            printf ( "%d %d", sizeof ( p ), sizeof ( q ) ) ;
      }

(17)  #define NULL 0
      main( )
      {
            struct node
            {
                int data ;
                struct node *link ;
            } ;
            struct node *p, *q ;

            p = malloc ( sizeof ( struct node ) ) ;
            q = malloc ( sizeof ( struct node ) ) ;

            p->data = 30 ;
            p->link = q ;
            q->data = 40 ;
            q->link = NULL ;
```

```
            printf ( "%d ", p->data ) ;
            p = p->link ;
            printf (" %d", p->data ) ;
        }

(18)    #define NULL 0
        main( )
        {
            struct node
            {
                struct node *previous ;
                int data ;
                struct node *next ;
            }

            struct node *p, *q ;

            p = malloc ( sizeof ( struct node ) ) ;
            q = malloc ( sizeof ( struct node ) ) ;

            p->data = 75 ;
            q->data = 90 ;

            p->previous = NULL ;
            p->next = q ;
            q->previous = p ;
            q->next = NULL ;

            while ( p != NULL )
            {
                printf ( "%d\n", p->data ) ;
                p = p->next ;
            }
        }

(19)    #define NULL 0
        main( )
```

```
        {
            struct node
            {
                int data ;
                struct node *next ;
            } ;
            struct node *p, *q ;

            p = malloc ( sizeof ( struct node ) ) ;
            q = malloc ( sizeof ( struct node ) ) ;

            p->data = 10 ;
            q->data = 20 ;
            p->next = q ;
            q->next = p ;

            while ( p != NULL )
            {
                printf ( "%d\n", p->data ) ;
                p = p->next :
            }
        }

(20)    main( )
        {
            struct a
            {
                int i ;
                char ch[2] ;
            } ;
            union b
            {
                int i ;
                char c[2] ;
            } ;
            printf ( "%d ", sizeof ( struct a ) ) ;
            printf ( "%d", sizeof ( union b ) ) ;
```

```
        }

(21)   main( )
       {
            union a
            {
                int i ;
                char ch[2] ;
            } ;
            union a u ;

            u.i = 256 ;
            printf ( "%d %d %d", u.i, u.ch[0], u.ch[1] ) ;
       }

(22)   main( )
       {
            struct a
            {
                long int i ;
                char ch[4] ;
            } ;
            struct a s ;

            s.i = 512 ;
            printf ( "%d %d %d", s.ch[0], s.ch[1], s.ch[3] ) ;
       }

(23)   main( )
       {
            union a
            {
                int i ;
                char ch[2] ;
            } ;
            union a u ;
```

```
                u.ch[0] = 3 ;
                u.ch[1] = 2 ;
                printf ( "%d %d %d", u.ch[0], u.ch[1], u.i ) ;
        }

(24)    main( )
        {
                struct a
                {
                    int i ;
                    int j ;
                } ;
                struct b
                {
                    char x ;
                    char y[3] ;
                } ;
                union c
                {
                    struct a aa ;
                    struct b bb ;
                } ;
                union c u ;

                u.aa.i = 512 ;
                u.aa.j = 512 ;

                printf ( "%d %d ", u.bb.x, u.bb.y[0] ) ;
                printf ( "%d %d", u.bb.y[1], u.bb.y[2] ) ;
        }

(25)    main( )
        {
                struct a
                {
                    int i ;
```

```
                int j ;
            } ;
            struct b
            {
                char x ;
                char y ;
            } ;
            union c
            {
                struct a aa ;
                struct b bb ;
            } ;
            union c u ;

            u.aa.i = 256 ;
            u.aa.j = 512 ;

            printf ( "%d %d ", u.aa.i, u.aa.j ) ;
            printf ( "%d %d", u.bb.x, u.bb.y ) ;
        }
```

(26)   ```
        main( )
        {
            union
            {
                unsigned long l ;
                unsigned int d[2] ;
                char ch[4] ;
            } a ;

            strcpy (a.ch, "ABC") ;

            printf ("%s\n", a.ch) ;
            printf ("%u %u\n", a.d[0], a.d[1]) ;
            printf ("%lu", a.l) ;
        }
```
```

Answers

Answers to [A]

(1)   *Output*

Error message: Lvalue required in function main

Explanation

The error message is obtained for the simple reason that we tried to assign a value to **e.name**. By mentioning **e.name** we get the base address of the array **name[ ]**, and question doesn't arise of assigning anything to this base address, as its a constant value. Since on the left hand side of = a variable should occur rather than a constant, the compiler flashes an error message saying 'Lvalue required in function main'. Incidentally, an lvalue is something which can change, or in other words, a variable.

(2)   *Output*

Error message: Declaration syntax in function main

Explanation

Let us check the type declaration first. Here we find the structure name missing. This is perfectly alright, as you may recall that if we want to skip giving the structure a name, we must declare the variables along with the type declaration. Thus the type declaration is fine. Then where lies the error? The error is that the **struct** variable **a** is declared twice; the first time along with the type declaration, and then again in the initialisation statement.

(3) *Output*

Error message: Declaration syntax in function main

Explanation

At the time of declaration of structure type, we declared **v[2]** outside **main( )**. **v[2]** is therefore allotted **extern** storage class. Once external storage class is associated with **v[2]**, we can't initialise it using the keyword **static**, which refers to **static** storage class. The compiler recognises the illegal declaration and flashes the error message.

(4) *Output*

Error message: Pointer required on left of -> in function f
Error message: Variable required on left of . in function g

Explanation

The function **f( )**, called from **main( )**, is sent the **struct** variable **var**, which is collected in **v**. The **printf( )** in **f( )** attempts to print the structure elements using the arrow operator with **v**, wherein lies the first error. On the left of the arrow operator, there must always be a pointer to a structure. On the other hand, function **g( )** collects a pointer to a structure, which it uses in conjunction with the dot operator. The dot operator must always be preceded by a structure variable, never a pointer. Hence the second error message.

(5) *Output*

Ransacked Ransacked
Ransacked Ransacked

Explanation

The program clearly brings out how the treatment varies for a string and a structure. **str1[ ]** and **s1.str** are both initialised to store "Ransacked". For copying the contents of one string to another, we have to use the function **strcpy( )**. However, the copying of structure elements is a simple affair: saying **s2 = s1** does the trick. For printing strings, only the name of the string needs to be mentioned, while for accessing the structure elements the dot operator should be used.

(6)   *Output*

```
1401 1403 1407
1 3.140000 Everything looks rosy
```

Explanation

In the elements **num** and **f** of the structure, 1 and 3.14 are stored. For assigning contents to the third element of the structure, i.e. the array **mess[ ]**, **strcpy( )**, the string copy function is used. Why use a string function for this? Could we not have said:

```
m.mess = "Everything looks rosy" ;
```

like when we assigned values to **num** and **f**? The answer is an emphatic NO! Unlike **m.num** and **m.f**, **m.mess** signifies an address, and a base address at that. Hence, it can't ever occur on the left hand side of the assignment operator. In other words, **m.mess** is not an lvalue.

The first **printf( )** prints the addresses of the three elements within the **struct**. The output goes to show that the elements of a **struct** are stored in contiguous memory locations. Address of **m.num** is found to be 1401. Since an **int** occupies two bytes in memory, address of the **float, m.f**, is 1403. Finally, the address of the array **mess[ ]** is 1407. This is four bytes ahead of the address of **m.f** as a **float** is a four-byte entity.

The second **printf( )** prints out the three elements of the structure.

(7)   *Output*

abhijeet nagpur

Explanation

Structures can be nested. That is, a structure may comprise of other structures, which in turn may be hosting other structures, and so on. Here, the third element of **struct emp** is **struct address a**, which has two elements of its own: a **char** string **city[ ]** and a **long int pin. a** has been declared as a variable of the type **struct address**, and **e**, of the type **struct emp**. While initialising **e**, care must be taken to provide the values in keeping with the order in which the elements have been declared in the structure.

Through the **printf( )**, the name is printed out using **e.name**. Since the dot operator is used for accessing an element of a structure, it means to access an element of a structure which itself is a part of another structure, the dot operator should be used twice. Hence "nagpur", an element of variable **a**, which in turn is an element of variable **e**, is printed using **e.a.city**.

(8)   *Output*

1004 1014 1016
1020 1030 1032

Explanation

v[ ] has been declared as an array of structures. Understand that though each structure consists of dissimilar datatypes, more than one similar structures are capable of forming an array. The word 'similar' is important here, as that is the only criterion Dennis Ritchie set for constructing an array of any datatype.

The output verifies that elements of an array of structures, in keeping with the tradition of arrays, are stored in contiguous memory locations. The address of the zeroth element of the zeroth structure is 1004. As this is a **char** array of size 10, ten bytes are used by it. Next, at 1014, the **int** of the zeroth structure is stored. After leaving 2 bytes for **v[0].i**, the **float v[0].b** occupies bytes 1016 to 1019. Immediately after this, the next structure of the array is stored, as the outputted addresses 1020, 1030, and 1032, justify.

(9)   *Output*

N B
Nagpur Bombay

Explanation

struct a comprises of **char** array **ch[ ]** and a **char** pointer **str**. **s1**, a variable of type **struct a**, is initialised next. Here "Nagpur" gets stored in the array **ch[ ]**, and "Bombay" gets stored starting from the address contained in **str**.

In the first **printf( )**, **ch[0]** signifies the zeroth element of the array **ch[ ]**. Since this array is within a **struct**, a dot operator, preceded by the structure variable of that type must be used. Thus, **s1.ch[0]** refers to the zeroth element of the array **ch[ ]**.

As this array has been assigned the string "Nagpur", the first character 'N' is printed out.

Next, ***s1.str** signifies the value at address contained in **s1.str**. Since this is the address at which 'B' of "Bombay" is stored, the **printf( )** prints out a 'B'.

The next **printf( )** outputs both "Nagpur" and "Bombay", as **s1.ch** denotes the base address of the former, and **s1.str**, that of the latter string.

(10) *Output*

```
Raipur Jaipur
aipur aipur
```

Explanation

At the outset, **struct a** is declared to comprise of a character array **ch[ ]** and a character pointer **str**. Next, **s2** is declared as a variable of type **struct b**, which is made up of a **char** pointer **c** and another variable **ss1** of type **struct a**. While initialising **s2**, the base address of the string "Raipur" is assigned to **s2.c**, "Kanpur" is assigned to **s2.ss1.ch[ ]**, and the base address of "Jaipur" is assigned to **s2.ss1.str**.

Coming to the **printf( )**s now, the first one is supplied **s2.c** and **s2.ss1.str**. **s2.c** gives the base address of "Raipur", and **s2.ss1.str** gives the base address of "Jaipur". Since these base addresses are passed to **printf( )**, it promptly prints out the two strings.

The second **printf( )** uses incremented values of these addresses. On incrementing **s2.c** using the **++** operator, it now points to the next element 'a' of "Raipur". Similarly, on incrementing

s2.ss1.str, it points to the 'a' of "Jaipur". With these as starting addresses, the remaining strings are printed out.

(11) *Output*

Nagpur Nagpur Nagpur

Explanation

The zeroth and first elements of **struct s1** are a character pointer and an **int** respectively. The second element is what's new. It is a pointer to a structure. That is, **p** stores the starting address of a structure variable of the type **struct s1**. Next, **a[ ]**, an array of such structures is declared as well as initialised. During initialisation the base address of "Nagpur" is stored in **a[0].z**, 1 is stored in the element **a[0].i**, and **a + 1** is assigned to **a[0].p**. On similar lines, the remaining two elements of the array are initialised. **a[1].z**, **a[1].i** and **a[1].p** are assigned "Raipur", 2 and **a + 2** in that order, and "Kanpur", 3 and **a** are stored at **a[2].z**, **a[2].i** and **a[2].p** respectively.

What exactly do **a**, **a + 1** and **a + 2** signify? **a**, of course, is the base address of the array **a[ ]**. Let us assume it to be 4000, as shown in Figure 10.4. Locations 4000 and 4001 are occupied by the **char** pointer **a[0].z**, since a pointer is always two bytes long. The next two bytes are used to store the integer **a[0].i**, and then 4004 and 4005 are used by **a[0].p**. Similarly, the next 6 bytes store the first structure **a[1]**, and the 6 bytes after that contain **a[2]**, the second structure in the array.

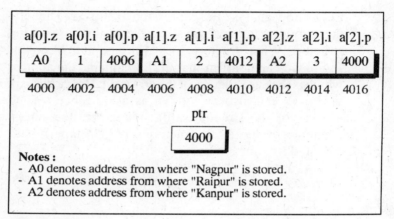

Figure 10.4

Now, when we say **a + 1**, we do not arrive at 4001, but at 4006. This is because on incrementing any pointer, it points to the next location of its type. **a** points to the zeroth structure in the array, i.e. **a[0]**. Hence, on incrementing **a**, it will point to the next immediate element of its type, i.e. the first structure **a[1]** of the array. Likewise, **a + 2** signifies the address of the second element **a[2]** of the array. Thus, **a[0].p** contains address 4006 (refer figure), **a[1].p** contains 4012, and **a[2].p** stores 4000.

A **struct** pointer **ptr** is now set up, which is assigned **a**, the base address of the array.

In the **printf( )**, **a[0].z** denotes the address from where "Nagpur" is stored. Hence "Nagpur" gets printed out.

Since **ptr** contains the address of **a[0]**, **ptr->z** refers to the contents of element **z** of the array element **a[0]**. Thus **ptr->z** gives the address A0 (refer figure) and this address happens to be the base address of the string "Nagpur". Hence "Nagpur" gets printed out.

Let us now analyse the expression **a[2].p->z**. The left side of the arrow operator always represents the base address of a structure. What structure does **a[2].p** point to? Looking at the figure we can confirm that **a[2].p** contains the address 4000, which is the base address of the array **a[ ]**. Hence the expression **a[2].p->z** can also be written as **a->z**. Since **a** is the base address of the structure **a[0]**, this expression refers to the element **z** of the zeroth structure. Thus, "Nagpur" gets printed for the third time.

(12) *Output*

```
0 agpur
1 aipur
2 anpur
```

Explanation

The example deals with a structure similar to the one we just encountered. Picking up from the **for** loop, it is executed for 3 values of **j**: 0, 1 and 2. The first time through the **for** loop, **j** is equal to zero, so the first **printf( )** prints --**a[0].i**. Since the dot operator has a higher priority, first **a[0].i** is evaluated, which is 1. As -- precedes the value to be printed, 1 is first decremented to 0, and then printed out.

The second **printf( )** prints the string at address ++**a[0].str**. **a[0].str** gives the starting address of "Nagpur". On incrementing, it points to the next character, 'a' of "Nagpur", so starting from 'a', the remaining string "agpur" is outputted.

A similar procedure is repeated for **j = 1**, and then once again for **j = 2**, following which the execution is terminated.

(13) *Output*

agpur
Kanpur
Kanpur

Explanation

With a similar set up as in the previous two programs, we try to print some more combinations. Let us tackle them one by one. The following figure should prove helpful in analysing these combinations.

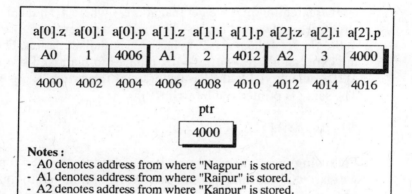

Figure 10.5

```
++( ptr->z )
```

ptr holds the base address of the array of structures. We can also think of this base address as the address of the zeroth structure in the array. **ptr->z** thus signifies the element **z** of the zeroth structure, which is the starting address of the string "Nagpur". On incrementing this using **++** operator, we get the next address, that of 'a' in "Nagpur". Therefore the string is printed out 'a' onwards.

```
a[ ( ++ptr )->i ].z
```

Intimidating? Won't seem so after we have finished dissecting it. Starting from the parentheses, **++ptr** leads to contents of **ptr** being incremented. Currently **ptr** contains the address of the zeroth structure of the array **a[ ]**. This address, as per the figure, turns out to be 4000. Adding 1 to this address takes you 6 bytes further, and not 1, as you might be led to believe. This is so because on incrementing any pointer, it points to the next location of its type. Since **ptr** is a pointer to a structure, it skips as many bytes as the structure comprises of, and points to the following location. Our structure **s1** uses 2 bytes for the **char** pointer **z**, 2 for the **int i**, and 2 for the **struct** pointer **p**. Hence, on incrementing **ptr**, we get that address where **a[1]**, the next structure of the array begins. This address as per the figure is 4006. Now, **(4006)->i** is 2, as has been initialised earlier. Thus the expression **a[(++ptr)->i].z** reduces to plain and simple **a[2].z**, which yields the base address of the string "Kanpur". The same is printed out by **printf( )**.

a[--(ptr->p->i)].z

Following our strategy of crossing the bridges one at a time, we start with the inner parentheses. Moving from left to right, **ptr->p** is evaluated first. **ptr**, after getting incremented in the second **printf( )**, points to the first structure, **a[1]** of the array. The element **p** of this structure stores the address 4012, or in other words, the address given by **a + 2**. This address, as you would agree, is the base address of the second structure of the array. Thus the parentheses reduce to **(a + 2)->i**, or **4012->i**, which is 3. 3 is decremented to 2 by the **--** operator, and we realise that the expression that almost succeeded in putting us off was only a camouflage for **a[2].z**! This again yields the starting address of "Kanpur", and the same is therefore displayed once again.

(14) *Output*

Aditya
Aditya
Aditya

Explanation

struct s1 comprises of 2 pointers; one a **char** pointer and another, a pointer to **struct s1**. **arr[ ]**, an array of such structures, is declared and initialised. Next, an array of pointers to structures, **p[3]** is declared. What this means is that each element of array of **p[ ]** will hold the address of a structure of the type **struct s1**.

The first time in the **for** loop, **arr[0].ptr** is assigned to **p[0]**, which is the zeroth element of the array of pointers to structures. **arr[0].ptr** contains the address 4004 as per the figure given below. Likewise, **p[1]** is assigned the address 4008 and **p[2]**, the address 4000.

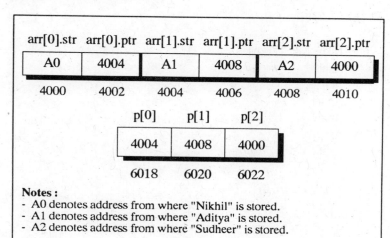

Notes :
- A0 denotes address from where "Nikhil" is stored.
- A1 denotes address from where "Aditya" is stored.
- A2 denotes address from where "Sudheer" is stored.

Figure 10.6

Following this, the **printf( )**s get executed. In the first one, the string at **p[0]->str** is printed. As **p[0]** is equal to 4004, the expression refers to the element **str** of the first structure, which stores A1, the starting address of "Aditya". Hence the name "Aditya" gets printed for the first time.

In the second **printf( )**, mentioning **p** gives the base address of the array **p[ ]**. This address according to the figure is 6018. Hence ***p** would give the value at address 6018, which is nothing but 4004. Thus **(*p)->str** evaluates to **4004->str**, which yields A1, the base address of "Aditya". This outputs "Aditya" once again.

Finally, let us analyse the expression ****p**. A quick glance at the figure would confirm that ***p** gives the address 4004, and ****p** therefore gives the address at 4004. This address this time too turns out to be A1. Thus "Aditya" gets printed out through this **printf( )**.

(15) *Output*

```
Nikhil Nikhil Nikhil
Akhil
Akhil
Anant
Anant
Akhil
nant
```

Explanation

You can by now take the setting up of the arrays of structures and pointers to structures in your stride. In the **for** loop the array **p[ ]** is set up with the addresses 4004, 4008 and 4000, as per the following figure.

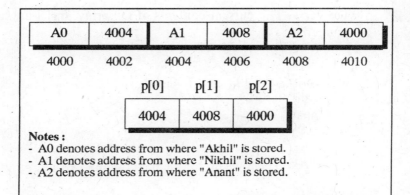

Notes :
- A0 denotes address from where "Akhil" is stored.
- A1 denotes address from where "Nikhil" is stored.
- A2 denotes address from where "Anant" is stored.

Figure 10.7

In the first **printf( )**, **p[0]->str** is same as (**4004->str**). As 4004 denotes the base address of the first structure, **str** corresponds to the address A1, which is the base address of "Nikhil". Hence this **printf( )** prints the first string "Nikhil".

*p is another way of referring to the same element **p[0]** (as you would recall that **n[i]** is equal to ***(n + i)**). Thus, corresponding to ***p- >str**, "Nikhil" is outputted once again.

The third expression uses ****p**, which is equal to ***(p[0])**, i.e. ***(4004)**, which can also be expressed as ***(arr + 1)**. But the expression ***(arr + 1)** is same as **arr[1]**. Thus the expression ****p.str** can also be thought of as **arr[1].str**. As can be confirmed from the figure, **arr[1].str** gives A1, which is the base address of the string "Nikhil". Hence "Nikhil" gets printed through the **printf( )**.

After this, a function **swap( )** is called, which takes as its arguments the base addresses of two structures, **arr + 1** (as ***p** equals **arr + 1**) and **arr**. Hence, in **swap( )**, **p1** and **p2** have been declared as **struct** pointers. Using an auxiliary pointer **temp**, the strings at (**arr + 1**)->**str** and **arr->str** are exchanged. Thus, "Akhil" is now present where "Nikhil" was and vice versa. The current contents of the array **arr[ ]** are now changed to:

```
{
    { "Nikhil", arr + 1 },
    { "Akhil", arr + 2 },
    { "Anant", arr }
}
```

Thus, "Akhil" shows up for the next two **printf( )**s.

Let us now analyse the expression (***p**)->**next->str**. ***p->next** is same as **p[0]->next**. Since **p[0]** contains the address 4004, the term can be expressed as **4004->next**, which yields the address 4008. Next, **4008- >str** yields A2, the base address of "Anant". Hence the **printf( )** outputs "Anant".

After this, **swap( )** is called once again with arrguments **p[0]** and **p[0]->next**. This time **p[0]** contains the address 4004, while **p[0]->next** contains the address 4008. 4004 and 4008 represent the base addresses of the first and second structures of the array **arr[ ]**. In the function **swap( )** the strings in these two structures are interchanged. So the array now looks like:

```
{
    { "Nikhil", arr + 1 },
    { "Anant", arr + 2 },
    { "Akhil", arr }
}
```

With this changed array, let's look at the last set of **printf( )**s. The first of these is quite simple. **p[0]->str**, i.e. **4004->str** yields "Anant" in keeping with the latest contents of the array.

Next is the expression (***++p[0]**)**.str**. In the parentheses **p[0]** is incremented by the **++** operator. Thus, **p[0]**, storing (**arr + 1**), now contains (**arr + 2**). Now, ***(arr + 2)** can be expressed as **arr[2]**. Hence the **printf( )** prints **arr[2].str**, which yields "Akhil".

Not allowing ourselves to be impressed by the length of the last **printf( )**'s argument, we start within the parentheses, on the left of the arrow operator. ***p**, i.e. **p[0]**, having been incremented in the preceding **printf( )**, currently contains (**arr + 2**). Since the **->** operator enjoys a higher priority than the **++**, (**arr + 2**)**->next** gets evaluated next, yielding address **arr**. Now the **++** goes to work and we get the address **arr + 1**.

The expression can now be rewritten as **++(*(arr + 1)).str**. As ***(arr + 1)** is same as **arr[1]**, the expression is reduced to **++arr[1].str**. **arr[1].str** gives the starting address of "Anant". The **++** operator increments this so that the address of the first 'n' of "Anant" is reached. Since this is the address supplied to **printf( )**, the string is printed 'n' onwards. This corresponds to the last output "nant".

(16) *Output*

2 2

Explanation

p and **q** have been declared as pointers to structures of the type **struct node**. In the next statement we come across **malloc( )**, which is a standard library function. It reserves as many locations in memory as its argument specifies. Unlike arrays, which put aside a fixed number of bytes specified at the time of declaration, **malloc( )** can be given a variable as an argument, thus allowing flexibility in the size of memory to be allocated.

The **struct node** engages two bytes for **data** and two for **link**, hence the size of **struct node** is 4. Therefore when the calls to

malloc( ) are made, the argument that is passed is 4. Hence each time, **malloc( )** reserves 4 bytes in memory. These bytes would always be in contiguous memory locations. Having successfully reserved the bytes, **malloc( )** returns the base address of these 4 bytes. The base address returned during the first call to **malloc( )** is collected in **p** and the one returned during the second call, in **q**. As **p** and **q** are both 2-byte addresses, saying **sizeof(p)** and **sizeof(q)** results in 2 and 2 being outputted.

(17) *Output*

30 40

Explanation

p and **q** are returned the starting addresses of two slots of memory allocated by the two **malloc( )**s for structures of the type **struct node**. When we say **p->data**, we are referring to the first two bytes starting from the address in **p**, where 30 is assigned. In **p->link** is stored the address present in **q**, which is the base address of the area of memory allocated by the second **malloc( )**. In the structure starting from address contained in **q**, 40 and NULL are stored, having defined NULL as 0 prior to **main( )**. On printing **p->data**, we find the 30 stored there. Now we change the contents of **p** to **p->link**, so that **p** is now equal to **q**. Thus **p->data** now evaluates to 40, and on printing the same this time we get 40.

The arrangement of the datatypes in this problem conforms to the popular 'linked list' data structure. This arrangement is shown in the following figure, where the arrow represents the pointer to the next node.

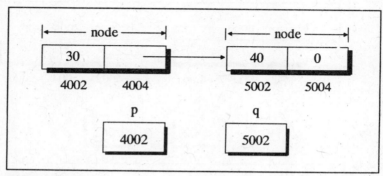

Figure 10.8

(18) *Output*

75
90

Explanation

The structure comprises of an integer **data** and two **struct** pointers, **previous** and **next**. The **malloc( )**s allocate 2 blocks of memory starting at addresses 4002 and 5002 as per the figure given below. The whole arrangement can be thought of as a chain of 2 structures. As the variable names suggest, **previous** of **p**, assigned NULL, indicates there is no structure prior to the one at **p. next** of **p** stores the address of the structure at **q**. Similarly, **previous** of **q** points to the structure preceding it in the chain, which is present at **p**, and **next** of **q** is assigned NULL, signifying there are no more structures after the one at **q**. This arrangement is nothing but a 'doubly linked list'.

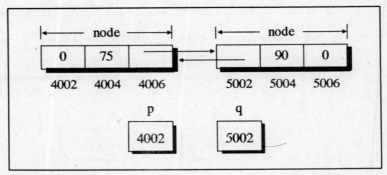

Figure 10.9

The body of the **while** loop is executed subject to the condition that **p** is not equal to NULL, i.e. 0. Since **p** contains 4002, this condition is satisfied for the first time, hence **p->data**, which is 75, gets outputted. Next **p** is assigned **p->next**, which is equal to 5002. This is as good as shifting **p** so that it now points to the next node. Since **p** now contains 5002, the condition in the loop would once again be satisfied, and this time around the **printf( )** prints out 90. In the next statement, **p->next** is assigned to **p**. But this time **p->next** contains 0 (NULL), so **p** is assigned the value 0. The condition in **while** now fails, and the program is terminated.

(19) *Output*

        10
        20
        10
        20
        10
        20
        ...
        ...
        ...

Explanation

p and **q** are declared as pointers to structures of the type **struct node**. With the use of **malloc( )**, two areas in memory, each of the same size as that of **struct node** are reserved. **p** and **q** collect the starting addresses of these areas. According to the figure, these addresses are 4002 and 5002. Now 10 and 20 are assigned to the **data** parts within the two structures. Next, **p->next** is assigned the contents of **q**, i.e. the address 5002, and **q->next** is assigned the contents of **p**, which is the address 4002.

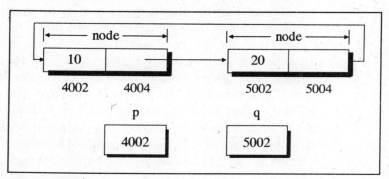

Figure 10.10

The **while** checks the contents of **p** for its execution. The first time since the condition is satisfied, **p->data**, which is 10, gets printed. Now **p** is assigned **p->next**, which is 5002. Thus **p** now points to the second structure. Hence the condition in **while** gets satisfied, and so this time **p->data** yields 20. After this **p** is assigned the value of **p->next**. Since **p** right now contains 5002, **p->next** this time turns out to be 4002 (refer figure). Thus **p** is assigned the address 4002, and **p** now points to the first structure. The integer **data** within the first structure stores 10, which again gets printed when the **printf( )** is executed. Once again the address 5002 is assigned to **p** through the statement **p = p->next**. Thus contents of **p** toggle between

4002 and 5002. And since **p** never becomes NULL, defined earlier as 0, the loop is an indefinite one.

(20) *Output*

4 2

Explanation

unions resemble structures is more than one ways. The methods for declaring, initialising as well as accessing elements of the **union** are exactly same as those used for structures. However, the resemblance is only skin deep. While in a structure each element uses different memory space, all the elements of a **union** refer to portions of the same slot of memory. Thus, **struct a** allots 2 bytes for **int i** and 2 more for **ch[ ]**. On the other hand, the **union** reserves a total of only 2 bytes. The first of the two bytes allotted to **int j** corresponds to **c[0]**, and the second to **c[1]**. Hence, the **sizeof** operator returns 4 for **struct a** and 2 for **union b**, and the same is seen in the output.

(21) *Output*

256 0 1

Explanation

In a **union** all elements refer to the same slot of memory. Thus, in **union a**, if 2 bytes, say 4501 and 4502, are allocated to **int i**, then **ch[0]** refers to location 4501 and **ch[1]**, to 4502.

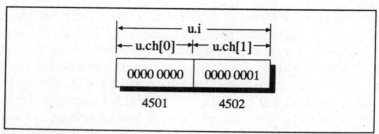

Figure 10.11

256, which is assigned to **u.i**, is 16-bit binary 0000 0001 0000 0000, and this is what is actually stored in memory when we say 256. Contrary to what we might expect, the first of the two bytes stores 0000 0000, and 0000 0001 is present in the second byte. This is because the lower 8 bits of an integer are always stored first, and then the higher 8 bits. That this is indeed so is shown by the result of the **printf( )**.

(22) *Output*

122 4 74

Explanation

s is a variable of the type **struct a**. Unlike a **union**, assigning a value to **s.i** does not mean that the other element in the structure, i.e. the **char** array **ch[ ]** is also set up. Hence, when we print out the contents of the array. we get all garbage values.

(23) *Output*

3 2 515

Explanation

Since each element of a **union** offers a different means of accessing the same portion of memory, initialising one element is necessary and sufficient for assigning a value to that portion. The following figure depicts the **union** variable **u** in memory. As can be observed, **u.ch[0]** is assigned 3, whose binary equivalent is 0000 0011, and **u.ch[1]** is assigned 2, i.e. binary 0000 0010. The same get printed through **printf( )** as 3 and 2. However, the output of **u.i** is not straight forward. This is because when an integer is stored in memory, its lower byte is stored before the higher byte. Therefore when **u.i** is printed, binary 0000 0010 0000 0011 is used rather than binary 0000 0011 0000 0010. Now binary 0000 0010 0000 0011 is equal to decimal 515. Hence **u.i** outputs 515.

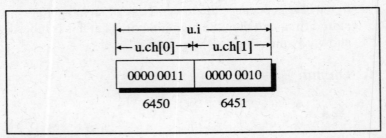

Figure 10.12

(24) *Output*

```
0 2 0 2
```

Here we have a **union** of two structures. The same four bytes of memory are made accessible by different names. For instance, bytes 6503 and 6504 can be accessed together by mentioning **u.aa.j**, or individually as **u.bb.y[1]** and **u.bb.y[2]**. Integer 512, which is 0000 0010 0000 0000 in binary, is stored in **u.aa.i** and **u.aa.j**. One look at the figure will tell you how the **printf( )** generates its output.

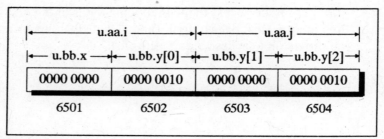

Figure 10.13

(25) *Output*

256 512 0 1

Explanation

union c unites a structure of type **struct a** and another of type **struct b**. The figure depicts the sort of arrangement that would be present in memory.

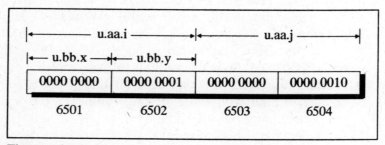

Figure 10.14

u.aa.i is assigned 256, i.e. binary 0000 0001 0000 0000, and **u.aa.j**, 512, i.e. binary 0000 0010 0000 0000. In keeping with the rule that the lower byte is stored first, 256 actually gets stored as 0000 0000 0000 0001, and 512 as 0000 0000 0000 0010. The first **printf( )** is straight forward. It prints out the two integers 256 and 512. In the second **printf( )**, **u.bb.x** and

u.bb.y provide access to the individual bytes of the first **int** in line, **u.aa.i**. Hence the output 0 and 1. Note that this **union** has no provision to access **u.aa.j** byte wise.

(26) *Output*

```
ABC
16961 67
4407873
```

Explanation

a is a variable which unites an **unsigned long l** (a 4 byte number), an integer array **d[ ]** and a character array **ch[ ]**. Into the character array **ch[ ]** is copied the string "ABC". On printing, we get this string as the first output.

a.d[0] refers to the first 2 bytes of the **union** and **a.d[1]** to the next 2. Since the ascii values of 'A' and 'B' are 65 and 66 respectively, the first 2 bytes contain 65 and 66 in that order. Taken as an **int**, the number in **a.d[0]** is the binary equivalent of 66 and 65 taken as a whole, as in an **int** the lower byte gets stored first. Binary equivalent of 66 is 0100 0010, and that of 65 is 0100 0001. So when **a.d[0]** is printed out using **%u**, the decimal equivalent of binary 0100 0010 0100 0001, 16961 is displayed. Similarly, while printing out **a.d[1]**, the next two bytes containing 'C' (decimal 67 or binary 0100 0011) and '\0' (decimal 0 or binary 0000 0000) are used. Hence the **printf( )** outputs 67, which is the decimal equivalent of 0000 0000 0100 0011.

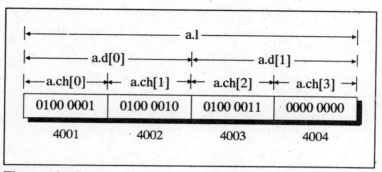

Figure 10.15

In the last **printf( )**, the 4 byte **a.l** is being printed, which is interpreted as 0000 0000 0100 0011 0100 0010 0100 0001, or talking in decimals, as 0, 67, 66 and 65. Taken as a whole, its decimal equivalent 4407873 is outputted.

11

Input and Output in C

I n an effort to keep C compact, Dennis Ritchie defined absolutely nothing for Input/Output (here onwards referred as I/O) in C. That's right - you read it right the first time! Then what are **printf( )** and **scanf( )** which we used consistently uptil now? These are called standard library functions. There is no dearth of such standard library functions that allow you to conduct all sorts of dialogues and monologues with C.

The I/O therefore, is entirely the responsibility of the Operating System. With different operating systems, the way I/O is done would obviously be different. Fortunately, keeping the standard library of functions common, the functions themselves have been written differently for different operating systems. Hence, we can use **printf( )**, **scanf( )**, or any other standard library function in any environment, say DOS or UNIX, and achieve the same result. This is what makes C programs portable.

The numerous library functions can be broadly classified as follows:

(a)   Console I/O functions - These receive input from the keyboard and write output to the VDU.

(b)   Disk I/O functions - These are to perform I/O operations on a floppy disk or a hard disk.

(c)   Port I/O functions - These functions are used to perform I/O operations on various ports.

The following sections deal with each of these categories one by one.

Console I/O Functions

Console I/O functions can be classified as formatted and unformatted. The basic difference between these two classes is that with the former class of functions, we can govern how the input is to be read from the keyboard, or how the output is going to appear on the screen.

printf( ) and **scanf( )** fall in the category of formatted console I/O functions. These can be used for reading and writing **chars**, **int**s, **float**s, as well as strings. The general form of **printf( )** is as follows:

```
printf ( "format string", list of variables ) ;
```

In the format string, we can use conversion specifications which begin with a % and escape sequences which begin with a \. The conversion specifications have already been dealt with at length in Chapter 6. As for the escape sequences, these are shown in the following figure along with the purpose of each.

Esc seq	Purpose	Esc Seq	Purpose
\n	Newline	\t	Tab
\b	Backspace	\r	Carriage return
\f	Formfeed	\a	Alert
\'	Single quote	\"	Double qoute
\v	Vertical Tab	\\	Backslash

Figure 11.1 Escape sequences

The **printf( )** allows us to format the output as we wish with the use of optional specifiers in the conversion specifications. For example, saying **%10d** in a conversion specification would ensure that the integer value is printed so that it is right aligned in a total of 10 columns, padding the empty columns, if any, on the left of the number with blank spaces. Similarly, using **%-8.2f** would mean that the **float** value is to have a total field width of 8 columns, and that it should be printed upto 2 decimal places. The minus sign indicates that within the 8 columns the **float** value should be left aligned.

Under the category of unformatted console I/O there are several functions for handling characters, integers and strings. However, there are no functions available for handling **floats** or **doubles** under this category. The following figures list out these functions along with their purpose.

INPUT		
Datatype	**Function**	**Purpose**
char	getch( )	Gets a character from the keyboard as soon as it is typed, no need to hit Enter
	getche( )	Similar to **getch( )**, except echoes the character on the screen
	fgetchar( )	Gets the character and echoes it on the screen, requires Enter key to be hit
	getchar( )	A macro, works similar to **fgetchar( )**
string	gets( )	Accepts a string until Enter key is hit

Figure 11.2a Unformatted Console Input functions

OUTPUT		
Datatype	**Function**	**Purpose**
char	putch( )	Prints the character on the screen.
	fputchar( )	Prints the character on the screen.
	putchar( )	A macro, works similar to **putch( )** and **fputchar( )**.
string	puts( )	Outputs a string to the screen.

Figure 11.2b Unformatted Console Output functions

Disk I/O Functions

We now come to how I/O is tackled with disks. Disk I/O is performed on entities called files. Accessing the disk every time a read or write operation is to be performed would be inefficient. Hence a buffer is used to hold the data in transit to and from a file. In a buffered read operation from a disk file, a fixed chunk of bytes is read from the disk into a buffer. The functions requesting data from the file actually read from the buffer. When the buffer has no characters left, it is automatically refilled by a disk read operation. A similar sequence occurs when writing to a file. The use of a buffer thus leads to efficient I/O on disk files because there are fewer disk accesses, which are much slower than reading from a buffer in memory. The Disk I/O functions are either High Level (also called standard I/O or stream I/O) or Low Level (or system I/O). The basic difference between them is that in the high level functions the buffer management is done by the functions themselves, whereas in low level functions this is the responsibility of the programmer.

There are a large number of functions available for Disk I/O. The following figure gives a ready reference of these with respect to the datatypes they handle.

Functions	Input / Output	Datatypes Handled	Level
getc( )	Input	characters	High
putc( )	Output	characters	High
fgetc( )	Input	characters	High
fputc( )	Output	characters	High
fscanf( )	Input	characters, strings, numbers, records	High
fprintf( )	Output	characters, strings, numbers, records	High
fread( )	Input	characters, strings, numbers, records	High
fwrite( )	Output	characters, strings, numbers, records	High
read( )	Input	chunks of bytes	Low
write( )	Output	chunks of bytes	Low

Figure 11.3 Functions for Disk Input/Output

The files that are to be accessed for I/O must first be opened. The function **fopen( )** is used to open a file in high level Disk I/O, whereas the function **open( )** is used in low level Disk I/O. Let us first look at **fopen( )**. Its syntax is:

```
fopen ( "file name", "mode" ) ;
```

A file can be opened in several modes, depending upon the operations we intend to perform on the file. The following figure gives the list of all the possible modes in which a file can be opened. Observe carefully how **fopen**( ) reacts when the file to be opened is present/absent on the disk.

Mode Text/Binary	Operation	Notes
"r"/"rb"	Reading from file	*
"w"/"wb"	Writing to file	** , ***
"a"/"ab"	Appending new contents at the end of the file	***
"r+"/"rb+"	Reading existing contents, writing new contents and modifying existing contents of the file	*
"w+/wb+"	Writing and reading	** , ***
"a+"/"ab+"	Reading existing contents, appending new contents at the end of file, cannot modify existing contents	***

```
  *    Returns NULL if file does not exist
 **    Overwrites the file if it already exists
***    New file is created if it doesn't exist
```

Figure 11.4 File Opening Modes

For opening files for low level I/O a function called **open**( ) is used. Like **fopen**( ) it takes as its argument the filename and the mode in which the file is to be opened. The file opening mode is however specified using the **O-flags** defined in the file "fcntl.h". These **O-flags** are shown in the Figure 11.5. What if we intend to open a file for reading in binary mode? In such a case we have to combine the **O-flags** using bitwise | operator. This operator is dealt with in detail in Chapter 12. The **open**( ) statement would look like:

```
open ( "temp.dat", O_READ | O_BINARY ) ;
```

When a new file is to be created, it is necessary to use the flag
O_CREAT.

Mode	Operation
O_APPEND	Opens a file for appending
O_CREAT	Creates a new file for writing (has no effect if file already exists)
O_RDONLY	Creates a new file for reading only
O_RDWR	Creates file for both reading and writing
O_WRONLY	Creates file for writing only
O_BINARY	Creates file in binary mode
O_TEXT	Creates file in text mode

Figure 11.5 O-flags for **open( )**

Once the files have been opened we may want to access the specific
part of the file. This is done by positioning the file pointer at the
desired position in the file. This can be achieved through functions
rewind( ) and **fseek( )**. **rewind( )** positions the file pointer right at
the beginning of the file. **fseek( )** in that sense is more versatile, since
it can place the file pointer virtually anywhere in the file. Its general
form is:

```
fseek ( file pointer, ± number of bytes, anchor ) ;
```

On calling **fseek( )** it positions the file pointer ahead (if +) or behind
(if -) the location specified by the anchor. The anchor can be:

(a)   SEEK_SET   -   Beginning of the file
(b)   SEEK_END   -   End of file
(c)   SEEK_CUR   -   Current position

Having opened the files, worked with them, we need to close them before exiting from the program. The function **fclose( )** does this for high level disk I/O, whereas the same is managed through **close( )** for low level disk I/O.

There are some standard file pointers that do not require the use of **fopen( )**. These correspond to devices like the keyboard and the display monitor, with which the communication is established at all times. That is, they are permanently open for reading or writing. These pointers are given in the following figure.

Pointer	Device
stdin	standard input device (keyboard)
stdout	standard output device (VDU)
stderr	standard error device (VDU)
stdaux	standard auxiliary device (serial port)
stdprn	standard printing device (parallel printer)

Figure 11.6 Standard File Pointers

Port I/O Functions

Having seen what Console and Disk I/O have to offer, let us now turn our attention to the Port I/O functions. With the earlier two forms of I/O we were able to access the keyboard, the VDU and the disks. However, they don't equip us to access peripherals like the speaker or the serial port. For instance, for generating a sound on the IBM PC compatible we would have to establish communication directly with the programmable peripheral interface chip present in the computer. In such cases Port I/O is the only option available. Thus, to beep the speaker we write data to the port associated with the PPI chip. The functions available under this category are given in the following figure.

Functions	Input/Output	Number of bytes accessed
inportb( )	Input	1
outportb( )	Output	1
inportw( )	Input	2
inportw( )	Output	2

Figure 11.7 Functions for Port I/O

inportb( ) and **outportb( )** are used for reading and writing 8 bit data from or to the port address specified as their arguments. As against this, **inportw( )** and **outportw( )** are used when we want to receive or send two bytes of data in a single call.

Exercise

[A]   What will be the output of the following programs:

(1)   main( )
```
       {
              static char str[ ] = "Academy" ;
              printf ( "%s\n%s", str, "Academy" ) ;
       }
```

(2)   main( )
```
       {
              float a = 3.14 ;
              printf ( "\na = %f", a ) ;
              printf ( "\na = %6.2f", a ) ;
              printf ( "\na = %-6.2f", a ) ;
              printf ( "\na = %6.1f", a ) ;
              printf ( "\na = %6.0f", a ) ;
       }
```

(3)   main( )
```
       {
              printf ( "%20s\n", "short leg" ) ;
              printf ( "%20s\n", "long leg" ) ;
              printf ( "%20s\n", "deep fine leg" ) ;
              printf ( "%20s\n", "backward short leg" ) ;
              printf ( "%20s\n", "legs all the same!" ) ;
       }
```

(4)   main( )
```
       {
              printf ( "Hello\nHi\n" ) ;
              printf ( "Hello\rHi" ) ;
       }
```

```
(5)    main( )
       {
            printf ( "Hello\b\b\b\b\b" ) ;
            printf ( "Hi!\b\b\bBye" ) ;
       }

(6)    main( )
       {
            printf ( "I\tam\ta\tboy" ) ;
       }

(7)    #include "stdio.h"
       main( )
       {
            static char str[ ] = "In the country of snake charmers..." ;
            char *s ;

            s = str ;
            while ( *s )
            {
                putch ( *s ) ;
                s++ ;
            }

            printf ( "\n" ) ;
            s = str ;

            while ( *s )
            {
                putchar ( *s ) ;
                s++ ;
            }
       }

(8)    #include "stdio.h"
       main( )
```

```
        {
            char ch ;
            int i;

            printf ( "Enter any number... " ) ;
            scanf ( "%d", &i ) ;

            fflush ( stdin ) ;

            printf ( "Enter any character... " ) ;
            scanf ( "%c", &ch ) ;

            printf ( "\n%d %c", i, ch ) ;
        }

(9)     #include "stdio.h"
        main( )
        {
            char str1[30], str2[30] ;

            printf ( "Enter a sentence\n" ) ;
            scanf ( "%s", str1 ) ;
            printf ( "%s", str1 ) ;
            fflush ( stdin ) ;
            printf ( "\nEnter a sentence\n" ) ;
            gets ( str2 ) ;
            printf ( "%s", str2 ) ;
        }

(10)    main( )
        {
            char name[20], sname[20] ;

            puts ( "Enter your name and surname\n" ) ;
            gets ( name, sname ) ;
            puts ( name, sname ) ;
            printf ( "%s %s", name, sname ) ,
```

```
        }

(11)   main( )
       {
            FILE *fp ;
            fp = fopen ( "TRIAL.C", "r" ) ;
            fclose ( fp ) ;
       }

(12)   #include "stdio.h"
       main( )
       {
            char str[20] ;
            FILE *fp ;
            fp = fopen ( strcpy ( str, "ENGINE.C" ), "w" ) ;
            fclose ( fp ) ;
       }

(13)   #include "stdio.h"
       main( )
       {
            FILE *fp ;
            char str[80] ;

            /* TRIAL.C contains only one line:
               Its a round, round, round world! */

            fp = fopen ( "TRIAL.C", "r" ) ;
            while ( fgets ( str, 80, fp ) != EOF )
                 puts ( str ) ;



(14)   #include "stdio.h"
       main( )
       {
            FILE *fp ;
```

```
        char c ;

        fp = fopen ( "TRY.C", "r" ) ;
        if ( fp = NULL )
        {
            puts ( "Cannot open file" ) ;
            exit(1) ;
        }
        while ( ( c = getc ( fp ) ) != EOF )
            putch( c ) ;

        fclose ( fp ) ;
}
```

(15)   ```
        # include "stdio.h"
        main( )
        {
            FILE *fp, *fs, *ft ;

            fp = fopen ("A.C", "r") ;
            fs = fopen ("B.C", "r") ;
            ft = fopen ("C.C", "r") ;

            fclose (fp, fs, ft) ;
        }
        ```

(16)    ```
        #include "stdio.h"
        main( )
        {
            char name [20], name1[20] ;
            int age, age1 ;

            printf ( "Enter name and age\n" ) ;
            scanf ( "%s %d", name, &age ) ;
            printf ( "%s %d", name, age ) ;

            printf ( "\nEnter name and age\n" ) ;
        ```

```
            fscanf ( stdin, "%s %d", name1, &age1 ) ;
            fprintf ( stdout, "%s %d", name1, age1 ) ;
        }
```

(17)   ```
        #include "stdio.h"
        main( )
        {
            char name[20] = "Sandeep" ;
            int salary = 1500 ;

            printf ("%s %d\n", name, salary) ;
            fprintf (stdout, "%s %d", name, salary) ;
        }
        ```

(18)    ```
        #include "stdio.h"
        main( )
        {
            static char str[ ] = "Triplet" ;
            char *s ;

            s = str ;
            while ( *s )
            {
                putc ( *s, stdout ) ;
                fputchar ( *s ) ;
                printf ( "%c\n", *s ) ;
                s++ ;
            }
        }
        ```

(19)   ```
        /* This program is stored in a file called PROB.C */
        main (argc, argv)
        int argc ;
        char *argv[ ] ;
        {
            printf ("%d\n", argc) ;
        ```
        ```

```
            printf ( "%s", argv[0] ) ;
        }
```

(20)   /* This program is stored in a file called PROB.C */
```
        main ( x, y )
        int x ;
        char *y[ ] ;
        {
            printf ( "%d\n", x ) ;
            printf ( "%s", y[0] ) ;
        }
```

(21)   /* Suppose this program is stored in the file PR.C and its correspond-
        ing executable file PR.EXE is executed at DOS prompt by saying,
        PR CAT DOG PARROT */

```
        main ( argc, argv )
        int argc ;
        char *argv[ ] ;
        {
            for ( i = 0 ; i < argc ; i++ )
                printf ( "%s\n", argv[i] ) ;
        }
```

(22)   main( )
```
        {
            char ch = 'z' ;
            static char str[ ] = "Zebra" ;

            putc ( ch, stdprn ) ;
            fprintf ( stdprn, "%s", str ) ;
            fwrite ( str, 5, 1, stdprn ) ;
            fputs ( str, stdprn ) ;
        }
```

(23)   #include"stdio.h"

```
main( )
{
    struct a
    {
        char city[10] ;
        int pin ;
    } ;
    static struct a b = { "Udaipur", 20 } ;
    static char c[ ] = "Bangalore" ;
    FILE *fp ;

    fp = fopen ( "TRIAL", "wb" ) ;
    fwrite ( &b, sizeof ( b ), 1, fp ) ;
    fwrite ( c, 9, 1, fp ) ;
}
```

[B]   Answer the following:

(1)   The requirement is that the program should receive a key from the keyboard. However, the key that is hit should not appear on the screen. Which of the following functions would you use?

    (a) getch( )
    (b) getche( )
    (c) getchar( )
    (d) fgetchar( )

(2)   Which of the following functions is most appropriate for storing numbers in a file?

    (a) putc( )
    (b) fprintf( )
    (c) fwrite( )

(3)   Which of the following functions is more versatile for positioning the file pointer in a file?

(a) rewind( )
(b) fseek( )
(c) ftell( )

(4)   Which of the following file opening modes would destroy the file being opened, if the file already exists on the disk?

(a) "w"
(b) "wb"
(c) "wb+"
(d) "rb+"
(e) "ab+"

(5)   Which of the following functions are ideally suited for reading the contents of a file record by record?

(a) getc( )
(b) gets( )
(c) fread( )
(d) fgets( )

[C]   Attempt the following:

(1)   Write a program which would remove all comments from a C program. Your program should be capable of removing comments which occur at the beginning of a statement, at the end of a statement as well as the comments which are split over multiple lines.

(2)   A file opened in Document mode in Wordstar stores each word with its last character being stored as the ascii value of the character plus 128. As against this a Non-document mode file is stored as a normal ascii file. Write a program which would convert a Document mode file into a Non-document mode file.

Answers

Answers to **[A]**

(1) *Output*

    Academy
    Academy

Explanation

We know that mentioning the name of a string yields the base
address of the string. When this base address is passed to
printf( ) it prints out each character in the string till it en-
counters '\0' sitting at the end of the string. A string written
within double quotes also gives the base address of the string.
This base address when passed to **printf( )** would result in
printing "Academy" once again.

(2) *Output*

    a = 3.140000
    a =   3.14
    a = 3.14
    a =   3.1
    a =   3

Explanation

The first **printf( )** uses the format specification for a **float**,
hence **a** gets printed as 3.140000, as by default a **float** is printed
with 6 decimal places. In the next **printf( )**, the number that
precedes the **f** in **%f** is an optional specifier, which governs
how exactly the variable is to be printed. 6.2 signifies that the

field width, i.e. the total number of columns that the value occupies on the screen, should be 6, and that the value should have 2 digits after the decimal point. Thus 3.14 is printed with blank spaces on the left, i.e. with right justification. For left justification, we use a minus sign with the specifiers, as is done in the next **printf( )**. It prints the value of **a** starting from the zeroth column, with only 2 decimal digits. The specification 6.1 prints 3.1 with right justification. In the last **printf( )**, 6.0 specifies zero decimal digits, hence only 3 is displayed right justified.

(3)   *Output*

```
          short leg
           long leg
      deep fine leg
 backward short leg
 legs all the same!
```

Explanation

The output is right justified, as the field width specified with each **%s** is plus 20. For each string, 20 columns are set aside, and the strings are printed with blanks filling up the remaining columns on the left.

(4)   *Output*

```
Hello
Hi
Hillo
```

Explanation

The escape sequence '\n', called new line, takes the cursor to the beginning of the next line. Hence with the first **printf( )** "Hello" and "Hi" are printed on consecutive lines. A '\r', on the other hand, takes the cursor to the beginning of the same line in which the cursor is currently present. Hence, having printed "Hello", the cursor is sent back at 'H', and then "Hi" is printed. The first two letters of "Hello" are therefore written over, and we get the output as "Hillo".

(5)   *Output*

Byelo

Explanation

The escape sequence '\b' stands for backspace, which takes the cursor to the previous character. In the first **printf( )**, "Hello" is printed, following which the cursor is positioned after 'o'. Now the 5 backspaces take the cursor to the letter 'H' of "Hello". The control now passes to the second **printf( )**, and "Hi!" is written over the first three characters of "Hello", resulting in "Hi!lo". Once again 3 backspaces are encountered, which take the cursor back at 'H' of "Hi!". Next "Bye" is printed on top of "Hi!". The 'lo' that is seen has persisted from the first **printf( )**'s "Hello", as it never got overwritten. Hence the output "Byelo".

(6)   *Output*

I   am   a   boy

Explanation

The message is printed with spaces inserted wherever the escape sequence '\t' occured. This sequence stands for a tab.

In our compiler, the tabs had been set up after every 5 columns, at 0 5, 10, etc. Hence, while executing **printf( )**, when '\t' is encountered, the cursor skips to the immediately next column which is a multiple of 5, and then prints the next word. Thus "I" is printed from the 0th column, "am" from the 5th, "a" from the 10th, and "boy" from the 15th column. Some compilers like Turbo C allow you to change the tab settings, so that the tab widths can be set up as desired.

(7)   *Output*

In the country of snake charmers...
In the country of snake charmers...

Explanation

putch( ) is an unformatted console I/O function, whereas **putchar( )** is a macro. However, their working is the same. They put the contents of the character variable supplied as their argument on to the screen. Having assigned to s the starting address of the string **str[ ]**, through the **while** loops, the value at address contained in s is printed out, then s is incremented so that it points to the next character. Hence, the string is printed out twice.

(8)   *Output*

Enter any number... 2
Enter any character... a
2 a

Explanation

We entered 2 and **a** and the same were faithfully outputted. Quite straight, that. What you might be wondering about is the statement **fflush (stdin)**. This statement empties the buffer before prompting us to enter a character. When we typed 2 and hit Enter, the buffer stored the ascii codes corresponding to 2 and the Enter key (carriage return) temporarily. Then the first **scanf( )** picked up the 2, as when an integer is to be read, whatever is typed prior to hitting Enter is treated as data. Thus 13, the ascii code of Enter still persisted in the buffer. Had we not said **fflush (stdin)**, the next **scanf( )** would have picked up this 13 as the character to be read, and not given us a chance to enter a character. Thus, by using **fflush( )** the contents of the buffer are first flushed out, so that the second **scanf( )** waits for us to type a character.

(9)   *Output*

```
Enter a sentence
Nothing succeeds like success.
Nothing
Enter a sentence
Nothing succeeds like success.
Nothing succeeds like success.
```

Explanation

The **scanf( )** suffers from the limitation that a maximum of only one word can be accepted by it. The moment a space (or a tab or a newline) is typed, **scanf( )** assumes you have finished supplying information, and hence ignores whatever follows. That's why, **str1[ ]** stores only "Nothing", as is proved by the first output. To overcome this limitation, we have an unformatted console I/O function called **gets( )**. It accepts whatever you type from the keyboard till the Enter key is hit. To be precise, **gets( )** accepts everything until a '\n' is encountered, which it replaces with a '\0'. Thus the entire string that we entered is obtained in the second output.

As in the previous program, **fflush( )** flushes out the current keyboard buffer contents. If not used, the Enter key present in the keyboard buffer would be read by **gets( )**. Since **gets( )** is terminated on reading an Enter key, you won't get a chance to supply the second sentence.

(10) *Output*

```
Enter your name and surname
Jaspal Bhatti
Jaspal Bhatti
Jaspal Bhatti ƒ5+yP~ƒdfG
```

Explanation

gets( ) and **puts( )** cannot take more than one argument at a time. Though no error message is displayed, whatever is typed before hitting Enter is accepted by the first argument **name[ ]**, and the second argument is simply ignored. Thus **name[ ]** stores the name "Jaspal Bhatti" and **sname** gets ignored in both **gets( )** and **puts( )**. That this is indeed so is proved by the output of **printf( )**, which prints "Jaspal Bhatti" corresponding to contents of **name[ ]**, and all garbage values for the string **sname[ ]**.

(11) *Output*

Error message: Undefined symbol FILE in function main

Explanation

FILE is a structure that is defined in the header file "stdio.h". Hence, for using this structure, including "stdio.h" is a must. Saying **# include "stdio.h"** before **main( )** would eliminate the error.

(12) *Output*

No output

Explanation

fp has been declared as a pointer to a structure called FILE
which has been defined in the header file "stdio.h". For accessing any file, we must first open the file in the proper mode using
fopen( ). We could easily have said **fopen ("ENGINE.C",
"w")** as "ENGINE.C" is the name of the file we want to open
in write mode. However, saying **fopen (strcpy (str, "EN-
GINE.C"), "w")** is another, though roundabout way of saying
the same thing. **strcpy( )** returns the base address of the string
str[ ], into which "ENGINE.C" has been copied. The same is
passed as argument to the function **fopen( )**, and "ENGINE.C"
gets opened in write mode. What we want to convey is that
fopen( ) needs a pointer to the name of the file we want it to
open. How we supply the same is entirely our prerogative.

(13) *Output*

```
Its a round, round, round world!
Its a round, round, round world!
 ... ..  .........  .........  .........  ........ .
 ... ..  .........  .........  .........  ........ .
```

Explanation

In the **while** loop, **fgets( )** reads a string of 80 characters from
the file indicated by **fp**, and returns a pointer to the string it
read. If it fails to read a string, as would be the case when the
end of file is reached, it returns a NULL, not EOF. Hence, we
must compare the returns of **fgets( )** with NULL and not EOF,

as the latter is never going to be returned. Thus the loop is an indefinite one.

(14) *Output*

Error message: Null pointer assignment

Explanation

Try opening any file using this program and the output would always be the same: "Null pointer assignment". In the **if** condition, instead of comparing **fp** and NULL, what the single = does is assign NULL to **fp**. Replacing the = with the comparison operator == would eliminate the bug. On removing the bug, the program would read the file character by character till the end of file is reached. Each character read would be displayed on the screen using the function **putch( )**.

(15) *Output*

No output

Explanation

Though you won't get any message here, what you aimed to do has not been done. Having opened the three files through calls to **fopen( )**, **fclose( )** goes to work. **fclose( )** can close only one file at a time. So after taking **fs**, the first argument in line, it paid no attention to the remaining two. Thus only the file "A.C" gets closed, while files "B.C" and "C.C" remain open. For closing the three files, we must call **fclose( )** three times. If we wish to close all the files through one call, we can make use of a function called **fcloseall( )**. This closes all the files that are currently open, except the standard files like **stdin**, **stdout**, etc.

(16) *Output*

    Enter name and age
    Raj 18
    Raj 18
    Enter name and age
    Sonia 21
    Sonia 21

Explanation

Here the first set of statements comprising of **printf( )**s and **scanf( )** is fairly simple. The **fscanf( )** **and fprintf( )** that follow next need some explaining.

fscanf( ), like **scanf( )**, is used for formatted reading of data. The only difference is that the former takes an additional argument, that of a file pointer. This pointer indicates to the **fscanf( )** from where the data is to be read, whereas **scanf( )** is capable of reading data only from the keyboard. In the call to **fscanf( )** the file pointer **stdin** is being used, which stands for standard input device, i.e. the keyboard. Since **stdin** is a pointer to a standard file, we do not need to use **fopen( )** to open it, as it is always open for reading. The counterpart of **fscanf( )** is **fprintf( )**. It too needs a file pointer as its first argument. Here the file pointer used is **stdout**, which stands for standard output device, i.e. the display monitor. Thus, using **stdin** in **fscanf( )** and **stdout** in **fprintf( )** makes them work like the familiar **scanf( )** and **printf( )** functions. Hence both the sets collect the names and ages from the keyboard and output them on the screen.

(17) *Output*

    Sandeep 1500
    Sandeep 1500

Explanation

fprintf( ), like its counterpart **fscanf( )**, requires as one of its arguments a file pointer. The argument sent here is **stdout**, which signifies the standard output device, i.e. the VDU. As standard devices are always open, we can access them without calling **fopen( )**. **name[ ]** and **salary** are initialised in **main( )** to store "Sandeep" and 1500. Both the **printf( )** and **fprintf( )** thus send the output to the screen, and we have "Sandeep" and 1500 printed onto the screen both ways.

(18) *Output*

```
TTT
rrr
iii
ppp
lll
eee
ttt
```

Explanation

The three statements within the **while** loop do the same job, i.e. to put the value at address contained in **s** onto the screen. What differs is how their arguments are specified. **putc( )**, unlike **fputchar( )** and **printf( )**, allows you to specify where the character is to be put. Here, **stdout** indicates the screen, hence the output of **putc( )** is sent to the screen. **fputchar( )** and **printf( )** are programmed to write to the screen alone, hence our output shows the triplets.

(19) *Output*

1

C:\PROB.EXE

Explanation

Having made an executable file PROB.EXE, we run this program by saying 'PROB.EXE' at the DOS prompt. Since we only mention one string, **argc**, the command line variable collects a 1. The other argument to **main( )**, **argv[ ]**, collects the pointer to this string. Through the program, **argc** on printing gives the 1 stored in it. The next **printf( )** prints out the string at the address contained in **argv[0]**. Since this address is the address of the name of the file along with its path, this string is printed out.

(20) *Output*

1
C:\PROB.EXE

Explanation

argc and **argv** are commonly used variable names assigned to collect the command line arguments. Here we have given the variable names as **x** and **y**, still we get the same result as with **argc** and **argv**. Hardly surprising, as Shakespeare pointed out ages ago, what's there in a name!

(21) *Output*

C:\PR.EXE
CAT
DOG
PARROT

Explanation

At the DOS prompt, four strings, PR.EXE, CAT, DOG and PARROT are passed to **main( )**. The base addresses of these strings are collected in the array of pointers to strings, **argv[ ]**. Hence in the **for** loop on printing the value at the addresses stored in **argv[ ]**, we get the strings mentioned at the DOS prompt.

(22) *Output*

Appears on the printer:

zZebraZebraZebra

Explanation

This program assumes that you have a printer connected to your machine. The argument **stdprn** is passed to all the four functions used in the program, indicating that the output should be directed to the printer. With the **printf( )**, we have no option but to write to the screen. This limitation is not encountered with **putc( )**, **fprintf( )**, **fwrite( )** and **fputs( )**. **putc( )** takes as its argument a character and prints 'z' onto the screen. After this the **fprintf( )** prints the string "Zebra", the base address of which has been passed to it. The function **fwrite( )** also outputs the string to the printer. To **fwrite( )** we supply the base address of the string to be written, the number of characters to be written (from base address onwards), the number of times the string is to be written and the device (**stdprn** in this case) to which it is to be written. Lastly **fputs( )** also outputs the string to the printer. Moral is, in all these functions which are used normally to write to a file, if the file pointer is replaced by **stdprn**, the output would be directed to the printer.

(23) *Output*

No output on screen

Explanation

The file "TRIAL" has been opened in write-binary mode by the **fopen( )** function. Once opened, the **fwrite( )**s write the contents of a structure and a string into it. This highlights the fact that **fwrite( )** is not only capable of writing structures, but strings as well. All that you have to provide to it is the base address of the data to be written, the number of bytes (from the base address onwards) to be written, number of times it is to be written and the file to which it is to be written.

Answers to **[B]**

(1)   (a)

getch( ) is the answer, as of the four it is the only one that does not echo the typed character. The functions **getche( )** and **fgetchar( )**, as well as the macro **getchar( )**, all print the typed character on the screen. **getchar( )** and **fgetchar( )** suffer from one more restriction. While using them, having entered a character, it has to be followed by hitting the Enter key. But for these subtle differences the working of all the four functions/macro is same.

(2)   (c)

putc( ) and **fprintf( )** are text mode functions. In text mode, the numbers are stored as strings. For instance, 20000, an **int**, which occupies two bytes in memory, would be treated as a string of characters '2', '0', '0', '0' and '0'. Naturally, this would occupy five bytes in the file, one for each character. Thus, three bytes would be wasted in storing a two byte number. On the other hand, **fwrite( )** is a binary mode function which writes numbers the way they appear in memory. That is, 20000 would be allotted two bytes while being stored in a file using **fwrite( )**. The saving of bytes brought about by using **fwrite( )** hence justifies our choice.

(3)   (b)

fseek( ) allows us to position the file pointer at the beginning of the file, at the end of file or at any other intermediate position which we specify. This facility however is not available with **rewind( )**, which can position the pointer only at the beginning of the file. The function **ftell( )** is of no use here, as all it does is to return the current position of the file pointer that is sent as its argument.

(4)   (a), (b), (c)

Whenever an existing file is opened in any of the first three modes, it is first erased completely and then the blank file is made available for writing. Hence care should be taken to use "w", "wb" and "wb+" only when we want to create a new file or when we can afford to loose the contents of the existing file.

(5)   (c)

getc( ) can read only one character at a time from a file. So it doesn't serve any useful purpose here since we want to read the file contents record by record. **gets( )** is still less useful since it accepts a string from the keyboard and not from the file. **fgets( )** would certainly allow us to read as many bytes as we specify, but would hardly prove to be ideal. In a record we may have an **int**, a **char**, a string, etc., and mind you all these would be read by **fgets( )** as one single string of as many characters as the record comprises of. And once the entire record is read as a string, separation of different fields of the record from the string would be a difficult task. Hence **fread( )** is the best choice, since it allows reading of a file record by record. Moreover, nothing special has to be done to segregate the field of the record once it has been read.

Solutions to **[C]**

(1)   *Program*

```
#include "stdio.h"
main ( argc, argv )
int argc ;
char *argv[ ] ;
{
    char ch1, ch2, source[30], target[30] ;
    FILE *fs, *ft ;

    if ( argc != 3 )
    {
        printf ( "Enter source and target filenames " ) ;
        scanf ( "%s %s", source, target ) ;
    }
    else
    {
        strcpy ( source, argv[1] ) ;
        strcpy ( target, argv[2] ) ;
    }

    if ( ( fs = fopen ( source, "r" ) ) == NULL )
    {
        printf ( "\nCannot open source file... Press any key" ) ;
        getch() ;
        exit ( 1 ) ;
    }
    if ( ( ft = fopen ( target, "w" ) ) == NULL )
    {
        printf ( "\nCannot open target file... Press any key" ) ;
        getch() ;
        fclose ( fs ) ;
        exit ( 2 ) ;
    }
```

```
while ( ( ch1 = getc(fs) ) != EOF )
{
    if ( ch1 == '/' )
    {
        if ( ( ch2 = getc( fs ) ) == '*' )
        {
            while ( 1 )
            {
                if ( ( ch1 = getc ( fs ) ) == '*' )
                {
                    if ( ( ch1 = getc ( fs ) ) == '/' )
                        break ;
                }
            }
        }
        else
        {
            putc ( ch1, ft ) ;
            putc ( ch2, ft ) ;
        }
    }
    else
        putc ( ch1, ft ) ;
}
printf ( "\nDone!! Press any key..." ) ;
getch() ;
fclose ( fs ) ;
fclose ( ft ) ;
}
```

Explanation

The program starts by checking whether the user has entered
the right number of arguments or not. **argc**, as we know,
collects the number of strings passed to **main( )** at the DOS

prompt. Comparing the contents of **argc** with 3, the right number of arguments, we first ensure that the proper parameters have been specified. Since **argv[ ]** contains the base addresses of the passed strings, we store the source and target file names in **source** and **target** respectively.

Having opened the file successfully with **fopen( )**, we come to the actual logic of segregating comments. The **while** loop first searches for the character '/' which marks the beginning of any comment. If a '/' is collected in **ch1**, the next character from the file is collected in **ch2** and checked whether it is a '*'. This is done in order to verify that a comment is indeed in the offing, and **ch1** did not read a solitary slash '/'. Having read "/*", the next two **if**s find when the ending "*/" are encountered. **while (1)** ensures that control remains in the loop till this ending syntax of a comment is reached. Thus, though the characters after "/*" are read from the source file, none get written into the target file. When the end of the comment is encountered, the **break** takes the control out of the inner **while** loop. After this whatever is read from the source is written to the target file as it is, till the next comment is met with.

(2)   *Program*

```
#include "stdio.h"

main ( argc, argv )
int argc ;
char *argv[ ] ;
{
    FILE *fs, *ft ;
    int ch ;
    char source[30], target[30] ;

    if ( argc != 3 )
    {
```

```c
        printf ( "\nEnter source and target filenames " ) ;
        scanf ( "%s %s", source, target ) ;
    }
    else
    {
        strcpy ( source, argv[1] ) ;
        strcpy ( target, argv[2] ) ;
    }

    if ( ( fs = fopen ( source, "r" ) ) == NULL )
    {
        printf ( "Cannot open source file... Press any key " ) ;
        getch( ) ;
        exit ( 1 ) ;
    }
    if ( ( ft = fopen ( source, "w" ) ) == NULL )
    {
        printf ( "Cannot open target file... Press any key" ) ;
        getch( ) ;
        fclose ( fs ) ;
        exit ( 2 ) ;
    }

    while ( ( ch = getc ( fs ) ) != EOF )
    {
        if ( ch >= 128 )
            putc ( ch - 128, ft ) ;
        else
            putc ( ch, ft ) ;
    }
    printf ( "\nDone!! Press any key..." ) ;
    getch ( ) ;

    fclose ( fs ) ;
    fclose ( ft ) ;
}
```

Explanation

The WordStar package has its special way of storing documents. It stores all the letters of the word as it is, except for the last letter. This letter is given an offset of 128. The ascii values from 128 to 255 correspond to graphic characters, hence the last letter of each word appears as a graphic character . Thus, to convert a WordStar file to an ordinary text file, all we need to do is restore all the last letters to their original values. In our program, whenever we encounter a graphic character, i.e. one having an ascii value more than 127, we subtract 128 from it and arrive at the character which must actually be present there.

12

Bits and Pieces

B y now we have dealt with most of the mainstream C. However, there are still a few loose ends to be tied up before you can go full steam ahead and use C for a variety of applications right from interacting with the hardware to designing sophisticated software. This chapter gives the finishing strokes with a brief discussion on bitwise operators, enumerated datatypes, bit fields, typecasting, the **typedef** keyword etc. Let us examine them one by one.

Bitwise Operators

Programming languages are byte oriented. But for getting down to the machine level, i.e. for interaction with the hardware, we must be able to access the individual bits of a byte. We do so with the help of Bitwise operators. These operators allow us to manipulate the individual bits of a byte. There are several bitwise operators available in C. Figure 12.1 shows these bitwise operators, and how they are put to work. Starting with any two 8 bit numbers, say **a** equal to 0100 1011 (decimal 75) and **b** equal to 1011 0010 (decimal 178), we examine how the bitwise operators function. We use a variable **c** for collecting the results of our operations.

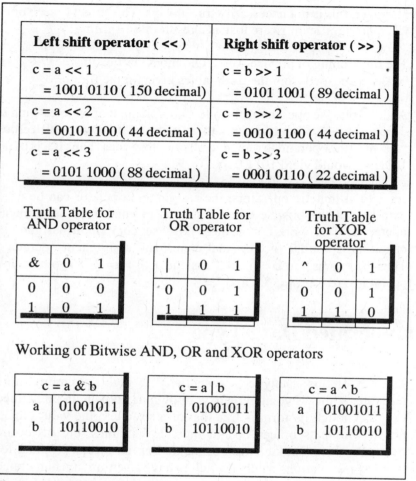

Left shift operator (<<)	Right shift operator (>>)

c = a << 1
  = 1001 0110 (150 decimal)
	c = b >> 1
	  = 0101 1001 (89 decimal)

c = a << 2
  = 0010 1100 (44 decimal)
	c = b >> 2
	  = 0010 1100 (44 decimal)

c = a << 3
  = 0101 1000 (88 decimal)
	c = b >> 3
	  = 0001 0110 (22 decimal)

Truth Table for AND operator

&	0	1
0	0	0
1	0	1

Truth Table for OR operator

|	0	1
0	0	1
1	1	1

Truth Table for XOR operator

^	0	1
0	0	1
1	1	0

Working of Bitwise AND, OR and XOR operators

c = a & b	
a	01001011
b	10110010

c = a | b	
a	01001011
b	10110010

c = a ^ b	
a	01001011
b	10110010

Figure 12.1 Bitwise Operators

Follow the figure carefully. On left shifting, all the bits are moved one position to the left, and on right shifting, to the right, with zeroes being placed wherever spaces are created on shifting of bits. Note that on left shifting **a** once, it gets multiplied by 2, and by right shifting **b** once, it gets divided by 2. Thus **c** stores decimal 150 and decimal 89 as a result of the operations **a << 1** and **b >> 1** respectively.

However, this is not necessarily true always. This effect is seen only when no significant 1s are lost as a result of bit shifting.

The functioning of bitwise AND, OR and XOR (exclusive OR) can be easily grasped from the truth tables given in the figure.

Another bitwise operator is the one's complement operator, which is denoted as ~. On applying this to an operand it converts all zeroes present in the operand to ones and all ones to zeroes. Thus if **a** is 0100 1011, **~a** would yield 1011 0100.

As with arithmetic operators, the assignment operator can be used with any of the bitwise operators to yield compound assignment operators. The working of these bitwise compound assignment operators is similar to the usual compound assignment operators. Thus the expression **b = b >> 2** is same as **b >>= 2**. The other such operators are **<<=, |=, &=** and **^=**.

Enumerated Data Type

The use of this datatype is essentially to make programs more readable. It allows you to create your own datatype with predefined values. Though its form is like that of a structure, the values mentioned within its braces do not indicate variables, but infact are constant values that the **enum** can take. For instance, a program for Railway reservations would do well to have an **enum**, or enumerated datatype of the following form:

```
enum rail
{
    firstclass,
    secondclass,
    ac
} ;
enum rail person1, person2 ;
```

Here **firstclass, secondclass** and **ac** are called enumerators, which are the values that the variable of the type **enum rail** can take. The next statement declares that **person1** and **person2** are variables of the type **enum rail**. These variables cannot take values other than **firstclass, secondclass** and **ac**. Internally, these values are treated as integers by the compiler. Hence, **firstclass** is interpreted as value 0, **secondclass** as value 1, and **ac** as 2. We can override these values by saying in the declaration:

```
enum rail
{
      firstclass = 20,
      secondclass = 30,
      ac = 40
} ;
```

or any numbers we want assigned.

The enumerated variables suffer from one minor weakness. The enumerated values cannot be used directly in input/output functions like **printf( )** and **scanf( )**. This is because these functions are not smart enough to understand that by 20 you mean **firstclass** or vice versa. You would agree that this limitation is quite sensible.

Typedef

Renaming datatypes with this keyword is another facility which helps in making lengthy or complicated programs easier to understand. For example, look at the following statement:

```
typedef long double F ;
```

Once this is done we can use the sweet and simple **F** wherever we intend to use **long double**. While declaring variables of this type, we can simply say,

```
F a, b, c ;
```

and **a, b** and **c** would be treated as variables of the type **long double**. This shortcut proves very useful when the names of datatypes are long and unweildy.

Typecasting

Typecasting allows us to explicitly convert the value of an expression or a variable to a particular datatype. If we want the result of 3 divided by 2 to be a **float** value, we can achieve this by saying (**float**) **3 / 2**. Of course, promoting either 3 or 2 (or both) to **float** by writing them as 3.0 or 2.0 would also serve the same purpose. But there may be instances when we want to use the value of the same variable as an **int** at a few places and as a **float** at others. In such cases typecasting is the only solution.

Bit Fields

If a variable is to take only two values 1 or 0, really speaking we need only a single bit to store it. Likewise, if a variable is to take values from 0 to 3, then two bits are sufficient to store these values. Then why sacrifice an entire integer when one or two bits would do? The reason is simple. C doesn't offer any one or two bit datatypes. However, when there are several variables whose maximum values are small enough to pack in a single byte, we can use 'Bit Fields' to store all these values in a single byte. For example, suppose there are four variables **a, b, c** and **d** such that **a** can take any one of the two values 0 or 1, **b** can take any value between 0 and 3, **c** can take any value between 0 and 7 and **d** can take any value between 0 and 15. This means that we need only one bit to store the value that **a** can take, two bits to store the value of **b**, three bits to store the value of **c** and four bits to store the value of **d**. Thus we need 10 bits altogether, which means we can pack all this information into a single integer, since an integer is 16 bits long. How to achieve this using bit fields is shown in the following program:

```
main( )
{
    struct num
    {
        unsigned a : 1 ;
        unsigned b : 2 ;
        unsigned c : 3 ;
        unsigned d : 4 ;
    } ;
    struct num n ;
    n.a = 0 ;
    n.b = 2 ;
    n.c = 5 ;
    n.d = 14 ;
    printf ( "%d %d %d %d", n.a, n.b, n.c, n.d ) ;
}
```

Observe the declaration **struct num**. The colon in the declaration tells the compiler that we are talking about bit fields and the number after it tells how many bits to allot to the field. Once we have established bit fields we can reference them just like ordinary structure elements - by using the '.' operator.

Pointers to Functions

We have studied about pointers to **char**s, **int**s, arrays, etc. Such pointers contain addresses of these entities, through which the entities can be accessed. Likewise, functions too can be invoked using their addresses. That is, we can have pointers to functions. Just like mentioning the name of an array gives the base address of the array, mentioning the name of the function yields the address of the function. Thus, the statement

```
printf ( "%d", demo ) ;
```

would print the address of the function **demo( )**. So far, for invoking a function we have used its name. The following program shows how a pointer can be used for calling a function **demo( )**.

```
main( )
{
    int demo( ) ;
    int ( *fpointer ) ( ) ;

    fpointer = demo ;
    ( *fpointer ) ( ) :
}
```

In the program, we declare the function as well as **fpointer**, a pointer to it. Having stored the address of **demo( )** in this pointer, we call the function with the statement

```
( *fpointer ) ( ) ;
```

Once the concept of pointer to a function is imbibed, it can be used as liberally as the ordinary char or int pointers. For example, a pointer to a function can be passed to another function, stored in an array, etc.

Exercise

[A]   What will be the output of the following programs:

(1)
```c
main( )
{
    int i = 32, j = 65, k ;
    k = i | 35 ;
    printf ( "k = %d\n", k ) ;
    k = ~k ;
    printf ( "k = %d\n", k ) ;
    k = j & j ;
    printf ( "k = %d\n", k ) ;
}
```

(2)
```c
main( )
{
    int i = 32, j = 65, k ;
    k = j ^ 32 ;
    printf ( "k = %d\n", k ) ;
    k = j << 2 ;
    printf ( "k = %d\n", k ) ;
    k = i >> 5 ;
    printf ( "k = %d\n", k ) ;
}
```

(3)
```c
main( )
{
    int a = 3, b = 2, c = 1, d ;
    d = a | b & c ,
    printf ( "d = %d\n", d ) ;
    d = a | b & ~c ;
    orintf ( "d = %d\n", d ) ;
}
```

```
(4)    main( )
       {
           int a = 0xff ;
           if ( a << 4 >> 12 )
               printf ( "Leftist" ) ;
           else
               printf ( "Rightist" ) ;
       }

(5)    main( )
       {
           int a = 10 ;
           if ( a & 8 == 8 )
               printf ( "Bit no. 3 is on" ) ;
           else
               printf ( "3 rd bit is off" ) ;
       }

(6)    main( )
       {
           int a = 12, i = 0 ;
           while ( a >>= i )
           {
               printf ( "a = %d i = %d\n", a, i ) ;
               i++ ;
           }
       }

(7)    main( )
       {
           int i = +1 ;
           while ( ~i )
               printf ( "vicious circles\n" ) ;
       }

(8)    main( )
```

```
        {
            int a = 0xa0, b = 0x0a, c, d ;
            c = a | b ;
            printf ( "c = %d", c ) ;
            d = a & b ;
            printf ( "d = %d", d ) ;
        }

(9)     main( )
        {
            enum code
            {
                add,
                delete,
                modify,
                unchanged
            } ;
            typedef enum code CODE ;
            CODE c, d ;
            c = add ;
            d = modify ;
            printf ( "c = %d d = %d", c, d ) ;
        }

(10)    main( )
        {
            enum status { low, medium, high } ;
            enum status rain ;
            rain = 0 ;
            if ( rain == low )
                printf ( "rain = %d", rain ) ;
        }

(11)    main( )
        {
            enum status { low = 10, medium = 20, high = 30 } ;
```

```
            enum status rain ;
            rain = medium ;
            if ( rain == 20 )
                rain++ ;
            printf ( "rain = %d", rain ) ;
        }


(12)    main( )
        {
            typedef struct
            {
                char name[20] ;
                int age ;
            } a ;
            a emp = { "Sunil", 30 } ;
            printf ( "%s %d", emp.name, emp.age ) ;
        }


(13)    main( )
        {
            struct address
            {
                char city[20] ;
                int pin ;
            } ;
            typedef struct address * ADDR ;
            ADDR addr ;
            static struct address a = { "Jodhpur", 20 } ;
            addr = &a ;
            printf ( "%s %d", addr->city, addr->pin ) ;
        }


(14)    main(')
        {
            printf ( "%f"  (float) ( (int) ( (float) ( (int)6.5/2 + 3.5 )) - 3.5 ) ) ;
        }
```

```
(15)  main( )
      {
          struct num
          {
              unsigned bit0 : 1 ;
              unsigned bit1 : 1 ;
              unsigned bit2 : 1 ;
              unsigned rest : 5 ;
          } ;
          union a
          {
              struct num n ;
              char ch ;
          } b ;
          b.ch = 32 ;

          printf ( "%d %d %d %d", b.n.bit0, b.n.bit1, b.n.bit2, b.n.rest ) ;
      }


(16)  main( )
      {
          int show( ) ;
          int ( *f )( ) ;
          f = show ;
          printf ( "address = %d\n", f ) ;
          ( *f )( ) ;
      }
      show( )
      {
          printf ( "Diamonds are forever" ) ;
      }


(17)  main( )
      {
          int show( ) ;
          int ( *f )( ) ;
```

```
        f = show ;
        display ( f ) ;
}
show( )
{
        printf ( "On the rebound..." ) ;
}
display ( ff )
int ( *ff )( ) ;
{
        ( *ff )( ) ;
}
```

```
(18)  main( )
{
        int i, fun1( ), fun2( ), fun3( ) ;
        int ( *f[3] )( ) ;
        f[0] = fun1 ;
        f[1] = fun2 ;
        f[2] = fun3 ;
        for ( i = 0 ; i <= 2; i++ )
                ( *f[ i ])( ) ;
}
fun1( )
{
        printf ( "Hail " ) ;
}
fun2( )
{
        printf ( "the " ) ;
}
fun3( )
{
        printf ( "viruses!" ) ;
}
```

Answers

Answers to **[A]**

(1)   *Output*

    k = 35
    k = -36
    k = 0

Explanation

Since **int**s are being considered, all the operations are carried out on 16-bit binary numbers. **i** stores 32, which is binary 0000 0000 0010 0000. On ORing it with 35, which is binary 0000 0000 0010 0011, each corresponding pair of bits is compared, resulting in 1 if at least one of the pair is a 1. The result is easily envisaged to be 35 itself.

The ~ operator gives the one's complement of its operand. On complementing **k**, which equals 35, the result is 1111 1111 1101 1100. This number is equivalent to decimal 65500, which lies outside the range of an **int**. Hence, after +32767, counting resumes at -32768, yielding -36.

Finally **i**, which is 32, on bitwise ANDing with 65 (binary 0000 0000 0100 0001) results in a zero. This is only natural, as 32 and 65 in their binary forms have no corresponding pair of bits as 1.

(2)   *Output*

    k = 97
    k = 260

k = 1

Explanation

The XOR operator ^ yields a 1 only if the 2 bits being compared are 0 and 1, else a 0 results. Thus, 65 and 32 yield 97, which is binary 0000 0000 0110 0001.

original value	65:	0000 0000 0100 0001
mask	32:	0000 0000 0010 0000
new value	97:	0000 0000 0110 0001

The second **printf( )** prints the value of **k**, which has been assigned the result of **j** left shifted twice. **j** is 65, i.e. 0000 0000 0100 0001. On left shifting twice, zeroes are appended on the right and **j** is transformed to 0000 0001 0000 0100, which is decimal 260.

Lastly, **i**, containing 32, is right shifted 5 times. The sequence of how the 16 bits are manipulated is:

32:	0000 0000 0010 0000
>>	0000 0000 0001 0000
>>	0000 0000 0000 1000
>>	0000 0000 0000 0100
>>	0000 0000 0000 0010
>>	0000 0000 0000 0001

After 5 right shifts, we get 1, which is assigned to **k**.

(3)   *Output*

d = 3
d = 3

Explanation

None of the bitwise operators change the value of the operands they act on. On saying **a | b & c**, the result is 0000 0000 0000 0011, i.e. decimal 3, which gets assigned to **d**. Note that bitwise **&** operator enjoys a higher priority than the **|** operator. When **a | b & ~c** is evaluated, **a, b** and **c** are still 3, 2 and 1 respectively. **~c** yields 1111 1111 1111 1110 and on ANDing it with 0000 0000 0000 0010 (decimal 2), we get 0000 0000 0000 0010. Finally, ORing this result with 3 again yields a 3.

(4)   *Output*

Rightist

Explanation

a contains hex ff, i.e. 0000 0000 1111 1111. Firstly the left shifting operation is carried out, changing the 16 bits to 0000 1111 1111 0000. Following this, right shift is executed 12 times, so that the latter 3 nibbles (a set of 4 bits is a nibble) are pushed out, and as many zeroes crop up on the left. As the 2-byte number is now 0, the **if** condition fails and the **printf( )** of the **else** block gets executed.

(5)   *Output*

Bit no. 3 is on

Explanation

In the binary equivalent of 8, only one bit is set to 1, which is bit number 3. On ANDing with **a**, which contains 10 (binary 0000 0000 0000 1010), only bit number 3 is copied as it is. All remaining bits are reset to 0, and for this reason 8 can be referred to as a mask. Hence the **if** condition reduces to **if (8 == 8)**. This is satisfied, therefore we get the output as 'Bit no. 3 is on'. This simple trick of checking what bits are on (or 1) is extremely useful in a variety of applications like calculating date and time for every file in the directory, or finding out the current file attributes etc.

(6)   *Output*

```
a = 12 i = 0
a = 6 i = 1
a = 1 i = 2
```

Explanation

In the **while** condition, **a** is right shifted **i** times and the result is assigned to **a** itself. Thus the condition **a >>= i** is same as **a = a >> i**. First time through the loop, **i** is 0, hence **a** remains unchanged. Since **a** is non-zero, the condition evaluates to true and the **printf( )** gives us our first output. The next time, **a**, i.e. 12 is right shifted once, as **i** has now been incremented to 1. 12 in binary is 0000 0000 0000 1100. On right shifting this by 1, we get 0000 0000 0000 0110, which is decimal 6. Note that if no significant 1s are lost on right shifting once, the number gets divided by 2. Hence **12 >> 1** yields 6, which is stored in **a**. Similarly, in subsequent executions of the loop **a** and **i** take values 6 and 1 respectively, and then 1 and 2, which are printed out through **printf( )**. Once **a** and **i** are 1 and 2 and the control reaches the **while**, **a** evaluates to 0. Hence the condition fails, and the loop is terminated.

(7)   *Output*

```
vicious circles
vicious circles
.......... ..........
```

Explanation

Firstly **i** is initialised to 1, and then in **while**, its complement is taken. **~1** is 1111 1111 1111 1110, which is also a truth value. Hence 'vicious circles' is printed for the first time and the control goes back to the **while**. Once again **~i** evaluates to the same value, 1111 1111 1111 1110. This so happens because **i** has remained unchanged, as **i**'s value can change only if **i** occurs on the left hand side of the assignment operator. Since the condition evaluates to true, the **printf( )** does its job once again. This goes on and on, as control has fallen in an indefinite loop, until we terminate the execution by typing either ctrl-C or ctrl-scroll lock.

(8)   *Output*

```
c = 170
d = 0
```

Explanation

a and **b** are made to store hex numbers a0 and 0a. These hex numbers are nothing but binary 0000 0000 1010 0000 and 0000 0000 0000 1010. On ORing them bitwise, the 2-byte number obtained is 0000 0000 1010 1010, which is decimal 170. On ANDing them, a zero results as in the binary representations of 0xa0 and 0x0a, no corresponding pair of bits happen to have both 1s. Hence the output.

(9)   *Output*

```
c = 0 d = 2
```

Explanation

The enumerated datatype **code** is declared to be capable of taking values **add, delete, modify** and **unchanged**. Using the **typedef** statement, two variables of this type, **c** and **d** are declared and initialised. **c** is assigned the value **add**, and **d**, the value **modify**. The **printf( )** then prints out the values of **c** and **d**. Did you expect **add** and **modify** to be printed? Well, this is one feature of an **enum** that takes away some of its usefulness. When values are defined for an **enum**, they are interpreted as integer values 0, 1, 2, etc. by default. Thus, **add**, which occurs first is assigned 0, **delete** is assigned 1, and so on. That is why, on printing the values of **c** and **d**, we get 0 and 2 respectively.

We can, if we want, change these assignment of values by explicitly saying so. For example, saying **add = 10** in the declaration would give the value of **c** as 10.

(10) *Output*

rain = 0

Explanation

rain is a variable of the type **enum status**, which is declared to be able to take values **low, medium** and **high**. In an **enum**, the values are interpreted as 0, 1 and 2 in that order. Hence, assigning 0 to **rain** is same as assigning **low** to **rain**. The **if** condition is therefore satisfied and we get our output.

(11) *Output*

rain = 21

Explanation

In this program we have overridden the default integer values that **low**, **medium** and **high** would have taken. We have set them to 10, 20 and 30. Thus, assigning **medium** to **rain** is same as assigning 20 to it. Hence the **if** condition is satisfied, and the **++** operator increments **rain** so that it now contains 21. The same is then printed out by the **printf( )**.

(12) *Output*

Sunil 30

Explanation

The **typedef** statement defines the structure in the program as **a**. Next, a variable of this type, **emp** is declared and initialised. Note how the **typedef** statement shortens the code used in the program. The structure elements are now accessed as usual using the dot operator, and we have the output as the values to which **emp.name[ ]** and **emp.age** were initialised.

(13) *Output*

Jodhpur 20

Explanation

In this case, we define **struct address *** as ADDR. Next, the variable **addr** is declared to be of this type, i.e. a pointer to the structure of the type **struct address**. The address of the structure variable **a** is assigned to this pointer, having first stored "Jodhpur" and 20 in **a**. On using the arrow operator with **addr**, the values of structure elements of **a** are printed out by the **printf( )**.

Note that C is a case sensitive language. Hence it treats **ADDR**
and **addr** as two different entities.

(14) *Output*

2.500000

Explanation

In the innermost parentheses, the expression is typecast to an
int. Hence, during division 6 is used instead of 6.5, which
results into 3, an **int**. To this is added 3.5, so that we have the
value 6.5. This result is typecast using (**float**), so that we now
have the value 6.500000, which is how a **float** is represented.
Once again, (**int**) typecasts this value to an integer, whence
the decimal part is truncated and the value is now 6. From this
value, we subtract 3.5, and thus are left with 2.5. This value is
finally typecast to a **float**, and hence the output displays this
as 2.500000.

(15) *Output*

0 0 0 4

Explanation

struct num is not an ordinary **struct**. The **:** sign indicates that
we are dealing with bit fields. In the declaration, **bit0**, **bit1** and
bit2 are assigned only 1 bit each. Hence we can conclude that
these variables are going to take not more than two values,
which can be represented by a 0 or a 1. Then, **rest** is assigned
5 bits, indicating that **rest** can represent a maximum of 2^5, i.e.
32 values. These declarations are made using the keyword
unsigned, as by default one bit is devoted to store the sign of

the number, and we do not want to store any sign information. Thus, a total of one byte is used by **bit0**, **bit1**, **bit2** and **rest**.

Next, a **union** of such a structure **n** and a **char ch** is declared. We know that assigning a value to one of the variables of a **union** automatically assigns a value to the other variable. This is because the same 8 bits that are used by **ch** are used for **struct n**. Thus, when we say **ch = 32**, the 8 bits are set up as shown in the following figure.

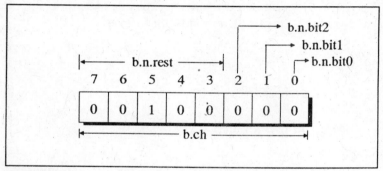

Figure 12.2

On printing **b.n.bit0**, **b.n.bit1** and **b.n.bit2**, we get the 0s stored here. Bit numbers 7, 6, 5, 4 and 3 store the information corresponding to **b.n.rest**. The contents here are 00100, which is the binary equivalent of decimal 4. Hence the last output is 4.

(16) *Output*

address = 528
Diamonds are forever

Explanation

This program demonstrates the use of pointers to functions. **f**, which is declared to be a pointer to the function **show( )**, is assigned the address of this function. The address of a function can be obtained by simply mentioning the name of the function. The **printf( )** in **main( )** prints this address, which may be something other than 528 when you run the program.

The last statement in **main( )** calls the function **show( )**. Instead of calling the function by name, we make use of the pointer to the function. As a result control goes to **show( )**, where the **printf( )** prints "Diamonds are forever".

(17) *Output*

On the rebound...

Explanation

To begin with, **f** is declared as a pointer to a function, which returns an **int**. Into **f** is stored the address of **show( )**. Now, this address is passed to another function **display( )**, where it is collected in **ff**. Hence **ff** is also declared to be a pointer to a function. From **display( )**, the function **show( )** is called by mentioning its address, and we get our output on the execution of the **printf( )** here.

(18) *Output*

Hail the viruses!

Explanation

Here we are dealing with an array of pointers to functions. To begin with, in the elements of the array **f[ ]** the addresses of functions **fun1( )**, **fun2( )** and **fun3( )** are stored. Next, with the

for loop, calls are made to each of these functions making use of their addresses. The first call results in "Hail " being outputted. Now, when **i** is 1, **fun2( )** is called, and "the " is printed. Finally, for **i** equal to 2, **fun3( )** gets called, and the **printf( )** here displays "viruses!".

13

Winding up...

Congratulations! Having reached this juncture, you have mastered the fundamental concepts of C and qualify as a C pro. Now that you're in the league, let me let you in on a secret: Work on something you love and you'll never have to work a single day of your life. State that before any C programmer and you'll see him emphatically nodding his head, agreeing heartily. Various persons enter the programming environment for as many reasons; they have some specific needs, or they want a short cut to a problem that is not manageable manually, or for the simple reason that they are curious, or whatever. But they have one thing in common - they stick around, programming more for fun than for the lifelong dividends it pays. Right from doing something as routine as keeping your bank accounts to calculating the precise moment to fire the Patriot, programming is the answer. And what better language than C? Not only has more than 90% of the UNIX operating system been written in C, it is also the prima donna of most of the applications on the world's foremost computers. Databases, spreadsheets, wordprocessors, games - you name it, and C does it effortlessly.

Accomodating 8 queens amicably

As an example, and in keeping with the brain-teasing problems in this book, here's a program that illustrates to what extent you can play around with C. Has it ever occurred to you how 8 queens could be placed on an 8 by 8 chess board so that none can take another? Knowing that the queens can advance in any and every direction they fancy, it is a challenge of sorts to come up with such a combination. But not to C. A few lines' program would provide you with more than 50 different ways to manage this, only one of which is shown here.

Figure 13.1 Combination of 8 queens on an 8 by 8 chess board

Instead of handing over the solution to you on a silver platter, I present its disguised version which can arrange from 4 to 99 queens on corresponding chess boards.

```
int v,i,j,k,l,s,a[99];
main( )
{
    for(scanf("%d",&s);*a-s;v=a[j*=v]-a[i],k=i<s,j+=(v=j<
s&&(!k&&!!printf(2+"\n\n%c"-(!!<<!j)," #Q"[l^v?(l^j)&1:2])&&
++l||a[i]<s&&v&&v-i+j&&v+i-j))&&!(l%=s),v||(i==j?a[i+=k]=0:++
a[i])>=s*k&&++a[--ij)
```

}

I'd advise you to reserve a quiet weekend to figure that out, if not more! For the present, lets ponder over another aspect of C, the linked list.

Reversing a Linked list

We had a brief introduction of the linked list in Chapter 10. While the elements of an array occupy contiguous memory locations, those of a linked list are not constrained to be stored in adjacent locations. The individual elements are stored "somewhere" in memory, rather like a family dispersed, but still bound together. The order of the elements is maintained by explicit links between them. For instance, this is how the marks obtained by different students can be stored in a linked list:

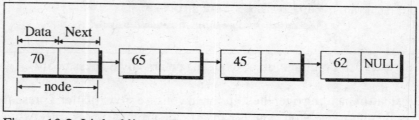

Figure 13.2 Linked list

Observe that the linked list is a collection of elements called nodes, each of which stores two items of information. One, an element of the list, and two, a link, i.e. a pointer or an address that indicates explicitly the location of the node containing the successor of this list element. In the figure, the arrows represent the links. The **Data** part of each node consists of the marks obtained by a student and the **Next** part is a pointer to the next node. The NULL in the last node indicates that this is the last node in the list.

With that information on linked lists put in a sufficiently responsive part of your brain, try developing the program to reverse all the links present in the list. For example, in the above figure, on reversing the link, the node with 62 in the **Data** part would become the first node in the linked list and the node with 70 in its **Data**, the last node. And if that isn't enough food for thought, how about writing a recursive function which will copy all the nodes in one linked list into another?

A Multiple Substitution Cipher

Security! It is possibly the costliest commodity today. None has been able to ignore it. No, not even the computers. In the world of computers there is an unending race to build stronger and stronger walls of defence around one's programs, so that one's software is protected from eavesdroppers with malicious intentions. There are several schemes in practice which encode your files in such a way that nobody can tamper with them. You were presented with the offset cipher earlier in the book, which is not very tough to break. A more potent scheme would be to offset different characters with different values. We can make use of three arrays **arr1[ ]**, **arr2[ ]** and **arr3[ ]**, in each of which all the 127 ascii characters (0 to 126) are stored in different sequences. While encoding, depending on the ascii value of the character read, the corresponding element from **arr1[ ]** is picked up and stored in the target file. When the same character occurs for the second time, we replace it with the corresponding element of the second array **arr2[ ]**, and when it is encountered for the third time, the appropriate character from **arr3[ ]** is substituted in the target file. Thus, for the same character, say 'A' (ascii 65), three different characters (**arr1[65]**, **arr2[65]** and **arr3[65]**) are substituted in turns. For decoding, just the reverse logic can be used. Writing this program would possibly turn out to be challenging. However, a more daunting task would be to hack this coding scheme, and figure out through a program, how to get back the original file from an encoded file. Want to give it a try? I would give you a clue - Think!

Manipulation of Sparse Matrices

A sparse matrix is one which has many of its elements as zeroes. There is no precise definition of when a matrix is sparse and when it is not, but it is a concept which we can all recognise intuitively. For example, if 24 elements of an 8 by 8 matrix are zeroes, then its certainly a sparse matrix. To save on memory space the sparse matrices are often represented using a 3-tuple form in which only the non-zero elements from the original matrix are stored.

The following figure shows a 5 by 5 matrix along with its 3-tuple representation. Observe that all the rows of the 3-tuple representation consist of three columns. Also, the three entries of the zeroth row represent the number of rows, number of columns and number of non-zero entries in the original matrix. In rows other than the zeroth row, column 0 and column 1 consist of row number and column number of the non-zero elements in the sparse matrix. Column 2 in all these rows consist of the value of the non-zero elements.

Sparse matrix					3 - tuple representation		
7	0	0	6	0	5	5	6
1	0	0	0	0	0	0	7
0	0	0	0	3	0	3	6
0	2	0	0	0	1	0	1
0	0	0	9	0	2	4	3
					3	1	2
					4	3	9

Figure 13.3 3-Tuple form of a Sparse matrix

The bigger the sparse matrix, more will be the saving in memory achieved by using the 3-tuple representation. Armed with that knowledge, get your grey cells going and cook up the logic for reading two matrices in their 3-tuple forms and compute their sum, product and transpose.

A parting thought

With all the exploring we have done as yet, you'll agree that C can be said to be a *laissez faire* language, with few encumbering rules to abide by. It allowed us to examine its various aspects in all their motley garbs. We picked up each topic in turn and experimented with it - in some cases performed nothing short of acrobatics with the entities that constitute C. The critics would pounce on this aspect of C as it may encourage illogical thinking. But that should hardly hinder a seasoned programmer, who can use this very leniency to his advantage. And that is the reason why C is so widely used. It leaves it to us to build upon and make the most of its potential. The only ignition we need is our imagination and we'll find C moulding and accomodating itself to whatever our mind conjures.

Appendix

Code	Char	Code	Char	Code	Char	Code	Char	Code	Char	Code	Char
0		22	§	44	.	66	B	88	X	110	n
1		23	¶	45	-	67	C	89	Y	111	o
2	⊞	24	∷	46	‿	68	D	90	Z	112	p
3	⊟	25	⇔	47	⌒	69	E	91	[	113	q
4	◖	26	↔	48	⋅	70	F	92	\	114	r
5	◀	27	▲	49	&	71	G	93	]	115	s
6	♣	28	▼	50	‰	72	H	94	↑	116	t
7	♦	29	✳	51	♪	73	I	95	↓	117	u
8	↔	30	♫	52	#	74	J	96	←	118	v
9	◆	31	↳	53	∷	75	K	97	→	119	w
10	·	32	⚥	54	—	76	L	98	a	120	x
11	○	33	○	55		77	M	99	b	121	y
12	◉	34	◉	56		78	N	100	c	122	z
13	○	35	◀	57	◀	79	O	101	d	123	{
14	◉	36	▶	58	▶	80	P	102	e	124	|
15	☼	37	↕	59	↕	81	Q	103	f	125	}
16	♀	38	⌐	60	⌐	82	R	104	g	126	~
17	↱	39	↑	61	=	83	S	105	h	127	↯
18	♪	40	↓	62	∨	84	T	106	i	128	Ç
19	∷	41	←	63	∨	85	U	107	j	129	ü
20	¶	42	→	64	?	86	V	108	k	130	é
21	§	43	+	65	A	87	W	109	l	131	ä

Code	Char	Code	Char	Code	Char	Code	Char	Code	Char	Code	Char
132	ä	154	Ü	176	░	198	╞	220	▄	242	≥
133	à	155	¢	177	▒	199	╟	221	▌	243	≤
134	å	156	£	178	▓	200	╚	222	▐	244	⌠
135	ç	157	¥	179	│	201	╔	223	▀	245	⌡
136	ê	158	₧	180	┤	202	╩	224	α	246	÷
137	ë	159	ƒ	181	╡	203	╦	225	ß	247	≈
138	è	160	á	182	╢	204	╠	226	Γ	248	°
139	ï	161	í	183	╖	205	═	227	π	249	∙
140	î	162	ó	184	╕	206	╬	228	Σ	250	·
141	ì	163	ú	185	╣	207	╧	229	σ	251	√
142	Ä	164	ñ	186	║	208	╨	230	µ	252	ⁿ
143	Å	165	Ñ	187	╗	209	╤	231	τ	253	²
144	É	166	ª	188	╝	210	╥	232	Φ	254	■
145	æ	167	º	189	╜	211	╙	233	Θ	255	
146	Æ	168	¿	190	╛	212	╘	234	Ω		
147	ô	169	⌐	191	┐	213	╒	235	δ		
148	ö	170	¬	192	└	214	╓	236	∞		
149	ò	171	½	193	┴	215	╫	237	φ		
150	û	172	¼	194	┬	216	╪	238	ε		
151	ù	173	¡	195	├	217	┘	239	∩		
152	ÿ	174	«	196	─	218	┌	240	≡		
153	Ö	175	»	197	┼	219	█	241	±		

Index

Diskette Order Form

Use this form to order sets of companion diskettes containing all the programs in **Exploring** C. The diskettes are 5 1/4", 360 KB floppies prepared for IBM PC compatibles running under DOS 2.0 or higher. The set of two diskettes sells for Rs. 200/- including packaging and forwarding and may be purchased by a Demand Draft only, drawn in the name of *BPB Publications, New Delhi*. Fill this form and mail it to *BPB Publications, B-14, Connaught Place, New Delhi - 110001, India*.

Diskette Order Form

Exploring C by Yashavant Kanetkar

Name _____ Company _____

Address _____

City _____ Pin _____ Phone _____

Place of Book Purchase _____

Number of sets orderd ____ (@ Rs. 200/-)

Total order amount Rs. _____

I am enclosing herewith DD no. _____ , dated _____

Exploring C Reader Feedback Card

Improvement in thoughts and actions is a continuous process. Inspite of taking all the care while scripting this book, we are well aware that there is always a scope for improvement. Your help in the appraisal of this book would be of utmost help to us when this book comes out in its second edition. Your suggestions would be most gratefully accepted. Please fill out this card and mail it to: **Exploring C Feedback, BPB Publications, B-14, Connaught Place, New Delhi - 110 001.**

1. How would you rate the contents of this book?
   ☐ Excellent   ☐ Very good   ☐ Good
   ☐ Fair   ☐ Poor   ☐ Below Average

2. What were the things you liked most about this book?
   ☐ Listings   ☐ Appendix   ☐ Examples
   ☐ Writing Style ☐ Figures   ☐ Cover
   ☐ Organization   ☐ Flowcharts   ☐ Price

3. What were the things you liked least about this book?
   ☐ Listings   ☐ Appendix   ☐ Examples
   ☐ Writing Style ☐ Figures   ☐ Cover
   ☐ Organization   ☐ Flowcharts   ☐ Price

4. Which topics did you find most difficult to understand?
   a)_____ b)_____c)_____

5. Any other comments that you have about this book:
   _____

6. In a nutshell, do you think you made the right decision in purchasing this book (yes/no)? _____

   Name   _____
   Address _____
   City   _____
   Pin   _____ Phone _____

Notes

Notes

Notes